ALSO BY DEB PERELMAN

Smitten Kitchen Every Day
The Smitten Kitchen Cookbook

smitten kitchen keepers

smitten kitchen keepers

new classics for your forever files

DEB PERELMAN

photographs by deb perelman

styled by barrett washburne

ALFRED A. KNOPF New York 2022

THIS IS A BORZOI BOOK
PUBLISHED BY ALFRED A. KNOPF

www.aaknopf.com

Knopf, Borzoi Books, and the colophon are registered trademarks
of Penguin Random House LLC.

Library of Congress Cataloging-in-Publication Data
Names: Perelman, Deb, author.
Title: Smitten Kitchen keepers :
new classics for your forever files / Deborah Perelman.
Description: First edition. | New York : Alfred A. Knopf, 2022. |
Includes index.
Identifiers: LCCN 2021060789| ISBN 9780593318782 (hardcover) |
ISBN 9780593318799 (ebook)
Subjects: LCSH: Cooking. | LCGFT: Cookbooks.
Classification: LCC TX714 .P4433 2022 | DDC 641.5 23/eng/20211—dc30
LC record available at https://lccn.loc.gov/2021060789

Book design by Cassandra J. Pappas

Jacket photograph by Deb Perelman
Food styling by Barrett Washburne

Manufactured in China
First Edition

In memory of my dad
Michael Rothberg
1940–2018

contents

introduction

I don't mean to be melodramatic, but I think this is the book I was always meant to write. Given that it's my third cookbook, this is a bit awkward. It would be like declaring a new child the one you got right, while your first two glare at you from across the room. To be clear, the first two weren't practice rounds. I'm very proud of them, and I'm overjoyed that so many of you have welcomed them into your kitchens. (I hope you know I'm back to talking about the cookbooks, not my kids, but if my children do wander into your kitchen, please send them home soon.) As I thought about what I wanted to do next, I rewound to the year 2006, and I remembered the central energy that drove me to create Smitten Kitchen in the first place. It was never to flex my cooking skills, which were just burgeoning at the time. It was never just to show you things you'd never seen before; I always bristled at innovation for the sake of newness when, as far as I'd tasted, the perfect pound cake didn't yet exist. It was

to create a place where I could collect all of the recipes worth repeating. I wanted my own forever files.

I was relatively new to cooking, but I kept running into duds. Even sixteen years ago, there were already too many recipes on the internet, and this made it hard to choose. When I tweaked a yellow cake so that it was perfectly crumbed, or found a method that ensured that my chicken would never come out dry, I wanted to shout it from the rooftops. I settled for a url.

It's unclear why I couldn't just be a person who was satisfied with a great lemon-cake recipe for my own repertoire and enjoyment. No, I also needed to make sure that nobody else ever made a different one; the thought of a friend making a mediocre lemon cake bothers me more than anything should. It's definitely something wired deeply into my personality. My father, who passed away in 2018, also couldn't keep an opinion to himself. He wrote many op-eds and letters to the editor; he was one of *those*. His strongest wish near the end was that I write a third cookbook. "Why, Dad? I wrote two. Can't I quit while I'm relatively ahead?" I asked more than once, but he loved the words "three-book deal" (even when I told him each book was individually pitched and negotiated, thanks to my fear of commitment). But something shifted around me when he passed, and when my son, who is now thirteen and reminds me so much of him (truly just brimming with strongly worded letters), wanted to know which of my recipes he could pull off,

I realized how much I wanted to be able to hand my kids a collection of recipes specifically written with making them forever in mind.

I don't mean basics—*shudder*—not a cell in my body is motivated to teach you how to make compound butter. Nor do I mean "the last hundred recipes you'll ever need" or something a clever marketer would cook up; imagine feeling that confidently clairvoyant about all of your future cooking needs! (I could never.) No, keeper recipes accumulate everything I've learned that makes shopping easier, cooking more doable and enjoyable, and food more reliably delicious. It's what happens when you've read every one of the 350,000 comments that have appeared with your recipes since 2006 and absorbed them into your brainwaves; I'm never not thinking about how a stranger will feel making a recipe of mine on spec in their kitchen, with free time they're not sure they have, just because it promised greatness.

Here's what I consider a keeper recipe: It's a brilliantly fuss-free lemon poppy seed cake. It's my favorite way to roast winter squash. It's an epic quiche. It's a slow-roasted chicken on a bed of unapologetically schmaltzy croutons. It's the last apple crisp I personally will ever make, and I hope you feel the same. And, as you might have seen coming, I now think that the perfect pound cake exists. I nominate each of these recipes for *your* forever files.

I hope you know I have tested and tested each recipe, and, in every place I could, removed every single hurdle possible—sifting, needing extra bowls or extra rising times, separating eggs, measuring zest, lopping off stray tablespoons of flours because I love even measurements—without compromising the result. When I brought a dish to the table, everyone eating it was grilled on texture, seasoning, and execution. (Dinnertime has been a real hoot around here.)

And that is because keepers are recipes I hope you'll keep around for good. I want you to make them, love them (I hope), and quietly envision a future in which this dish will play a recurring role, because it doesn't just fit into your repertoire—it belongs there.

I realize it now sounds like I'm talking about a life partner, and not, say, the zucchini and pesto lasagna I hope you'll make every summer. It might be because, in my mind, I find it impossible to say the word "keeper" without hearing the residents at the nursing home where I used to work (that story for another time) singsonging in their Yiddish accents about boyfriends they approved of:

"He's a *keeper*!"

But these recipes don't care about your partner status. They are here, first and foremost, to bring joy to *you,* the cook.

Now, please understand that making every single recipe in this book worthy of lamination is, uh, a tall order, the cause of a dozen gray hairs, and unequivocally the reason I took five years

(and a few begged-for weeks) to finish this book. I cannot promise that. I can tell you this was the goal; it was the guiding voice nudging me along as I embraced, rejected, and waded through five hundred–plus jotted ideas to whittle them down to this hundred. If it pays off, and if you find a few keepers here for your forever files, I will soar over the tall buildings around me with glee.

So much for not being melodramatic, eh?

using this book

weights and salt I've included weights for every ingredient in this book of 15 grams or more with the exception of salt, for which all weights of 3 grams (or 1 teaspoon) or more are listed. I do this because there are no two types (table, kosher, sea, flaky) or brands of salt that will impart the same saltiness per teaspoon, maddening as it may be for home cooks. There is absolutely no reason to seek out any particular brand or variety of salt if it's not what your store carries; any salt you keep around will effectively season any dish. However, Diamond Crystal, my go-to kosher salt, is lighter, and therefore less salty than all other kosher brands per teaspoon.

If you're trying to figure out the "right" amount of salt per dish when kosher salt is called for, you can either use the weight as a guideline, or try this: **If you're using any other brand besides Diamond Crystal, simply start by using half of what the recipe recommends, in spoonfuls, and add more to taste.**

liquids I'm using weights instead of volume measurements for liquids here, based on the understanding that people who weigh most ingredients in a recipe probably do not want to root around their kitchen cabinets looking for a tablespoon or liquid measuring cup to check liquid measurements.

nonstick spray Throughout the book, I call for "nonstick spray" to coat baking pans and more. I'm referring to spray cooking oils, such as Pam, but if you don't keep one around, you can coat any baking pan with butter, margarine, or shortening instead.

neutral oil Throughout the book, I also call for "neutral oil." This refers to any cooking oil without flavor—usually vegetable, canola, grapeseed, or corn oils, but there are others. If the recipe calls for frying, make sure the neutral oil you use is one that is safe for high-heat cooking (that is, will not smoke or burn). This information will be on the oil's label.

finely grated cheese I love zesters and rasp tools (often referred to by the brand name Microplane) for finely grating garlic, ginger, nutmeg, and citrus zest, but *not* for finely grating hard cheeses, such as Pecorino or Parmesan. One cup will be a fluffy cloud of cheese that weighs significantly less than a cup of Parmesan grated on a traditional box grater. So when I call for "finely grated" Parmesan, put away your Microplane and use the small holes on a box grater, or presume you'll need more than the suggested measurement by half.

aluminum-free baking powder I prefer this when baking. I find the flavor less "tinny" and, when fresh fruit is present (see: Peach Crumb Muffins [page 13]), you're less likely to find blue-green streaks near the fruit.

breakfast anytime

I sure have a lot of breakfast recipes for someone whose breakfast is just a giant cup of coffee most mornings. Let me explain! First and foremost, not being a weekday breakfast person turns out not to be acceptable grounds for not feeding breakfast to my offspring, who perplex me by being morning people. Buckwheat pancakes with chocolate chips and a cheesy single-egg sandwich that can be made while you're still half asleep are no accident. More recipes in this section fall into the more leisurely weekend breakfast category, or need not be limited to the morning hours at all. Zucchini Cornbread is picnic-perfect; Slumped Parmesan Frittata is great for lunch, brunch, or a light dinner. Peanut Butter, Oat, and Jam Bars are a coveted afternoon snack of all household age groups. The Breakfast Potato Chips, with or without Sheet Pan Eggs, make a frequent appearance on our dinner table. And you can bring me those Challah Cheesecake Buns at any hour of the day; I do not mind one bit.

sour cream and flaky cheddar biscuits

makes 9 biscuits plus 1 snack

2¼ cups (295 grams) all-purpose flour

1½ teaspoons baking powder

½ teaspoon baking soda

1½ teaspoons (4 grams) kosher salt

A few grinds of black pepper

Heaped ¼ teaspoon onion powder

12 tablespoons (170 grams, or 6 ounces) unsalted butter, diced

4 ounces (115 grams) sharp cheddar, cut into ¼-inch cubes (heaped ¾ cup)

¾ cup (180 grams) sour cream

Flaky salt, to finish

This is the kind of biscuit you might make once on a whim, but should you make the "mistake," as I did, of sharing it with family, friends, or perhaps an entire pre-kindergarten classroom, do know that it will not be the last time you make them—because puddles of crispy cheddar cheese you can pick off in salty, lacy chiplike flakes make an impression on people. Initially, I'd intended to add spinach (just a handful of fresh leaves, chopped harmlessly small) for more of a breakfast-in-one-hearty-cube effect, yet, strangely, nobody in the four-year-old set seemed pleased with this when I offered to do so next time. Having tested it both ways many times since, I've realized they're not wrong.

If you, like me, love an accordion-like biscuit, with layers that spring tall, begging to be pulled apart in small, buttery squares, then the quarter-then-stack technique here (which I first learned from the wonderful Claire Saffitz) is so gloriously simple, you won't want to make breakfast biscuits another way. With no fancy folds or turns, and not even a rolling pin required, this has not-really-a-morning-person, aka me, written all over it.

———————

Heat the oven to 400°F (205°C), and line a baking sheet with parchment paper.

In a large bowl, whisk the flour, baking powder, baking soda, salt, black pepper, and onion powder. Add the butter to the bowl, and use your fingers or a pastry blender to squash the pieces into flatter bits, pinching and tossing until the mixture has tiny clumps throughout. Stir in the cheddar, then the sour cream. (The mixture will seem crumbly, but it will come together, I promise.)

Flour your counter, and dump the dough and any unmixed floury bits onto it, kneading it once or twice to bring it together. Pat the dough into a 1-inch-thick square. Use a knife or bench scraper to divide it into quarters; then stack the quarters. Repeat this process, patting the dough into a thick square a second time, re-flouring the counter if needed, and stuffing any loose scraps of dough between the layers. →

Transfer the dough slab to the prepared baking sheet, and pat it into a ¾-inch-tall square. Place the tray in the freezer and keep it there for 7 to 10 minutes, until it's cool and semi-firm to the touch. Remove from the freezer. Use a sharp knife to trim ¼ inch from each side, and squish these pieces into a bonus biscuit you do not need to tell anyone about. Cut the newly trimmed large square into nine approximately 2-inch-square biscuits, and space them out on the sheet. Sprinkle with flaky salt. (If you'd like to bake them another day, freeze them at this point. Let them warm up at room temperature for 15 minutes—they will not fully defrost—before baking.)

Bake the biscuits for 16 to 19 minutes, until they are deep golden brown at the edges and some cheese is melted in crisp puddles around the edges. Eat right away.

peanut butter, oat, and jam bars

makes 12 bars

¼ cup (50 grams) neutral oil, olive oil, or melted butter

¼ cup (80 to 85 grams) honey or maple syrup

¼ cup (65 grams) peanut butter, any kind

1 teaspoon (3 grams) kosher salt

¾ teaspoon baking powder

1½ cups (150 grams) quick-cooking rolled oats

½ cup (65 grams) whole-wheat flour

½ cup (160 grams) jam, any kind

3 tablespoons (30 grams) roughly chopped salted peanuts

note If you need these bars to be peanut-free, use almond butter. If you need them nut-free, use sunflower-seed butter. For both versions, omit the chopped peanuts.

A common conversation in my family when we're eating something wonderful away from home is "Wait, you know how to make this? Why haven't you?" And they all glare at me and shake their heads in seemingly-joking-but-you-can-never-quite-tell disappointment. It's true, though. Why *haven't* I made nacho fries, Nutella-stuffed doughnuts, or those pork wontons in chili oil I never want to stop slurping? "Hours in the day!" I insist, but on the inside, I can't help but wonder (it's okay to use your Carrie Bradshaw voice here): Am I just stubborn? Bored? Have I fallen prey to that food-writer trait in which we are fatigued by what's already out there and must always chase new combinations that, at times, nobody has asked for?

Which brings me to: peanut butter and jelly, obviously the greatest of flavor combinations, which I took far too long to apply to breakfast bars, for no reason other than stubbornness. But then I was out-stubborned by my own daughter (that's my mother smirking in the background), who is so picky she rejected all of my granola-ish treats until I made them taste like the only sandwich she will eat. I hardly mind these thin, crisp bars, either; they're shockingly delicious, considering how earnest they read—no refined sugar, no white flour, not even dairy. And they're a cinch to make, as breakfast treats should be.

———————

Heat the oven to 350°F (175°C). Lightly coat an 8-by-8-inch baking pan with nonstick spray, then line it with two pieces of parchment paper in opposite directions, extending each sheet up the opposite sides to create a parchment sling.

In a large bowl, whisk together the oil, honey, peanut butter, and salt. Whisk in the baking powder; then stir in the oats and flour. Set aside ½ cup of this peanut-butter mixture, and press the remaining batter evenly across the bottom of the prepared pan; it will be a thin layer, but try the best you can to avoid making holes. Dollop the jam on top, and spread/nudge it almost to the edges. Sprinkle the reserved ½ cup peanut-butter mixture evenly on top, in smaller clumps for best coverage. Scatter with chopped peanuts. →

peanut butter, oat, and jam bars *(continued)*

Bake for 20 to 25 minutes, until nicely browned at the edges and golden across the top. Transfer to the fridge to chill; I find these easiest to cut when they are cold. Once they're cool and firm, tilt your pan and gently pull on an end of the parchment sling to slide the bars onto a cutting board. Use a sharp serrated knife to cut them into a four-by-three grid, making twelve bars. Store the leftover bars in the fridge for up to a week, or in the freezer, packed tightly with parchment between the layers, for up to 2 months.

my bodega-style egg-and-cheese

makes 1 sandwich

1 large egg

Kosher salt and freshly ground black pepper

2 teaspoons butter or oil

1 slice cheese, or a small pile of grated or crumbled cheese

Spoonful of sliced scallions, chives, crumbled bacon, or whatever else you want in your eggs

1 English muffin or roll, or 2 slices bread of your choice, toasted

Most New Yorkers have strong opinions on the classic bacon, egg, and cheese sandwich (BEC), and mine—since I'm a person who is constitutionally incapable of multitasking—is a mix of awe for the griddle cooks who make half a dozen egg sandwiches with special requests all at once like it's nothing; and gratitude for the bodegas that let me buy a warm breakfast sandwich, pet the cat-in-residence, and grab dish soap at the same time.

My order is always an egg-and-cheese on rye toast, and truly one of the most blessed things about New York City is that rye bread is considered a standard bread option. My only quibble with these sandwiches is that often the cheese isn't melted enough, either because it was not engineered with melting in mind (ghastly) or it was added as an afterthought. At home, however, my technique fixes this problem by pocketing the cheese in the center. If you're appalled by my choice of individually wrapped cheese, you can of course use any cheese that makes you happy, be it crumbled, grated, or sliced; you can add minced scallions, chives, or crumbled bacon, too—but I think cheese engineered with melting in mind deserves more credit. The awesome thing about this sandwich is that it's so easy, it requires no planning, and you can be eating these in approximately 3 minutes, which is exactly what I want to hear at 9:00 a.m. on a Saturday. This makes one single-egg sandwich, but you can also make it with two eggs and just cook it slightly longer.

———

Heat a medium-sized skillet, preferably nonstick, over medium-high heat. Beat one egg with ½ teaspoon of water, a couple pinches of salt, and a few grinds of black pepper until just blended.

Melt the butter in your pan or brush it with oil, to coat it thinly. Pour in the egg, and roll it around so it coats the pan, as a thin crêpe would. Immediately place your cheese and optional other fillings in the middle. Cook for 30 to 45 seconds, or until the egg is lightly set but not browned underneath. →

my bodega-style egg-and-cheese *(continued)*

Fold the part of the egg closest to you over the cheese, as if you were folding the first section of a business letter. Repeat this on the three remaining "sides," forming a small square, or you can aim for more of a rectangle if that's the shape of your bread. Leave the folded egg-and-cheese in the center of the skillet to cook for another 30 seconds, then slide it onto your muffin or one slice of toast. Top the sandwich with the other piece of toast, if using, cut in half, and eat immediately. Notice a couple sets of eyes gazing at you, perhaps wondering where their sandwiches might be. Repeat a couple more times and not even mind, because it's so easy.

peach crumb muffins

makes 12 muffins

3 medium-large (1 to 1½ pounds, or 455 to 680 grams, total) ripe, even very ripe, peaches

8 tablespoons (½ cup, 4 ounces, or 115 grams) unsalted butter, melted

¾ cup (150 grams) granulated sugar

1 teaspoon (3 grams), plus a pinch, kosher salt

2¼ cups (295 grams) all-purpose flour, divided

1 cup (230 grams) plain yogurt, any variety

2 large eggs

2 teaspoons baking powder

½ teaspoon baking soda

½ teaspoon ground cinnamon

½ teaspoon ground ginger

note These also taste great with ½ teaspoon ground cardamom added. You can use other stone fruit here, too—nectarines, plums, or apricots—but be sure you have 1½ cups chopped, plus slices for decoration.

Have you ever noticed, how shall I say this politely, a gap between the kinds of muffins that catch our eye in a coffee-shop case—tall, craggy, rich, bronzed—and the kind we most often make at home—brown, squat, with vague promises of wholesomeness? Consider this muffin something of a redemption. This is my bakery-est muffin, but one that tastes phenomenal, and it wants to go to potlucks and picnics and showers and brunches with you. It unapologetically wants to be the thing that disappears first.

For as long as I can remember, I've been pursued by a vision of a peach muffin that was the Platonic ideal of a peach crumble's worth of fruit stuffed into a sturdy muffin base. The peaches would be fanned on top, and baked skin-on, leaving fuchsia streaks around them. The crumbs would actually adhere. But, because I'm still me, I wanted the sweetness in check, and I wanted to do all this in as few steps as possible. Over three peach seasons, and forty-plus testing rounds (if we know each other in real life, I've shoved these in your hands but told you they weren't good yet; thanks for being polite about it), I can finally say that I could not be happier to get them into your hands.

———————

Heat the oven to 375°F (190°C). Line twelve standard muffin cups with paper liners, or coat with nonstick spray.

Halve, pit, and thinly slice the peaches. Set twenty-four to thirty-six slices aside for decoration; if the slices are longer than the muffin cups, trim them down. Chop the remaining peach slices into small pieces. You need only 1½ cups; the rest are snacks.

Mix the butter, sugar, a pinch of salt, and half of the flour (1 cup plus 2 tablespoons, or 145 grams) in a large bowl until it forms a clumpy mixture. Remove 6 semi-packed tablespoons (about 115 grams) and set it aside; this will be your crumbs. Add the yogurt and eggs to the big bowl of crumbs, and whisk to combine; it's okay if it doesn't get totally smooth. Add the baking powder, baking soda, cinnamon, and ginger, and whisk well. Stir in the remaining flour and chopped peaches just until the flour disappears. $\rightarrow$

peach crumb muffins *(continued)*

Spoon the muffin batter into the prepared cups; it will fill them nearly to the top. Arrange two or three fanned slices of peach on top of each. Divide the reserved streusel over the muffins, using it up. Nudge any that spills off back onto the cups of batter.

Bake for 20 to 22 minutes, or until a toothpick inserted under the peach slices comes out batter-free. Let the muffins rest in the baking tin for 5 minutes before removing. Eat these warm or at room temperature.

do ahead Leftover muffins keep for 2 days at room temperature; I like to keep them in their baking pan but uncovered. The peach slices on top keep things moist, but the air keeps the crumbs from getting mushy.

slumped parmesan frittata

serves 4, or 6 as part of
a spread

2 tablespoons (30 grams)
unsalted butter

1 large shallot, minced
(about ½ cup)

Kosher salt

1½ tablespoons cornstarch

10 large eggs

Freshly ground black pepper

1 cup (235 grams) whole
or low-fat milk

1 cup (100 grams, or 3½ ounces)
finely grated Parmesan, plus a
spoonful for garnish

2 teaspoons red-wine vinegar

1½ tablespoons (20 grams)
olive oil

1 cup (6 ounces, or 170 grams)
cherry tomatoes, halved

2 cups (2 ounces) mixed salad
greens

1 tablespoon chopped fresh
herbs (parsley, mint, chives)
(optional)

Over the years, as the time of day when I served frittatas moved from breakfast to lunch to dinner, my frittatas got busier and busier—every speck of the pan cluttered with potatoes, bacon, greens, and more. I love them, but this version goes intentionally, abruptly in the other direction. Here, the busiest parts aren't buried in the eggs but heaped on top, where they keep their crunch and provide a bright contrast. The frittata departs from the usual in other ways, too. Tired of starting frittatas on the stove and playing guessing games about the right moment to switch them to the oven, I chose to make this one entirely in the oven. It's so much easier that way, much harder to over- or undercook. Weary of frittatas sticking to my ovenproof skillets, no matter how buttered or well seasoned, I bake this in a sling of pleated parchment paper, and it always releases cleanly; plus, I love the edges it creates. A little bit of cornstarch provides a silky, rich texture. I use more milk than would ever be traditional to keep it tender, and flavor it only with a shallot cooked in butter, sharp Parmesan, and black pepper, which also turns out to be all it needs. By design, it comes out of the oven puffed and dramatic and then deflates a little, leaving a perfect spot in the center for the kind of sharp breakfast salad that is the best complement to all frittatas. The sides sigh a bit, and I love how rustic it looks, served right on the parchment. Can a frittata be a centerpiece? This one is pleading its best case.

———————

Heat the oven to 425°F (220°C). Line a 9-inch round cake pan with a 12-inch square of parchment paper, pressing it into the bottom and pleating it as much as necessary to line the sides. It will be "rustic"—just go with it.

Melt the butter in a small frying pan over medium heat. Reserve 1 tablespoon of the shallot, and set it aside. Add the remaining shallot and a pinch of salt, and cook, stirring, until the shallot is soft and just golden at the edges, about 5 to 7 minutes. Scrape it into a large bowl and let cool. $\rightarrow$

Stir the cornstarch into the shallot until the cornstarch disappears, then add the eggs, 1¼ teaspoons salt, and an arm-fatiguing number of grinds of pepper, and whisk to combine. Whisk in the milk; then stir in the cheese. Pour the egg mixture into the prepared pan, and bake the eggs for 18 to 20 minutes, until just set.

While the frittata bakes, prepare your salad. Add the reserved raw shallot to an empty bowl with the red-wine vinegar. Set aside and let it rest for 5 minutes. Add the olive oil and tomatoes, toss to coat, and season them well with salt and pepper.

Remove the frittata from the oven, and let it cool in the pan on a rack for 5 minutes. Use this time to add the salad greens to the tomatoes, tossing to coat them evenly. Lift the frittata by the parchment, using two hands, and transfer it to a serving plate. Heap the salad in the center, garnish with salt, black pepper, herbs, if using, and the remaining spoonful of Parmesan. Cut the frittata into wedges, and serve.

chocolate chip buckwheat pancakes

makes 18 small pancakes

1 tablespoon (15 grams) unsalted butter, melted, plus more for pan

½ cup mashed banana, from 1 large (about 8 ounces, or 225 grams, unpeeled), very ripe banana

¾ cup (170 grams) buttermilk, plus more as needed

1 tablespoon (15 grams) brown or granulated sugar

1 large egg

½ teaspoon vanilla extract

½ teaspoon kosher salt

1 teaspoon baking powder

1 teaspoon baking soda

1 cup (150 grams) buckwheat flour

½ cup (85 grams) semisweet chocolate chips

Why challenge myself to create a 100-percent buckwheat pancake that's not dry or brittle or tastes like something you "ought" to eat? Because buckwheat is delicious: nutty and almost faintly tangy, with a silky-but-hearty crumb. It deserves a spotlight, and it shouldn't have to share it with wholesome proclamations. To drive this point home, I've added chocolate chips. Okay, fine, I added chocolate chips because I have children, and because the combination of buckwheat, chocolate, and banana is one of my favorites. The recipe is one-bowl, and the yield is on the low side, just enough for us four, because, to be completely honest, I don't like standing in front of a pan flipping pancakes for very long, and certainly not before I've had my coffee. And, while we're being honest, I need to tell you one final thing: buckwheat pancakes love butter. We're not going to go restaurant-style, with a soup ladle per pan, but I do recommend a hearty pat. When you bite into the kind of crisp-edged pancake you can only get from buckwheat, you'll know why.

Whisk together 1 tablespoon melted butter, banana, and ¾ cup buttermilk in a large bowl. Whisk in the sugar, egg, vanilla, and salt. Sprinkle the surface of the batter with baking powder and baking soda, and whisk it thoroughly to combine. Add the flour and chocolate chips, and mix until they disappear. The batter should be on the thick side, but if it seems closer to cookie dough, add 1 to 2 more tablespoons of buttermilk, until you get a looser consistency.

Heat a large nonstick skillet over medium heat and coat the pan with a very generous pat of butter. Scoop the pancakes to your preferred size— a 2-tablespoon scoop makes 3-inch pancakes—giving them room to spread. Cook until bubbles appear on the surface and the edges look slightly dry, about 2 to 3 minutes. Flip and cook the pancakes until they're set and turning a shade darker underneath, for another 2 minutes. Reduce the heat to medium-low if the pancakes are darkening too quickly. Transfer them to a platter, and repeat with more butter and the remaining batter.

Leftovers, which I do not believe you'll have, reheat well on a baking sheet in a 350°F (175°C) oven.

breakfast potato chips and sheet pan eggs

serves 2 to 4

Olive oil

1 teaspoon (3 grams) kosher salt, plus more for eggs

Many grinds of black pepper

½ teaspoon mild or hot smoked paprika

½ teaspoon onion powder

1 pound (455 grams) Yukon Gold potatoes, unpeeled, sliced ⅛ inch thick

4 large eggs

note Cooking times here are *all* about thickness. If your potatoes are paper-thin going in, they'll cook faster; if they're closer to ¼ inch thick, they'll cook slower. If you'd like to make these without the eggs, that's fine; the potatoes need 5 to 8 minutes baking time once flipped.

I think the world would be a better place if we all accepted that sometimes we just want potato chips for a meal, "balance" and "forks" be damned. They're . . . a vegetable, right? (Shh, don't tell me.) These breakfast potatoes embrace this urge. Over the years, I've made and loved every kind of breakfast potato, from hash browns to home fries and even giant breakfast latkes, but these are the ones I make that get snatched from the pan, because potato chips for breakfast are fun. Here the potatoes are baked, not fried. Except for the need to cut them thin, they're low-fuss. Sprinkling them with salt, pepper, paprika, and onion powder makes them taste especially home-fries-ish. When you drop in a couple eggs for the last 5 minutes, it becomes a true sheet-pan breakfast. As they bake, the eggs attach to a halo of chips around them, perfect for plucking off and dipping into the egg at the table.

Heat the oven to 400°F (205°C). Line a half-sheet (13-by-18-inch) pan with parchment paper, and drizzle it with olive oil. Combine the salt, pepper, paprika, and onion powder in a small dish, and sprinkle half over the oiled parchment. Arrange the potatoes in a single, slightly overlapped layer on the parchment. Drizzle them with a little more oil, and use your fingers or a brush to help it coat the potatoes more evenly. Sprinkle with the remaining spices. Bake for 20 minutes, or until some of the potatoes are golden underneath or at their edges. Flip the potatoes; I use a large spatula or tongs and rearrange them, as needed, for even cooking. Return the pan to the oven and cook for 3 to 4 minutes; then take the pan out once more, and push the potato chips into four open-centered nests, leaving a 3-inch space in the middle of each. Crack an egg into each opening, sprinkle with additional salt and pepper, and return the pan to the oven for 4½ to 6 minutes, or until the whites are set and yolks are still soft. Give the pan a shimmy to see if the white part of the egg is shaking; if it is, put the pan back in for another minute. Slide the eggs and any chips around them onto plates, and eat right away.

zucchini cornbread and tomato butter

makes 9 servings

butter

1 cup (6 ounces, or 170 grams) cherry or grape tomatoes, halved (lengthwise if grape)

½ teaspoon kosher salt

Freshly ground black pepper

½ cup (4 ounces, or 115 grams) unsalted butter, cold

bread

¼ cup (2 ounces, or 55 grams) unsalted butter, melted

⅓ cup (70 grams) neutral oil or olive oil

2 large eggs

2 teaspoons (6 grams) kosher salt

½ cup (115 grams) buttermilk

1 cup (6½ ounces, or 185 grams) packed coarsely grated zucchini

½ cup (70 grams) fresh or frozen corn kernels (no need to defrost if frozen)

½ cup (45 grams, or 1½ ounces) minced scallions (white and green parts)

½ teaspoon baking soda

1¼ teaspoons baking powder

¾ cup plus 2 tablespoons (125 grams) cornmeal

1⅓ cups (175 grams) all-purpose flour

Much as I love cinnamon, brown sugar, and passing cake off as breakfast, it is unclear to me why it has been considered an official statute of the summer baking handbook that zucchini in baked goods must be sweet. I believe this cornbread to be equally worthy of your warm-weather baking canon: a savory loaf that enlists the peak-season garden trifecta of zucchini, tomatoes, and corn, plus also scallions, should you have stuck some in soil. For a summer breakfast, we love this bread fresh (or toasted, if leftovers) with scrambled eggs and grilled bacon. I also like it for picnics and potlucks—it goes so well with a salad and meat-and-cheese spread. Mostly, I love that it's quintessentially summery and almost impossible to mess up.

———————

Heat the oven to 350°F (175°C). Lightly coat a small (about 1-quart) baking dish with butter or a nonstick spray.

Start the tomato butter: Arrange the tomatoes cut side up and bake for 40 to 45 minutes, until they are softened and beginning to shrivel. Transfer them to a blender or food processor, and blend with ½ teaspoon kosher salt and many grinds of black pepper until smooth. Leave them in the work bowl until they are lukewarm.

Meanwhile, make the cornbread: Lightly coat an 8-inch square baking pan with nonstick spray. For easier removal, you can line it with a piece of parchment that extends up two sides of the pan. In a large bowl, whisk the butter, oil, eggs, and salt together. Add the buttermilk, and whisk to combine. Mix in the zucchini, corn, and scallions. Sprinkle the baking soda and baking powder over the batter, and mix it in thoroughly. Add the cornmeal and flour, and mix only until they disappear.

Pour the batter into the prepared pan, spread it until smooth, and bake for 28 to 33 minutes, or until a toothpick inserted into the center comes out batter-free. (It bakes at the same temperature as the tomatoes and can join them in the oven if the tomatoes aren't done yet.) Transfer the zucchini bread to a cooling rack. →

zucchini cornbread and tomato butter *(continued)*

Finish the butter: Cut the butter into chunks, and add it to the tomatoes in the blender or food processor. Blend until evenly combined and whipped, scraping the machine down a few times with a spatula. Adjust the seasoning to taste.

To serve: Cut the cornbread into squares, and serve with tomato butter alongside, for spreading.

notes

- I like the combination of butter and oil here for crumb and flavor, but you can use all of one or the other if that's your dietary preference or grocery necessity.
- No, we are not going to wring out the zucchini; I wouldn't do that to us, but especially to me; plus, the moisture here is essential.
- I use a medium-grind cornmeal, but just about any kind will do.
- I did not feel the need to add cheese, but you absolutely can—usually 6 ounces coarsely grated cheddar does the trick.
- The cornbread can also be baked in a 9-inch cast-iron skillet or a 9-inch round cake pan; the baking time will be about the same.

caramelized cinnamon sugar french toast

serves 4

2 large eggs

1 cup (235 grams) milk, whole or low-fat

One 12-ounce (340-gram) baguette, cut on an angle into 1-inch slices

3 tablespoons (45 grams) butter, salted or unsalted

½ cup (100 grams) granulated sugar

2 teaspoons ground cinnamon

note This recipe is great with either unsalted or salted butter; use the latter if you prefer a saltier note in French toast.

In my first cookbook, I vowed, after discovering baked French toast, that I would never, ever fry it again. Why stand over a hot stove, dipping and flipping and trying to keep the first slices warm while the last ones cook, when you could just put the pan into the oven and walk away? From there we made a cinnamon-toast French-toast casserole, which remains a favorite for entertaining. At home on a Sunday morning, though? I've been holding out on you for too long.

Once I started making French toast with baguettes, I never looked back. It's in part practicality—baguettes are inexpensive and go stale as soon as you blink, perfect for resuscitating the next morning—but I also love the contrast: the slight saltiness of a baguette against a sugary coating, the crispness of the crust against the plush center. When these custard-soaked, cinnamon-sugar-dipped baguette slices bake on a buttered sheet pan at high heat, they caramelize all over and slightly hollow in the center, reminding me of the churros we've eaten in Spain, and if there is any better reason to get out of bed on a weekend morning, well, I don't believe you.

Heat the oven to 425°F (220°C). In a large bowl, beat the eggs and milk until evenly combined. Add the bread, and toss a few times so all the pieces are coated. Set aside for 10 minutes.

While the egg/bread mixture rests, line a rimmed half-sheet (13-by-18-inch) pan tightly with foil, which will ensure that no caramelized sugar gets left behind. Add the butter to the pan, and place it in the oven until the butter melts, about 3 minutes. Remove it from the oven, and roll the butter around to coat the foil evenly.

Combine the sugar and cinnamon in a medium bowl, and remove 1 tablespoon of the mixture, setting it aside. Use a fork to lift the bread from the egg mixture, letting the excess drip off. Quickly roll the bread in the larger bowl of cinnamon sugar, so it's lightly coated on all sides. Place the bread on the buttered baking sheet, and repeat with the remaining slices, spacing them out. $\rightarrow$

caramelized cinnamon sugar french toast *(continued)*

Bake for 9 to 10 minutes, or until the slices turn a deep golden brown underneath. Flip them, and bake for 3 to 5 minutes on the second side, aiming for the same color. Remove the pan from the oven, and sprinkle the slices with the reserved cinnamon sugar. Transfer the French toast to a serving plate within the first couple minutes it's out of the oven, or the melted sugar will fuse them to the foil. (If this happens, just rewarm in the oven until the sugar releases.)

Serve exactly as is—seriously, these need nothing on top—but my family doesn't agree, so we often add chocolate spread and berries.

three breakfast salads

I love breakfast salads. I quietly bristle at the way most breakfast menus make you choose sides—the salty (bacon, sausage, eggs, bagels and lox) or the very sweet (doughnuts, sticky buns, the cereals my kids beg me for, like I once begged my own parents)—when what I love the most is the middle ground: something fresh and bright. As part of a decadent brunch spread, it's an oasis. As a weekend staple along with the kid-pleasing pancakes and French toast, it offers some balance. For a home breakfast when I'm not craving anything heavy, it hits the spot. Though most of my breakfast salads come from a very cheffy, culinarily advanced place I call "whatever we have around, arranged on a plate," I return to these three again and again. I hope you use them as a jumping-off point for whatever is in your fridge.

honeydew with avocado and almonds

serves 2

½ cup (70 grams) almonds, roughly chopped

¼ cup (50 grams) olive oil

Flaky sea salt

Aleppo or another flaked red pepper

½ medium honeydew melon (2 to 2½ pounds, or about 1 kilogram), peeled, seeded

1 medium-large firm-ripe avocado

Juice of 1 lime

½ teaspoon ground sumac

Combine the almonds with olive oil in a small skillet, then turn the heat to medium. Cook, stirring, for 2 to 3 minutes, or until the oil is bubbling and the almonds are toasted. Keep a close eye on them; raw almonds may be able to handle more time, but roasted almonds will need less. Remove from the heat before the biggest pieces are golden, and pour them into a small bowl. Season with a couple pinches of salt and pepper flakes and set aside.

Cut the honeydew into eight wedges, and cut each wedge into narrow, thin slices. Halve the avocado, remove the pit, and cut the flesh into thin slices. On a large plate, arrange the melon and avocado. Squeeze lime juice over the fruit, and season the whole plate with salt, pepper flakes, and sumac. Spoon the almonds and olive oil over the top.

citrus with radishes and hazelnuts

1 large watermelon radish, or 4 or 5 red or breakfast radishes

2 tablespoons (25 grams) olive oil, plus more to taste

2 tablespoons (30 grams) lemon juice, plus more to taste

Kosher salt and freshly ground black pepper

2 large oranges, any variety

¼ cup (40 grams) hazelnuts, toasted, loose skins removed, coarsely chopped

Halve (or quarter if radish is very large) radish lengthwise and thinly slice. Place the radish slices in a bowl with 2 tablespoons olive oil, 2 tablespoons lemon juice, several grinds of black pepper, and a couple generous pinches of salt.

Trim all the peel and pith from the oranges; then—holding the peeled fruit over the bowl of radishes—use a sharp knife to cut citrus segments from their membrane and drop them into the bowl. Squeeze out any remaining juice from the citrus membrane. Add the hazelnuts, and stir to combine with the radishes and dressing. Add more olive oil, lemon juice, salt, or pepper, to taste.

tomatoes with cottage cheese and bagel seeds

serves 1 or 2

¾ pound or 340 grams cherry tomatoes (2 cups), halved, or large tomatoes in wedges

Olive oil

Coarse sea salt

Freshly ground black pepper

1 cup (220 grams) full-fat cottage cheese

1 teaspoon sesame seeds

1 teaspoon poppy seeds

½ teaspoon dried minced onion or garlic, or ¼ teaspoon of each

In a bowl, toss the tomatoes with 1 tablespoon olive oil, a few pinches of salt, and a few grinds of black pepper. Let the tomatoes marinate for 5 minutes. Meanwhile, use the back of a spoon to spread the cottage cheese smoothly on a plate. Drizzle with olive oil, and season with coarse sea salt and black pepper. Spoon the tomatoes and any juices over the cottage cheese, and sprinkle the top with sesame seeds, poppy seeds, dried onion and/or garlic, and more salt and pepper as needed.

note This is an homage to my late grandma Helen, who, every morning, ate a toasted, scooped-out bagel filled with cottage cheese and a slice of tomato on top. You can, of course, use a prepared everything-bagel seeds mix here instead, if you have it around.

bialy babka

makes 1 loaf, or 8 to 10 slices

dough

4 tablespoons (2 ounces, or 55 grams) unsalted butter, melted

6 tablespoons (90 grams) whole or low-fat milk

1¾ teaspoons instant yeast

1 tablespoon (15 grams) granulated sugar

1½ teaspoons (4 grams) kosher salt

1 large egg, plus 1 large egg yolk

2¼ cups (295 grams) all-purpose flour

filling

2 tablespoons (1 ounce, or 30 grams) unsalted butter

1½ pounds (680 grams) yellow onions, diced

1½ teaspoons (4 grams) kosher salt

2 teaspoons poppy seeds, plus more to finish

A bialy—Yiddish shorthand for *bialystoker kuchen,* hailing from Białystok, Poland—is a palm-sized chewy roll with an indentation filled with cooked onions and poppy seeds. Warm from the oven, spread with butter, it is, to me, simple bliss. A bialy babka is elaborate bliss. It's what happens when you take those same flavors and ribbon and twist them through a stretchy, rich dough, then bake it into a perfectly proportioned loaf—with way more than a pinch of onion per serving, hooray. The ingredient list isn't long, hard to procure, or pricy, but what comes out of the oven is something of unbelievable beauty, aroma, and flavor—a favorite fall baking project.

You can slice it and eat it warm, either plain or spread with butter or cream cheese (and even lox). You can eat a slice toasted with a bowl of soup, as we sometimes do for dinner, or for breakfast the next day, with an egg. Want to make a French Onion Babka? Sprinkle 1 to 2 cups of grated cheese (such as Comté, baby Swiss, or Gruyère) on the onions before you roll it. But you must believe me, this needs nothing extra to be savory perfection.

———————

Make the dough: In the bowl of a stand mixer, whisk together the butter, milk, yeast, sugar, salt, egg, and yolk until blended. Add the flour, and use a dough hook to bring the mixture together and knead on low speed for 5 to 7 minutes, until the dough is stretchy but soft. Transfer it to an oiled bowl, cover tightly with plastic, and set aside for 1½ to 2 hours in a warm spot, until just about doubled—it will grow from about 2 cups to about 4. Additional advice: If your kitchen runs cold, or things seem to be moving very slowly, heat your oven to 200°F (95°C) for a few minutes, turn it off, place your bowl in there, and let it stay there for the remainder of the rising time. It should move along more quickly.

(For a longer rise, or to finish baking the following day, you can chill the dough in the fridge. Just remember to take it out about 1½ hours before baking, so it has time to warm up again before you roll it out.)

While the dough rises, cook your onions: Melt the butter in a large sauté pan over medium heat. Add the onions, toss to coat them in the butter, →

bialy babka (*continued*)

and cover the pot. Reduce the heat to medium-low, and let the onions slowly steep for 12 to 15 minutes, stirring once or twice. You can walk away.

Uncover the pot, raise the heat slightly, and stir in the salt. Cook the onions, stirring every 5 minutes, for another 20 to 30 minutes, until they are golden brown and very tender and sweet. No need to fully caramelize them, as you would for onion soup, which would take much longer. Raise the heat to medium-high, and cook the onions until they get a little dark at the edges, about another 5 minutes. Transfer them to a plate, and spread them out so that they cool faster.

Assemble the babka: On a large, well-floured counter, roll out the dough until it is about 12 inches wide on the side closest to you and as far away from you as you can make it when rolling it very thin, likely 10 to 14 inches. Spoon and then spread the onions over the dough in an even layer; then sprinkle the onions with 2 teaspoons poppy seeds. Roll up the dough with the filling, rolling it away from you into a tight coil. Transfer the coil to a parchment-lined baking sheet or board, place it in your freezer, and let it chill for 5 to 10 minutes. (You will be able to cut it in half much more cleanly if the dough has been chilled.) While it's there . . .

Prepare the pan: Coat a standard loaf pan with butter or nonstick spray, and line the bottom and two sides with a sling of parchment paper for easier removal.

Finish shaping the babka: Remove the dough from the freezer, and use a serrated knife to cut the log gently lengthwise into two long strips; lay them next to each other, cut sides up. Lift one side over the next, forming a twist and trying to keep the cut sides facing up (because they're pretty). Don't worry if this step seems messy; it will be gorgeous regardless. Transfer the twist to your prepared loaf pan.

Let the dough proof again: Cover the pan with the same plastic wrap you used earlier, and let it rise another 45 minutes at room temperature. You won't see much of a change in the size, and that's fine; we're just letting the dough relax a little.

Heat your oven to 350°F (175°C). $\longrightarrow$

bialy babka *(continued)*

Bake the babka: Sprinkle the babka with a few extra pinches of poppy seeds. Bake for 40 to 45 minutes, until a skewer inserted into the center doesn't feel like it's hitting sticky/rubbery dough, or until the internal temperature is 185°F (85°C). If the onions get too brown on top (mine did), you can cover the babka with foil for the last few minutes, but unless they fully burn, it will taste great regardless.

Serve the babka: Let it cool for 10 to 20 minutes, then cut it into thick slices with a serrated knife. Leftovers keep at room temperature for a few days; I usually wrap it in foil. Gently toast slices to rewarm.

challah cheesecake buns

makes 12 buns

dough

2 large eggs, plus 1 large
egg yolk

¼ cup (50 grams) granulated
sugar

½ cup (115 grams) butter,
melted, then cooled, plus more
for the mixing bowl

⅔ cup (155 grams) milk,
any variety

3¾ cups (490 grams) all-purpose
flour

1 packet (2¼ teaspoons,
or 7 grams) instant yeast

1¼ teaspoons (4 grams) kosher
salt

filling and assembly

8 ounces (225 grams) cream
cheese, softened

⅓ cup (65 grams) granulated
sugar

¼ teaspoon vanilla extract

¾ cup (240 grams) raspberry
jam, or another that you prefer

1 large egg, beaten with
1 teaspoon water for wash

Poppy seeds, for sprinkling

glaze (optional)

2 cups (240 grams)
confectioners' sugar

3 to 4 tablespoons
(45 to 60 grams) lemon juice

My father grew up in the Bronx, and he told me that after school they'd sometimes go to the corner deli and get cream-cheese-and-jelly sandwiches. He spoke wistfully of these days, when nobody balked at putting a 1-inch-thick slab (or so he dramatically remembered it) of cream cheese on a sandwich, with no ruminations about cholesterol or arteries. Since then, I've always associated this combination with him, but felt the part he left out of the story is that cream cheese and jam together taste like cheesecake, or one of those cheese Danishes I never see enough anymore. Challah bread, stretchy and enriched with eggs and oil, is a close cousin to brioche, and I've had fun tweaking it to make breakfast buns with the easiest and most forgiving dough you could possibly imagine. The filling will seem messy as you roll and slice it, but, no matter how crooked they look going into the pan, they are stunning when they emerge from the oven the next morning, glossed to a high challah shine. A lemon glaze is optional but delicious here, especially because the buns aren't heavily sweetened.

Make the dough: Whisk together the eggs, yolk, granulated sugar, butter, and milk in the bottom of a stand-mixer bowl. Add the flour, yeast, and salt, and mix with the dough hook on low until it comes together; then let the machine knead it for about 5 minutes. Scrape the dough onto a lightly floured counter, and leave it there just long enough so you can coat a mixing bowl with oil; return the dough to the oiled bowl, cover it loosely, and let it rise until doubled, about 2 hours.

For the filling and assembly: Butter a 13-by-9-inch (or equivalent size) baking dish, or coat it with nonstick spray.

Combine the cream cheese, granulated sugar, and vanilla in a medium bowl (I just use a fork to mix this).

On a very well-floured counter, roll out the dough into a rectangle about 16 inches wide on the side facing you and as far away from you as it comfortably goes, usually 13 to 15 inches. $\rightarrow$

challah cheesecake buns *(continued)*

Spread the cream cheese mixture all over the rolled-out dough. Dollop the jam over it, and spread it smooth. Roll the dough into a snug spiral; it will stretch to about 18 inches wide.

Cut the log very gently—it's going to be a soft mess, so use a sharp serrated knife or flavorless dental floss—into 1½-inch segments. Arrange all the pieces in the prepared baking dish. Brush the tops of the buns with the egg wash, and cover with plastic wrap.

From here, you can opt for one of two schedules: Refrigerate the buns overnight, along with the leftover egg wash (both covered), or you can chill the buns for just 30 minutes and bake them right away. If you're using the overnight method, remove the buns from the fridge in the morning and let them warm up for 30 minutes before baking; if you're using the faster chill, no need to give them warm-up time.

Heat your oven to 350°F (175°C).

Brush the tops of the buns with a second coat of egg wash, and sprinkle with poppy seeds. Bake until the buns are bronzed all over and have an internal temperature of 190°F (90°C), about 30 minutes. Let cool slightly before serving.

For the glaze, if using: Whisk the confectioners' sugar together with 3 tablespoons lemon juice until smooth, drizzling in an additional tablespoon of lemon juice if needed to loosen the glaze. Drizzle this over the warm buns, or serve it alongside with a spoon.

blueberry pancake cobbler

serves 4

2 cups (565 grams) fresh blueberries

Grated zest and juice of ½ lemon

4 tablespoons (2 ounces, or 55 grams) unsalted butter, melted

½ teaspoon kosher salt

6 tablespoons (75 grams) granulated sugar, divided

6 tablespoons (85 grams) whole milk or buttermilk

½ teaspoon vanilla extract

1 teaspoon baking powder

¼ cup (35 grams) whole-wheat flour

½ cup (65 grams) all-purpose flour

¼ cup (60 grams) hot water

notes

- This cobbler is on the petite side, serving my family of four in moderate portions, but it can easily be doubled in an 8-by-8-inch or 2-quart baking dish to give more servings, or tripled in a 9-by-13-inch or 3-quart baking dish.

- You can also make this entirely with either whole-wheat or all-purpose flour.

- Buttermilk or regular milk works here; buttermilk provides a bit more of a pancake-y tang.

- This is easily veganized with a nondairy fat (margarine or oil) and milk (almond, oat, or soy).

I'm keenly interested in the place where baked fruit desserts and breakfast might intersect, even if I must nudge them there. What is the difference, after all, between an oaty crisp topping on seasonal fruit after dinner and an oaty granola topping on seasonal fruit early in the day? Sugar level? Proportion of whole grains? Ice cream? Impudence?

For example, a classic cobbler is often topped with a cakelike batter that one (fine: me; I mean me) might liken to a pancake. Here, it's poured over blueberries that are syrupy and slightly tart—like a blueberry compote you'd pour over breakfast pancakes, but inverted. The pancake topping is mostly whole wheat, not too sweet, and a cinch to make. And, in a little twist I can never resist, it's finished with a hot sugar crust. I first learned of these crusts in a recipe from Renee Erickson, the Seattle author and chef, who coats her peach-cobbler batter with sugar and warm water. It feels all wrong to do until you see what happens in the oven: it develops a crisp lid, as on a great crème brûlée, that we've been tapping our spoons through for several blueberry seasons now.

Heat the oven to 350°F (175°C). Line a rimmed baking sheet with foil to catch the drips. Place blueberries in a 1-quart baking dish, and toss with lemon zest and juice.

In a medium bowl, whisk together the butter, salt, 4 tablespoons of the sugar, all of the milk or buttermilk, and vanilla. Thoroughly whisk in the baking powder. Add the flours, and stir just until they disappear. Dollop this batter over the berries, and use a knife or small offset spatula to spread it as evenly across the berries as you can. Sprinkle with the remaining 2 tablespoons sugar; then drizzle the hot water evenly over the sugar.

Place the baking dish on the foil-lined baking sheet, and bake for 30 minutes, until the berries are bubbling in their juices, the top is cracklylooking, and a toothpick inserted into the pancake topping comes out batter-free. Eat right away, as is, or finished with a dollop of plain yogurt or a drizzle of cold cream.

salad

snow peas with pecorino and walnuts

serves 2 or 3

½ pound (225 grams) snow peas

3 tablespoons (40 grams) olive oil, plus more if needed

1 tablespoon (15 grams) white-wine vinegar

Kosher salt and freshly ground black pepper

2 tablespoons (15 grams) finely grated Pecorino cheese, plus more for garnish

¼ cup (30 grams) chopped walnuts, lightly toasted

I've spent most of my cooking life only using snow peas in stir-fries. I was severely missing out. At the late NoMad restaurant one birthday dinner, I had them raw and finely julienned in a salad so juicy and crisp, well, it was the exact reason I love to go to restaurants: to leave inspired. At home, I sleuthed on the internet until I learned that the secret to getting those snow peas so crunchy was a soak in ice water. (Yes, I realize every restaurant cook is probably rolling his or her eyes right now that I didn't already know this trick.) Even the softest, most sleepy-looking snow peas suffocated in tight plastic wrap at the grocery store are magically revived this way. At the restaurant, the snow peas were tossed with pancetta, cooked onion, mint, and lemon juice, but at home, where simpler preparations are the only ones I'll actually make a habit of, I use toasted, chopped walnuts for crunch, and a simple dressing of olive oil, vinegar, and grated sharp Pecorino. The result is the kind of salad that I put out on the dinner table while I finish up everything else, and the bowl is empty by the time we all sit down. If you fear this might happen to you, go ahead and preemptively double it.

Soak the snow peas in a bowl of ice water for 10 to 20 minutes. Drain and pat dry with a towel. Gather the peas in small stacks at a time, and cut them lengthwise into thin ribbons. (If you'd like the pieces more bite-sized, you can cut them at an angle in the other direction.)

Whisk the olive oil, vinegar, ½ teaspoon salt, many grinds of pepper, and 2 tablespoons grated Pecorino in a large bowl. Add the snow peas and walnuts, and toss to coat evenly. Taste the salad; add more salt, pepper, or olive oil if needed. Transfer to a serving bowl, leaving no dressing behind. Use a peeler to shave more Pecorino on top. Eat immediately.

sesame asparagus and carrot chop

serves 2 or 3, ostensibly

½ pound (225 grams) asparagus (½ bundle)

½ pound (225 grams) slim carrots, mixed-color if you can find them (about 1 bundle)

2 tablespoons (30 grams) unseasoned rice vinegar

Kosher salt

2 tablespoons (25 grams) mayonnaise

2 teaspoons toasted sesame oil

2 teaspoons sriracha

2 teaspoons low-sodium soy sauce

1 large firm-ripe avocado, diced

Toasted black and/or white sesame seeds, for garnish

When I cannot bear winter produce for one minute longer, this is the salad I make. It's a vividly colored crunchy, nutty, and spicy mix of asparagus, carrots, and avocado, springlike vegetables that, rather conveniently in a place where "spring" vegetables may not emerge from the soil until spring is two-thirds over, taste pretty great from the produce we find at the grocery store. I know that mayo is a highly controversial ingredient, but mayo seasoned with toasted sesame oil and soy sauce is a whole other thing, a thing I refuse to believe anyone wouldn't want to lick from a spoon. It's rivetingly good. Here, it dresses the crunchy vegetables and rich cubes of avocado in a way that lightly coats them but, I promise, doesn't scream "mayo salad" in any way. This is one of my favorite lunch salads, and you should not believe the serving suggestion at all: the recipe is just for you.

———————

Hold the asparagus by the tough end (no need to snap it off) and carrots by the stem end, and cut each diagonally into thin slices. Place these in a large bowl, and dress with rice vinegar and a few pinches of salt.

Combine the mayonnaise, sesame oil, sriracha, and soy sauce in a small bowl, whisking until smooth.

When you're ready to eat the salad, add the dressing to the asparagus and carrots, and stir to coat evenly. Add the diced avocado, and gently fold it in. Taste for seasoning, and add salt and more sriracha to your liking. Finish with the sesame seeds.

cucumber salad with garlicky dill yogurt

serves 2 to 4

yogurt

1½ cups (345 grams) plain, unsweetened Greek-style yogurt

1½ tablespoons chopped fresh dill, plus more for garnish

1 large garlic clove, minced

¾ teaspoon kosher salt

Freshly ground black pepper

cucumbers

1 pound (455 grams) small Persian (or larger seedless) cucumbers, unpeeled

½ small red onion, very thinly sliced

1 tablespoon (15 grams) plain or white-wine vinegar

2 tablespoons (25 grams) olive oil

½ teaspoon kosher salt

Freshly ground black pepper and/ or red-pepper flakes, to taste

This is what happens when your favorite part of tzatziki is the cucumbers, so you amplify them until they're dramatic, crunchy, and fork-spearable. The proportions are upended, and the cucumbers, lifted out of the yogurt, are encouraged (you encourage your cucumbers, don't you?) to be their coldest and most refreshing selves, erasing, I hope, any bad memories of the softer, swimming-in-dressing-style cucumber salad. These cucumbers are tossed in vinegar and oil with some thinly sliced red onion, and the sharp garlic-and-dill yogurt dressing stays underneath, with no chance to make anything soggy. If my balcony garden is overflowing with mint, I sometimes add to the yogurt an amount of mint equal to the dill.

———————

Mix the yogurt with the dill, garlic, salt, and many grinds of black pepper.

Cut the cucumbers in half lengthwise into 4 to 6 wedge-shaped slices (you'll have fewer for smaller cucumbers, more for bigger ones). Cut the wedges into 1-to-1½-inch lengths on a diagonal, and add them to a big bowl with the onion, vinegar, olive oil, ½ teaspoon kosher salt, and pepper.

When you're ready to eat the salad, spoon the yogurt sauce into a wide bowl or rimmed plate, and swirl it so it covers the bottom. Spoon the cucumbers and onions over the top. Finish with extra dill, and eat right away. If you'd prefer a mixed, creamy salad, remove the seeds from the cucumbers to avoid sogginess.

two-bean salad with basil vinaigrette

serves 2 as a meal,
or 4 as part of a spread

½ pound (225 grams) regular green beans or skinnier haricots verts

One 15.5-ounce (440-gram) can large white beans, drained and rinsed

½ medium fennel bulb, trimmed and thinly sliced (115 grams, or 1 cup)

2 tablespoons (25 grams) drained capers

1½ cups (30 grams) fresh basil leaves

1 teaspoon smooth Dijon mustard

2 tablespoons (30 grams) red- or white-wine vinegar

5 tablespoons (70 grams) olive oil

Kosher salt and freshly ground black pepper

½ cup (50 grams) Parmesan, chopped into mixed-sized rubble (optional)

Right after your smiling faces—sorry, that was grimacingly twee— a bowl of this salad is the thing I want to see most on a blanket at a summer picnic. Why? It's a marinated salad that is excellent fresh or, later, cold or at room temperature. Long beans, short beans, something crunchy, an herb dressing—this is an oasis of summer freshness and texture. The cheese is optional, in case you wish to keep it dairy-free or just want to home in on the fresher ingredients. The crunch is not, but there's some flexibility here as to how you get to it. The star is the basil vinaigrette, which is what happens when you crave pesto but want the acidity of a vinaigrette. It goes well on everything in the summer, so, if you have an overflowing basil plant about to flower, whack it down and make a big jar of this dressing. Your tomatoes, grilled summer squash, and even grain or lentil salads will thank you.

If you do not care for fennel, you can replace it here with 1 cup of thinly sliced celery. Oh, you don't like celery, either? Try half a white onion, thinly sliced. No raw onion, eh? You could add some thinly sliced radishes, because crunch is important here. But I think you are missing out on the fennel.

———————————

Trim the green beans, and cut them into large segments. In salted water, boil the green beans for 2 minutes (1½ minutes for haricots verts), until crisp-tender, heavier on the crisp. Drain the beans, and plunge them into ice water to cool them fully. Drain again, pat them dry on a towel, and place them in a large bowl. Add the white beans, fennel, and capers.

In a food processor or blender, combine the basil, Dijon mustard, and vinegar until the herbs are well chopped. With the machine running, drizzle in 5 tablespoons olive oil in a thin stream. Season very well with salt and black pepper; then add more vinegar and/or oil to taste. You might need to scrape the machine down a few times to get all of the leaves minced.

Pour the vinaigrette over the beans and turn to coat them in the bowl. Add the cheese, if using. Taste, and adjust seasoning.

endive salad with apple matchsticks

serves 4

1 large sweet-tart apple,
such as Honeycrisp, Pink Lady,
or Braeburn

1 medium lemon

1 tablespoon (15 grams) olive oil

Kosher salt and freshly ground
black pepper

¼ cup (50 grams) mayonnaise

2 ounces (about ⅓ to ½ cup,
or 55 grams) Danish blue cheese,
crumbled or in ½-inch pieces,
divided

1 small garlic clove, minced

½ cup (115 grams) buttermilk

4 medium-large Belgian endives,
ends trimmed, leaves separated

½ cup (45 grams) roughly
chopped smoked or salted
roasted almonds

¼ cup (20 grams) minced fresh
chives

note For a chopped salad—
Category 1!—you can also
slice your endives crosswise
into 1-inch-thick segments and
separate them, then toss the
ingredients in a big bowl; this
makes for less drama and more
fork-friendliness.

Might I air a tiny, petty salad grievance? Salads should be composed of small enough pieces to spear on a fork and fit into your mouth, or they should be fork-and-knife salads, or they can be portable salads, scooped onto something that can be lifted by hand. Eating salad, one of my favorite things, would be much easier if every salad knew what team it was on. With that said, this is a Category 3 salad. It's also a very stubborn salad, or perhaps its creator is. I know, from the number of times I've explained it to people (an editor, a spouse, friends, and a twelve-year-old) as their faces tried valiantly to keep up enthusiastic smiles, that there is deep skepticism around these ingredients. Despite these odds, I am uncowed, determined that it can win you over if you give it a chance. It's inspired by the classic, overdue-for-a-comeback-tour 1990s combination of apples, blue cheese, and walnuts, except here I use smoked almonds, because I love their intense saltiness against the sweet and lemony apples. The blue-cheese dressing isn't the thick kind for hot wings and iceberg wedges, but blended and thinned into a pourable vinaigrette, perfect for puddling in endive leaves. Champagne-tower-ing the leaves most dramatically is inspired by the way they serve their endive salad at Estela, a small but perfect restaurant on Houston Street. If you can find one green and one red endive, you're in for a particularly stunning display. Rather than apologizing here for the impracticality of eating a tower of dressed full-sized leaves, I encourage you to roll up your sleeves and delight in the fork-free snack before you.

Halve the apple and remove the core; then cut it into thin matchsticks by slicing each half in thin slices in one direction, then turning the stack of slices on its side, and cutting it in thin slices again. In a bowl, toss the apple slices with the juice of half the lemon, 1 tablespoon olive oil, and a pinch of salt.

In a bowl, whisk together the mayo, all but 1 tablespoon of the crumbled blue cheese, and the garlic until smooth; then whisk in the buttermilk, a splash at a time, to form a thin dressing. Add 1 tablespoon juice from the second half of the lemon, ¼ teaspoon salt, and more black pepper →

than seems necessary. We're looking for a lighter and more vinaigrette-textured blue-cheese dressing, one that pours easily. Add more lemon juice, salt, or pepper to taste.

Arrange the endive leaves, cupped side up, on a round dinner plate in a single layer. (You won't use them all yet.) Pinch or spoon some of the apple slices into each endive cup, drizzle with a little dressing, and garnish with some of the almonds and chives. Season the layer with more salt and black pepper. Repeat in a second layer on top, and then a third if needed, to use up all of your ingredients; then sprinkle with the reserved 1 table-spoon blue cheese and serve.

deli pickle potato salad

serves 4 to 6

1½ pounds (680 grams) small red potatoes

Kosher salt

½ medium white onion, very thinly sliced

3 tablespoons (45 grams) pickle brine, from jar

1 teaspoon spicy mustard, plus more to taste

3 tablespoons (40 grams) olive oil

1 teaspoon nigella seeds (see headnote)

Freshly ground black pepper

⅔ cup (4 ounces, or 115 grams) half-sour or kosher dill pickles quartered lengthwise and thinly sliced

3 tablespoons chopped fresh dill

This is me, pleading the case for potato salads untethered from the summer months. Welcome as they are at a barbecue, I also like them for lunch, straight from a bowl or with a sandwich, and with dinner. If you go ahead and boil a bag of small potatoes as soon as you bring them home (and before they sprout, what feels like twenty-four hours later) and keep them cold in the fridge, they're far more useful, and, yes, I just described food that's cooked as more useful than food that's raw. (Next, I suppose, I will explain that water is wet and not dry.) But with small potatoes in particular, whether you want to smash-roast them in a pan or chop them into home fries or fork-crush them with a ranch-y dressing (see page 194), once they're boiled, you're 75 percent there.

My favorite quick way to use them is with a sharp, mayo-free vinaigrette. Depending on what's in season, I might add segments of parboiled asparagus, green beans, or fennel, but let's say it's January, and the brightest thing in your fridge is a container of half-sour kosher dills from the Pickle Guys on Grand Street? This is the lucky outcome. Everything else in here falls in the category of Things I Like with Potatoes and Pickles, but I suppose only the nigella seeds, sometimes called black caraway and/ or charnushka, will raise eyebrows, so let me explain. Though they look like black sesame seeds, nigella seeds have a stronger flavor, a bit oniony; they're often seen on two other deli staples, Jewish rye or pumpernickel breads. Here, I love the accent they provide. But don't go crazy tracking them down: this salad is good without them, too.

Place the potatoes in a medium saucepan, and cover them with 1 inch of well-salted cold water. Bring to a boil, and cook for 20 minutes, or until a skewer or paring knife easily pierces a potato. Drain them and plunge them into ice water, letting the potatoes hang out there until they're cool. Drain again, and chill them until needed. The potatoes will keep in the fridge for up to 5 days.

Meanwhile, mix the onion, brine, and 1 teaspoon salt, and set this aside for 15 minutes, during which the onions will soften and mellow slightly. Whisk in the mustard, then the oil and nigella seeds, if using. →

deli pickle potato salad *(continued)*

Season well with black pepper, and more salt as needed. Taste, and if it's not zippy enough—remember, we want this to season a whole bowl of very neutral, absorbent potatoes—add more pickle brine and/or spicy mustard to taste. Halve the cooled potatoes and add them to the dressing, along with the pickles and dill. Stir to coat.

You can eat this right away, let it harmonize at room temperature for an hour or two, or keep it in the fridge for up to 4 days. (But not if your potatoes were already 5 days old, okay? Then eat it sooner.)

double shallot egg salad

serves 2

1 medium-large shallot
(3 ounces, or 85 grams)

2 tablespoons (30 grams)
red-wine vinegar

Kosher salt

Pinch of granulated sugar

4 large eggs, cold from fridge

Neutral oil

2 tablespoons (25 grams)
mayonnaise

1 teaspoon smooth Dijon
mustard

Freshly ground black pepper

Hot smoked paprika (see note)

1 tablespoon minced fresh chives

Four crispbread crackers

note If you don't have hot
smoked paprika, use sweet
smoked paprika and some
cayenne. Or simply use regular
paprika and cayenne.

I would like to make it absolutely clear that this is not my everyday egg salad. Quick-pickling shallots is one thing, but frying them? That's a bit much for a Tuesday lunch, although I will also tell you, as a life-long procrastinator, I love making it for lunch on Tuesdays, especially as deadlines—perhaps even this one—loom. When I searched deep inside my heart for egg salad the way I wished it always tasted, the way I wanted to eat it forever, this vision came to me fully formed and wouldn't let go its grip until I'd made it, at which point I realized I was now doomed to frying shallots whenever I wanted egg salad, because nothing else would taste as good again. Fortunately, it only takes 5 minutes.

So what's the point? This is the egg salad I'm going to make for you if I know you like egg salad and you're swinging by for lunch. While the core of it is as straightforward and fuss-free as egg salad should be—a simple salad, lightly dressed—the toppings make it dressy: shallots that are crispy and salty, bright-pink pickled gems, with fresh chives and spicy paprika. You're worth the extra step(s), I can just tell.

———————

Halve the shallot widthwise. Cut one half into a small (¼-inch) dice—you'll have about 2 tablespoons—and place it in a small bowl. Pour the red-wine vinegar over it, and add one big pinch of kosher salt and a smaller pinch of sugar. Stir, and set aside while you prepare the rest of the salad, or at least 20 minutes. (Pickled shallots keep for 2 or 3 days in the fridge.)

Bring a medium pot of water to a boil. Gently lower in the eggs, and boil for exactly 10 minutes. Drain, and immediately plunge the eggs into ice water; let them rest in the water for 10 to 15 minutes.

While the eggs chill and the shallot pickles, very thinly slice the second half of the shallot and add it to a small puddle of oil, enough to semi-submerge the shallot, in your smallest frying pan (I use 2 tablespoons oil in a 6-inch frying pan; a large pan will require more oil). Turn the heat to medium, and watch, stirring, flipping (I find this easiest with a fork), until the shallot is evenly browned. Drain it, on a paper towel, and immediately, while it's still piping hot, season with salt. →

double shallot egg salad *(continued)*

In a medium bowl, combine the mayo, Dijon mustard, ¼ teaspoon salt, and several grinds of black pepper. Peel and chop your eggs, and add them to the dressing, stirring gently until the eggs are evenly coated. Taste, and adjust seasoning if needed. Scoop the egg salad onto four crispbreads on a platter, and sprinkle each with paprika, pickled shallots, chives, and crispy shallots.

farro salad with roasted tomatoes

serves 4 to 6

4 cups (about 680 grams) cherry or grape tomatoes

Olive oil

Kosher salt

1 cup (215 grams) uncooked farro

1 large garlic clove

1 tablespoon dried oregano

Freshly ground black pepper

¼ cup (60 grams) red-wine vinegar

3 ounces (85 grams) crumbled salty cheese, such as ricotta salata or feta

½ cup (85 grams) cured black olives, pitted, then roughly chopped

Handful of fresh basil or mint leaves, thinly sliced

note No farro? Use barley or another grain you love; pearl couscous works, too. If you can find Sicilian dried oregano, it's my favorite here. Gaeta olives are great here, but use any kind you like.

As someone who also might have been briefly cool in the 1990s but rarely since, I have a soft spot for sun-dried tomatoes. When sun-dried tomatoes were good, they added an essential chewy, sweet-sour accent to salads and pasta. By the time everyone sent them packing, they were more often tinny, artificial, and—wait—is that soggy rehydrated oregano in the jar? Blergh. But, rather than trying to rewind the clock to their original glory, I prefer to turn to something I bet all of us in the 1990s would have been delighted to see: reliably sweet, fresh cherry and grape tomatoes in every grocery store, year-round.

Halved and slow-baked in the oven, these seasonless tomatoes concentrate into something that tastes almost like tomato candy. Combined with salty cured olives, sharp crumbled cheese, and a dried-oregano vinaigrette (inspired by the one in Nancy Silverton's wonderful chopped salad) that reminds me, in the best possible way, of the Good Seasons Italian dressing mixes of my childhood, these make a salad base perfect for pasta, beans, or, my current favorite iteration, farro. The chewy, nutty grains against the intense tomato bites make a fridge-ready lunch dream, even better on days two and three.

Roast the tomatoes: Heat the oven to 300°F (150°C). Cover a half-sheet baking pan with parchment paper. Cut each tomato in half (lengthwise if using grape tomatoes), and arrange them, cut side up, in a single layer on the prepared sheet. Drizzle lightly with olive oil (about 2 to 3 tablespoons), and sprinkle with salt (about 1 teaspoon). Bake for approximately 90 minutes, until somewhat shriveled and dry to the touch but not fully dehydrated. Set the tomatoes aside until needed, letting them cool.

Meanwhile, cook the farro: Bring the farro, 4 cups water, and 1 teaspoon salt to a boil. Once it's boiling, reduce the heat to a simmer, and cook the farro, uncovered, until tender, about 15 to 20 minutes. If any extra water remains, drain it. Set the farro aside to cool.

Make the dressing: Roughly chop the garlic on a cutting board, then add oregano, 1¼ teaspoons salt, and a few grinds of black pepper. Mince the mixture with your knife until it's a fine paste. Transfer it to a large →

farro salad with roasted tomatoes *(continued)*

bowl, whisk in the vinegar, then slowly drizzle in ¼ cup oil, whisking the whole time. Taste, and adjust as needed; you might need more salt or vinegar. Season well with pepper. You want a strongly flavored dressing that won't get lost in that big bowl of ingredients.

Assemble the salad: Add the farro to the dressing, and stir to coat evenly. Stir the roasted tomatoes, cheese, and olives into the farro, and toss gently to combine. Add extra salt and pepper to taste. Finish with the herbs.

The salad can be eaten right away, but will keep in the fridge for up to 4 days.

the big green little gem salad

serves 4

1 small garlic clove

1-ounce (30-gram) chunk Parmesan or Pecorino cheese

½ cup toasted, salted sunflower seeds

1 sun-dried tomato, dried, or oil-packed and patted dry

Kosher salt and freshly ground black pepper

2 tablespoons white-wine vinegar, plus more to taste

½ teaspoon smooth Dijon mustard

6 tablespoons (75 grams) olive oil

4 heads (8 to 10 ounces) Little Gem lettuce, washed and dried

note This recipe makes double the rubble that you'll need, but I'm always happy to have it in the fridge for future salads.

As someone who loves to suggest we serve meals with a big green salad, I find it rather galling that you won't find a single recipe titled "big green salad" in either of my two previous cookbooks, or on my website. I know this disconnect comes from a place of not confidently believing anyone really needs a prescriptive recipe for a green salad—isn't it just salad greens with oil, vinegar, and maybe a smidge of Dijon mustard?—but when I responded to a reader who had asked for basic guidance on a simple salad, paragraphs spilled out of me, and I realized that, while the concept may be simple, having made hundreds of big green salads in my life has left me teeming with opinions on how to make them better, and, for better or worse, I'm incapable of keeping cooking advice to myself.

Greens: My go-to salad greens are smaller heads of lettuce, often called "Little Gems," a cross between romaine and butter lettuce, which have the perfect balance of crunch and leafiness, while holding dressing well. However, the best lettuce for *your* salad will always be whatever you like the most, or whatever looks the freshest at the store. When they're in season, I love chicories, especially those beautiful speckly pink ones you might find at a greenmarket, and will always add them as an accent.

Cleaning: I dislike salad spinners; I don't have space for a clunky, single-use object that still, after spinning, leaves me with damp leaves. Instead, I dip-swish my lettuce in very cold tap water, lift it out (don't drag your lettuce across the bottom of the bowl or it will re-collect deposited grit) a handful at a time, shake it a couple times, and spread the leaves out in one layer on my largest absorbent kitchen towel (or two, if necessary). Once all of my lettuce is on the towel, I loosely roll it up like a cigar, grab the ends tightly, and shake, shake, shake it vigorously for 20 to 30 seconds; it can handle it. (If you're not in a rush, you can even leave it in this towel roll for a bit on a counter.) When you unroll it, you'll have perfectly washed and dried lettuce, and no highly specific devices required.

Dressing: White-wine or champagne vinegars are my go-to, and they're fairly mild, so I go heavier on them than you might see in →

more classic vinaigrette formulas. My second favorite is sherry vinegar, which can have more of a bite, so adjust accordingly. I use whatever olive oil I have around, but if you have one that is a bit more fruity, rich, or delicate, this is a great place to use it: the flavor will not be cooked out. Because acidity ranges from vinegar to vinegar, almost all vinaigrettes need to be adjusted to taste, so don't be afraid to. If my salad is heavier on the aforementioned chicories, which lean bitter, I might add ½ teaspoon honey to the dressing for balance.

When to mix: The best way to get a salad ready now but eat it later without its getting soggy is to make the dressing in the bottom of your bowl and pile your washed, dried leaves on top. Only toss it in the minutes before you are ready to eat it.

On dry dressing: You can stop right here and have a perfect green salad, but when I have time to do a little extra, I love to make a dry mixture of sharp ingredients that taste amazing in salads—aged cheese, nuts or seeds, garlic, oh, and even the sun-dried tomato I mocked a few pages ago (just one per salad is the only correct amount)—to sprinkle on the lightly dressed leaves. To do this, I sprinkle the dressed leaves layer by layer on the serving platter, ensuring that no leaves are left crunch-free. The mixture clings wonderfully to them and turns a big green salad into what is actually the best salad ever.

On a cutting board with your sharpest knife, finely chop the garlic, then add the Parmesan and sunflower seeds and reduce the mixture to a breadcrumblike rubble. Mince the sun-dried tomato, and add it to the cheese and seeds. Place this in a small bowl, season with salt, if needed, and black pepper, and set aside.

In the bottom of your largest bowl, which you can rest on a damp towel for greater stability, whisk together the vinegar and mustard. Drizzle in your olive oil in a thin stream, whisking the whole time. Season with salt and freshly ground black pepper. Taste the dressing, and add more vinegar to taste, if needed. Pile the lettuce leaves on top, but don't mix it yet.

When you're ready to assemble and serve the salad, wash your hands well and use them—they're truly the best tool here to ensure that the dressing distributes perfectly—to toss the lettuce with the dressing, evenly coating each leaf.

On your serving plate or wide bowl, spread out a layer of dressed leaves. Sprinkle them lightly with the sunflower-seed mixture, and season the whole layer with a little salt and a few grinds of black pepper. Repeat with more layers, the dry mixture, and more salt and pepper until all ingredients are used up.

Eat right away.

soups and stews

ginger garlic chicken noodle soup

serves 4 to 6

soup

2 pounds (905 grams) boneless, skinless chicken thighs

6 garlic cloves, thinly sliced

3-inch piece ginger, peeled, finely chopped

1 bundle (6 to 8 ounces, 170 to 225 grams) scallions, thinly sliced, whites and greens separated

4 teaspoons (11 grams) kosher salt

Freshly ground white or black pepper

10 cups (2.4 kilograms) water

8 ounces (225 grams) dried curly (in a brick) or other dried ramen-style noodles

1 cup (135 grams) sliced carrot, cut into thin matchsticks (about ½ full-sized carrot)

finish

¼ cup (60 grams) black rice vinegar (see note)

¼ cup (60 grams) soy sauce

2 tablespoons (25 grams) toasted sesame oil

Crispy chili oil, to taste

On a cold winter weekend day when nobody wants to go outside, there are few better things than a pot of chicken noodle soup, quietly simmering on the stove while my family, in all likelihood, is glued to another *Star Wars* marathon. But on a cold winter weekend day when nobody wants to go outside but we also don't want to spend the afternoon long-cooking a pot of bone broth? This, this is the soup we make.

One of my favorite discoveries of the last few years was that I didn't actually need to make, to buy, or even to build-from-bouillon chicken stock to make chicken noodle soup. It turns out that just simmering boneless, skinless chicken thighs with aromatics in salted water creates a gentle but delicious soup-building base. With ginger, garlic, scallions, and a punchy seasoning added at the end, all efforts to explain calmly how much I love this soup fall short. This is the first recipe I worked on for this book, and, for us, the very definition of a keeper. A deeply flavored chicken noodle soup you can make in 45 minutes is one we're going to want to make as often as possible.

A few things here are key: Chicken thigh cutlets have more fat than breast cutlets, and the richness helps build a more flavorful soup here. Adding the soy sauce, vinegar, and sesame oil at the end as a salty, robust finish, versus cooking them into the broth, keeps them from getting lost in the soup. This gives it a bit of a hot-and-sour-soup note, too, which is also finished with vinegar.

Bring the chicken, garlic, ginger, scallion whites (reserve greens), salt, pepper, and water to a boil in a 4-to-5-quart pot. Reduce the heat to medium-low, and simmer, uncovered, stirring occasionally, until the chicken is very tender and cooked through, about 15 minutes.

While the soup simmers, whisk together the vinegar, soy sauce, and sesame oil in a bowl, and add as much or as little chili crisp as your heart desires. (Mine desires a lot, but, to keep the less spice-inclined kids happy, we use just a smidge and add more to our bowls at the table.) →

ginger garlic chicken noodle soup *(continued)*

Remove the chicken with tongs, and transfer it to a cutting board. Add the noodles and carrot to the broth, following the cooking-time estimate on your noodles' package directions. Use two forks to shred the chicken into bite-sized pieces. Once the noodles are done, return the chicken to the pot, and rewarm for 1 minute. Taste, adjusting seasoning if needed.

Divide the soup between bowls. Add a handful of scallion greens, and drizzle each bowl with 1 tablespoon of the soy-sauce mixture, adding more to taste.

notes

- Deeper in color and flavor, black vinegar (also sold as black rice vinegar and Chinkiang vinegar) should be very easy to find in an Asian grocery store or online, and I love it here for flavor and color. Should you seek it out, you can also use it for the Soy-Glazed Tofu with Crisped Rice (page 129), which helps give it that dark glaze.

- Cook the noodles in the soup right before you want to serve it, or they will keep "drinking" the broth until there's little left.

simple black bean chili

serves 2 to 4

1 medium poblano, halved, seeds removed

1 jalapeño or habanero chili, halved, seeds removed

1 medium white onion, trimmed, cut into 8 wedges

2 large garlic cloves, unpeeled

2 tablespoons (30 grams) vegetable oil, divided

1½ teaspoons (4 grams) kosher salt

1 teaspoon chipotle chili powder, or 1 tablespoon chipotle purée from a can

2 teaspoons ground cumin

1 teaspoon dried oregano

One 14.5-ounce can (1½ cups, or 410 grams) crushed tomatoes, fire-roasted if you can find them

Two 15.5-ounce cans (each 1¾ cups, or 440 grams) black beans, drained and rinsed

Water, if needed

Handful of chopped fresh cilantro leaves

Juice of ½ lime

Sour cream, sliced scallions, avocado, pickled jalapeños, for garnishes

note If you've got access to a grill, you can char the base vegetables there instead.

As a devoted bean eater, I have made my share of vegetarian chilis, tuning out my Texan friends who balk at the beans, tomatoes, absence of dried chilis, and even beef in what I have the audacity to call chili. I'd always build it like a soup, sautéing ingredients in oil and then adding the tomatoes, beans, and spices for a long simmering time—but the day I decided to build it the way I make salsa, charring the onion, garlic, and hot peppers under the broiler and blending them as a base for the chili, changed everything. While this added more steps, it didn't add much more time—I make it most often on weeknights—and it imbues even bland canned beans with a much more layered, complex flavor than anything I've made before. By the time it's blended, you're three-quarters of the way to your chili. On the stove, it's a simple season-and-simmer operation, and takes just 15 minutes. While it simmers, I pull out whatever we've got in the fridge to turn into what we call taco fixings—quick-pickled red onion, sliced avocado, cilantro, crumbled cheese, limes, and some hot sauce for the grown-ups. Everyone heaps their bowls with whatever they like, and I am happy I've convinced everyone to eat what I want most: a bowl of beans for dinner.

Broil your peppers and garlic: Heat your broiler, if you have one, or your oven to its highest temperature. On a small foil-lined baking sheet, toss the peppers, onion, and garlic with 1 tablespoon oil, and broil or roast until the ingredients are blackened in spots, 5 to 10 minutes.

Blend your veggies: Carefully remove the garlic cloves from their skins and transfer them to a blender or food processor, along with the remaining charred ingredients. Pulse the machine until they're well chopped but not puréed.

Finish it off on the stovetop: In a large saucepan, heat the remaining tablespoon of oil over medium-high heat. Once it's hot, add the ingredients from the blender, plus salt, chipotle, cumin, and oregano, and cook for 2 minutes, stirring. Add the tomatoes, and simmer for 4 to 5 minutes. Add the black beans, and bring it back to a simmer. If the chili looks $\rightarrow$

dry, add ¼ to ½ cup water to loosen it. Simmer for 5 minutes. Taste, and adjust seasonings and spices to the level you like.

Off the heat, stir in cilantro and lime juice. Ladle the chili into four small or two large bowls, and garnish with your choice of toppings—shown here with sour cream, avocado, and scallions, plus some off-screen tortilla chips on the side for "the kids" to crumble in.

winter squash soup with red onion crisp

serves 6

1 large or 2 small red onions

Vegetable or another neutral oil

4 garlic cloves, thinly sliced, divided

1-inch piece ginger, peeled, thinly sliced

1 teaspoon ground cumin

Red-pepper flakes, to taste

Kosher salt

2 pounds (905 grams) peeled, seeded winter squash, in 1-inch cubes

One 13.5-ounce (400-gram) can full-fat coconut milk, well shaken

2 cups (475 grams) vegetable broth, plus more as needed

¼ cup (15 grams) dried coconut flakes

Lime juice, to taste

Big handful of fresh cilantro or flat-leaf parsley, chopped

My extremely radical—although I'm not sure why it has to be—belief about being a person who cooks in a household full of people who are all picky but in different ways (this cook included) is that, as much as humanly (and humanely) possible, one should ignore the picky contingent and just make what you want. Wait, let me explain. I'll start with the kids. I love them, but when they tell me they don't like something, often what they mean is they just want something else for dinner (pizza, perhaps), or that they're not hungry, which, of course, is not the same thing. Imagine missing out on a decade of something you loved to eat over such irrationalism! Now, let's say it's a spouse who decided they didn't like, say, winter squash with coconut milk—but isn't that just due to one bad cream-and-cinnamon squash soup years ago, a soup that tasted like pie?

What I am trying to say is that I made this spiced soup one fall day because it was the only thing I was craving, despite worrying that everyone was going to hate it, but also knowing that, some days, the only things I can rally to cook are the things I want to eat the most. And everyone finished it. These stories do not always end so well—sometimes they end with hastily assembled peanut butter sandwiches—but I will absolutely take the risk, because when it works we can increase the number of dishes everyone agrees on by a single, solitary recipe. Thank you for coming to my Deb Talk.

———

Prep your onions: Finely dice (into ¼-inch pieces) a total of ¼ cup onion, and set it aside. Thinly slice the rest.

Prepare the soup: Heat 2 tablespoons oil in a large pot over medium heat. Add the thinly sliced onion, three of the garlic cloves, all of the ginger and cumin, ¼ teaspoon red-pepper flakes (or adjust to taste), and 1 teaspoon kosher salt, and sauté until tender, about 8 to 10 minutes. Add the squash, and cook in the onion-spice mixture for 1 minute. Add the coconut milk and broth, and scrape up anything stuck to the bottom of the pot. Bring the soup to a simmer. Reduce heat to keep it simmering, cover the pot, and cook until the squash is very tender, about 20 minutes. →

Working in batches, purée the soup in a blender, or you can use an immersion blender to do it right in the pot. If the soup is very thick, you can thin it now with additional broth. Season with more salt to taste.

Make the topping: Heat 1 tablespoon oil in a small skillet over medium-high heat. Add the reserved diced red onion, the coconut flakes, and two pinches of red-pepper flakes, and cook, stirring almost the whole time, until the onion and coconut are a shade darker, about 4 to 5 minutes. Add the remaining garlic, and continue to cook until garlic, onion, and coconut are golden brown and crisp, about 2 minutes more. Season with salt, and scrape the crisp into a bowl.

Ladle the soup into bowls, and finish each with a squeeze of lime juice, a spoonful of the red-onion crisp, and some cilantro.

essential french onion soup

serves 6 to 8

3 tablespoons (45 grams) unsalted butter

3 pounds (1.4 kilograms) yellow onions (see note), halved, thinly sliced

Kosher salt

¼ cup (60 grams) dry sherry, vermouth, or white wine (optional)

2 quarts (8 cups, or 1.9 kilograms) beef, chicken, or vegetable stock, the more robust the better

1 bay leaf, and a few sprigs fresh thyme (optional, and, honestly, I rarely bother)

Freshly ground black pepper

One ¾-to-1-inch-thick slice of bread for each bowl of soup

1 garlic clove

¼ cup (20 grams) grated Gruyère, Comté, or a mix of Gruyère and Parmesan, per toast

Minced fresh chives and/or flat-leaf parsley, to finish (optional)

French onion soup is not just a forever favorite of mine; it's what I consider a core recipe in my arsenal because it aligns with so much that I think is important in cooking: It's totally budget-friendly (and downright cheap) to make. It's made from buy-anywhere ingredients and very few of them—99 percent of the flavor comes just from onions, cooked very slowly, transformed by a technique you need no advanced cooking skills to master. And it has a depth of flavor that is unparalleled by almost anything else I know how to make.

Up until a few years ago, I only made it one way: Julia Child's. But, through repetition and real life, I've tweaked it a bit to make my favorite soup even more perfect for me: more onions for heartiness, and nixing the small amount of flour, which didn't seem necessary for the soup body, especially with the higher proportion of onions.

And I try to keep it as doable as possible, because I remember how daunting even so-called simple recipes were when I started cooking. Don't have ovenproof bowls? Make a casserole of it, like a giant pot pie. You can also broil individual cheese toasts and float them on the soup. Want it vegetarian? Use a good dark vegetable stock, or a mushroom broth. Cannot possibly imagine spending an hour or longer frequently attending to caramelizing onions? Sigh, I'm sorry, but that's the whole soup, where all of the magical flavor comes from. I find I can trim off a little of the hands-on stirring time by using a lid at first, but do know, as you're attending to the later stages more carefully, as your kitchen smells like heaven on earth, that the remainder of the recipe is virtually hands-off, and ends with charred-edge melted cheese toasts, as noble a cause as any.

Caramelize your onions: Melt the butter in the bottom of a 5-to-6-quart saucepan or Dutch oven over medium heat. Add the onions, toss to coat them in butter, and cover the pot. Reduce the heat to medium-low, and let them slowly steep for 15 minutes. They don't need your attention.

Uncover the pot, raise the heat slightly, and stir in the salt—I start with between 2 and 3 teaspoons of kosher salt. Cook the onions, stirring →

notes

- Because this is a rich soup, I use 12-ounce (or 1½-cup) ramekins/baking dishes. However, I know some people prefer it in 16-ounce or 2-cup bowls, in which case, you might end up with only six servings.

- I always start with an onion or two more than I need, because, given the vagaries of buying onions from grocery stores in the middle of winter, I never know when I'll get one that is banged up inside (except, reliably, any time I don't buy extras).

essential french onion soup *(continued)*

every 5 minutes (you might be fine checking in less often in the beginning, until the water in the onions has cooked off and they feel like they're sticking more to the pot), for about 40 to 90 minutes longer.

(What? I know, this range is crazy. Stoves vary so much, even my own. If your onions are browning before 40 minutes are up, reduce the heat to low, and if it's still cooking too fast, try a smaller burner. The longer you cook the onions, the deeper the color, the more complex the flavor, but when you're happy with it, you can stop—the ghost of Julia Child will not haunt you or anything.)

Make the soup: Onions are caramelized when they're an even, deep golden brown, sweet and tender. Add the sherry or vermouth, if using, and scrape up any onions stuck to the pan. Cook until the liquid disappears. Add the stock, herbs (if using), and a lot of freshly ground black pepper, and bring the soup to a simmer. Partially cover the pot, and simmer for 15 to 20 minutes. Taste, and adjust seasoning as needed; discard bay leaf, and thyme sprigs, if you used them.

While the soup is finishing, heat your broiler (if you don't have a broiler, heat your oven as hot as it goes). If your bread is fresh and soft, toast it lightly, until firm. Gently rub each slice of bread with the raw garlic clove. Line a baking sheet with foil, and arrange the soup bowls/vessels on top.

To finish: Ladle the soup into bowls. Place a piece of toast (trimming the edges if needed) on each bowl. Sprinkle it with cheese. Run the bowls under the broiler until the cheese is melted and brown at the edges. Garnish with chives or parsley, if you wish.

slow-simmered lentils with kale and goat cheese

serves 4

¼ pound (115 grams) kale, preferably lacinato or dinosaur kale (half a standard bunch)

3 tablespoons (40 grams) olive oil, divided

1 small yellow onion, diced small (¼ inch)

3 garlic cloves, minced

1 tablespoon (15 grams) tomato paste

1 cup (150 grams) small green lentils (ideally French du Puy), rinsed

2½ to 3 cups (590 to 710 grams) vegetable broth, the more robust the better

Kosher salt

Freshly ground black pepper

2 tablespoons (30 grams) sherry vinegar or red-wine vinegar

4-ounce (115-gram) log goat cheese, cut into 1-inch (2.5-centimeter) segments

Thick slices country or sourdough bread, toasted or grilled, for serving

note I prefer tiny, dark-green lentils du Puy most of all here, because they stay intact as they cook.

This is the kind of recipe I had always wished was in my arsenal when I began cooking: a fairly simple way to turn a box of lentils into a luxurious vegetarian weekday meal with simple ingredients. I might have missed the window on *my* early cooking days, but I think I've got a chance of indoctrinating my son, who said things like "Wow, lentils are good," and "I thought I didn't like lentils," and "You should make these more often," the first time I made them, and helped himself to seconds—not exactly what I expected from a middle-schooler. If it's puddles of melted cheese that make this magic happen, then puddles of cheese will be standard in this recipe. I hardly mind one bit.

———————

Strip the leaves from the stems of the kale, and tear the leaves into bite-sized chunks. Thinly slice the stems.

Place 2 tablespoons of the olive oil in a medium-sized heavy pot (like a Dutch oven—you'll need a lid) over medium heat. Add the kale stems, onion, and garlic, and cook until the onion is translucent and beginning to soften, 4 to 5 minutes. Add the kale leaves, and cook until they soften down, 1 to 2 minutes. Add the tomato paste, and cook for 1 minute; then add the lentils, 2½ cups broth, 1 teaspoon kosher salt, and many grinds of black pepper. Bring to a boil; then reduce to a very low simmer, and cover. Cook for 60 minutes, until the lentils are tender but not collapsed. If the lentils look thirsty, like they may dry out before they cook through, add the last ½ cup broth.

Remove from the heat, and stir in the sherry vinegar. Make little divots in the lentils with a spoon, and drop a piece of goat cheese into each. Replace the lid, and let the lentils rest for 4 to 5 minutes, until the goat cheese has softened. Drizzle with the remaining tablespoon of olive oil. Serve, scooped onto grilled bread.

cozy chicken and dumplings

serves 6

stew

2½ to 2¾ pounds (1.15 to 1.25 kilograms) bone-in, skin-on chicken breasts

Kosher salt

Freshly ground black pepper

A pinch or three of red-pepper flakes, to taste (optional)

4 tablespoons (55 grams) unsalted butter, divided

3 large ribs celery, diced (about 1½ cups, or 210 grams)

3 medium carrots, diced (about 1½ cups, or 215 grams)

1 large yellow onion, diced

¼ cup (60 grams) dry sherry or white wine (optional)

⅓ cup (45 grams) all-purpose flour

1 quart (950 grams) chicken broth

1 cup (235 grams) milk, any kind

1 bay leaf

1 teaspoon minced fresh thyme leaves

¾ cup (105 grams) frozen green peas (optional)

¼ cup minced fresh herbs of your choice (I like parsley, chives, and dill), divided →

This is the dish my husband requests the most, but for years I was terrifically resistant to making it because my previous go-to recipe was too fussy—leeks, tarragon, a long cooking time, and a whole lot of peas. It took one of those face-biting twenty-degree weeks in January, and no desire to make a special trip to the store, for me to finally start making it the way it always should have been: a rustic, easy chicken stew with lots of carrots, celery, and peas, only if you love them. I much prefer dark meat, but my husband always requests white, which is how I learned that this is actually quite perfect with white meat, not remotely dry or flavorless, as I might have assumed. Giant cloud dumplings that fully cover the pot are nonnegotiable. The result is the most warming thing, and it's always done in under 90 minutes—coziness without a long commitment feels like unlocking a new level of winter thriving.

———

Make the stew: Season chicken on both sides with salt, freshly ground black pepper, and, if using, red-pepper flakes.

Heat a large (5-to-6-quart) heavy pot, such as a Dutch oven, over medium-high heat, and melt half of the butter in it. Arrange half the chicken pieces skin side down and cook until a nutty golden brown underneath, about 5 minutes. Turn pieces over and brown on the second side. Transfer chicken to a plate and repeat with the remaining butter and chicken, adding it to the plate with the first pieces.

Add the celery, carrots, and onion to the empty pot, season well with salt and pepper, and cook until partially softened, about 7 minutes. Add the sherry or wine, if using, scraping up any stuck bits, and cooking until the liquid disappears. Stir in the flour. Stir in the broth, milk, bay leaf, and thyme. Return the chicken to the pot, and season with additional salt and pepper. Cover, and simmer over medium heat until the chicken is just cooked through (it will have more cooking time in a moment) and tender, 20 to 25 minutes. Remove the chicken with tongs, and set it on a cutting board. Use two forks to shred the chicken into bite-sized pieces, discarding the skin and bones. Discard the bay leaf, and return the chicken to →

dumplings

1 cup (235 grams) milk, any kind

3 tablespoons (45 grams) unsalted butter

1½ teaspoons (4 grams) kosher salt

1 tablespoon baking powder

1¾ cups (230 grams) all-purpose flour

the pot to rewarm. Stir in peas, if using, and add 3 tablespoons of the minced herbs. Taste for seasoning (this will be your last chance to get it right), adding more salt and pepper as needed. (I usually need a total of 2 to 3 teaspoons of kosher salt for the stew.)

Make the dumplings: Heat the milk, butter, and salt in a medium bowl in the microwave, or in a medium pot over medium-high heat, just until the butter melts. Thoroughly whisk in the baking powder; then stir in the flour. Scoop golf-ball-sized portions of the soft dough (with either a soup spoon or a cookie scoop), and drop them, one at a time, over the top of the stew. Reduce the heat to low, cover, and cook until dumplings cover the surface, having doubled in size, about 15 minutes. If you can bear it, let the soup rest for 5 minutes before serving. Sprinkle with the remaining tablespoon of herbs, and divide between soup bowls.

notes

- I actually love these dumplings with buttermilk, but was loath to ask you to use two different kinds of milk in the same recipe when dumplings are also excellent made with regular milk. If you've got buttermilk around and want to use it here, however, use the same amount as of regular milk, but drop the flour in the dumplings to 1⅔ cups, because buttermilk is thicker.

- Why brown the chicken if you're just ultimately going to remove the skin and bones? Flavor. Bone-in, skin-on parts have much more flavor and cook up far less dry than cutlets. Browning the skin releases delicious schmaltz into the pan, which flavors the whole dish. However, if you absolutely insist, you can make this with boneless breast or thigh cutlets. Just use less chicken (1¾ to 2 pounds), and cook it for just 15 to 20 minutes.

creamy tomato chickpea masala

serves 4

3 tablespoons (45 grams) neutral oil, butter, or ghee

1 large yellow onion, minced

2-inch piece ginger, peeled, and minced or grated

2 garlic cloves, minced or grated

Kosher salt

1 teaspoon ground cumin

1 teaspoon ground turmeric

½ teaspoon garam masala

1 teaspoon ground coriander

½ to 1 teaspoon ground cayenne or mild chili powder

2 tablespoons (35 grams) tomato paste

One 14.5-ounce can (410 grams) diced or crushed tomatoes, or 1¾ cups small-diced fresh tomatoes

3½ cups (two 15.5-ounce or 440-gram cans) cooked chickpeas, drained, rinsed (see note)

2 to 4 tablespoons (30 to 60 grams) heavy cream

Handful of roughly chopped fresh parsley or cilantro (optional)

Rice, for serving

I grew up in an area of New Jersey with a large South Asian population. Though I know my affinities for cumin, coriander, turmeric, and ginger were planted by the incredible aromas at friends' houses while their moms cooked dinner—and the rotis puffing on the stove we'd ooh and aah over—I didn't have the confidence to try my favorite dishes at home until well into my twenties. Conveniently or coincidentally, I worked two blocks from Kalustyan's, a spice-and-specialty wonderland, making it easy to stock up. I have hardly wanted to stop for one minute since. This is a dish I'd been craving for years but I couldn't find the exact recipe I was looking for. So I took parts of a few of my favorites—a chicken curry from Chetna Makan; a chana masala from Madhur Jaffrey; and dal makhani, a black-lentil-and-red-kidney-bean curry enriched with butter and cream—and adjusted everything to get to what I'd envisioned, which is a more tomato-forward and lightly creamy take on makhani chole (butter chickpeas). The result is so warming, spiced, and lush, I had to stop writing this headnote midway to add ingredients for this to my grocery list, because thinking about it again made me crave it so much. I hope it has this kind of effect on you, too.

In a medium-large (3-quart) heavy pan with a lid, heat the oil over medium-high heat. Once it's hot, add the onion and cook for 5 to 7 minutes, until the onion is browned at the edges. Add the ginger and garlic, and cook for 1 minute more. Add 1 teaspoon salt, cumin, turmeric, garam masala, coriander, and cayenne, to taste, and cook for 2 minutes. Add the tomato paste, and cook until it is one shade darker, 1 to 2 minutes. Add the tomatoes, stirring up any stuck bits, season with another 1½ teaspoons salt, and bring to a simmer, stirring. Cook the tomatoes until they begin to break down and look saucy, mashing them a bit with your spoon if needed, which takes between 4 and 8 minutes. (Fresh tomatoes cook down faster.) Add 1¼ cups water, stir to combine, and reduce the heat to the lowest simmer. Cover, and cook for 5 minutes; then add chickpeas, and cook for another 10 minutes, until they have slightly softened. →

creamy tomato chickpea masala *(continued)*

If the chickpea mixture looks dry or thick, add more water to loosen. Taste, and adjust the seasoning if needed. Remove from the heat, and stir in 2 tablespoons cream. Gaze at the color and ask yourself if you're in more of a red, orange, or pink mood today. If the last, add the remaining 2 tablespoons cream. Finish with herbs, if using, and serve with rice.

notes

- I sometimes add some toasted paneer or halloumi cubes here as luxurious croutons. Cut an 8-ounce package of paneer or halloumi into 1-inch pieces. In a large nonstick skillet, heat 1 tablespoon of a neutral oil over medium heat. Cook the cheese until it's golden underneath, then flip and lightly brown on the second side. Add to the pot of chickpeas—the warmth will keep them soft—right before serving.

- The biggest debate in my household over this dish is whether it should be entirely chickpeas (my favorite) or one part chickpeas and one part cauliflower (my husband's). Both are excellent. If you'd like to add cauliflower, reduce the chickpeas to one can, the water to 1 cup; then add 3 cups cauliflower chopped into ½-to-1-inch pieces (about 1 pound total, from half a large head). Add the cauliflower when you add the water, and give it 10 minutes to begin softening before adding the chickpeas. The dish is done when the cauliflower is at your desired level of tenderness.

clam chowder with bacon croutons

makes 8 cups, serving 4 to 6

6 pounds (2.7 kilograms) cherrystone clams

Kosher salt

6 ounces (170 grams) thick-cut bacon, diced medium (½ inch)

2 cups (4 ounces, or 115 grams) medium-diced sourdough bread

2 tablespoons (30 grams) unsalted butter

1 tablespoon (15 grams) olive oil

1 large rib celery, diced

1 medium sweet onion (such as Spanish), diced

2 medium garlic cloves, minced

1 teaspoon chopped fresh thyme

Freshly ground black pepper

½ cup (115 grams) dry white wine (optional)

3 tablespoons (25 grams) all-purpose flour

1½ pounds (680 grams) Yukon Gold potatoes, peeled if you wish, cut into ½-inch pieces

1 bay leaf

½ cup (120 grams) heavy cream

3 tablespoons minced fresh chives

note It never hurts to buy a few extra clams in case some don't open. (This is a normal occurrence, and you always discard those unopened clams.) If all do, nobody has ever complained about too much clam in their chowder.

Most of my fantasy of what adulthood would be like came from watching *Barefoot Contessa* episodes, in which Ina cooks simple, perfect meals in her sunny kitchen, and a cast of friends stop by to share jokes and snacks. But have you ever tried to make actual plans with friends in real life? A simple "We should get dinner!" can take forty-two texts to put on the calendar three weeks later, and still need to be rescheduled at the last minute because something came up. But I think I've cracked the code. Almost without fail, when I tell friends I've made too much layer cake or am drowning in netted bags of clams—more on that in a moment—my buzzer rings in under ninety minutes, and it's all I ever wanted.

Although, hmmm, does Ina hand out gritty 5-pound sacks of cherrystones as door prizes? Thanks to a totally minor, could-happen-to-anyone (right?) grocery mishap while testing this recipe, I'd ordered 4 pounds but received 22 pounds of cherrystone clams. I barely have the fridge space for a spare cantaloupe, so I begged friends to take them off my hands. Later that evening, as one friend shared a picture of the clam pizza he'd made and another was slurping linguine alle vongole, I shared that the clam chowder had finally come out perfectly, and it was a bit like a needle screeching off a record. They had not been aware that there was a Deb-makes-clam-chowder-for-a-crowd option they could have forced my hand on if they'd just waited. I mean, would you rather pick up raw clams, or a container of warm chowder with bacon and sourdough croutons as a door prize? I promise, I've made it right since.

And this is what all of that fuss was about, what I consider the perfect clam chowder. My hunt is over—with no canned broth (we make our own when we steam the clams), busy like a stew, seasoned with a conviction of black pepper, and, this is absolutely key for me, no soggy pieces of bacon. Instead, we crisp it, and then make sourdough croutons in the renderings, for a crunchy soup-finish that's the best thing since oyster crackers. The serving size here is just for us, but don't worry: it scales well to whatever volume of clams, or friends, shows up on your doorstep that day. →

Clean the clams: Rinse and scrub them gently with a brush to remove any excess debris. Combine 3 tablespoons kosher salt and 1½ quarts water in a large bowl, and add the clams. Soak for 15 to 20 minutes; then scoop the clams out of the water (leaving the sandy debris in the bowl). Rinse again under cold water.

Cook the clams and make your broth: Bring 3 cups water to a boil in a large pot with a lid, or the 5-quart Dutch oven or soup pot you'll be using for the chowder. Carefully add the cleaned clams, cover the pot, and cook until the clams just open, about 8 to 10 minutes. Discard any clams that haven't opened. Use a large slotted spoon to transfer the clams to a large bowl, leaving the cooking water behind. Pour the water through a fine-mesh strainer into a measuring cup. If you don't have 4½ cups of liquid, add water until you do. This will be your clam broth. If you're using the same pot for the chowder, rinse it well to ensure no grit has stayed behind.

Pull the meat from the clams, and chop it into ½-inch pieces. (You should have 1½ cups.) Discard the shells.

Make the bacon croutons: Scatter the bacon in the bottom of your cold soup pot, then turn heat up to medium-high. Cook, stirring, until the bacon is evenly browned and crisp, about 5 to 7 minutes. Use a slotted spoon to transfer the bacon bits to paper towels to drain. Add the sourdough to the bacon fat, and crisp it, turning frequently, until it's golden all over. Season with salt. Transfer to a bowl, and add the bacon; set aside for serving.

Add the butter and olive oil to the pan, and once the butter is melted, cook the celery, onion, garlic, and thyme until soft, for 6 to 8 minutes. Season lightly with salt, and more heavily with pepper. Add the wine, and simmer, scraping up any stuck bits. Stir in the flour, and cook until it's golden, for 2 minutes; then gradually whisk in the clam broth. Add the potatoes, bay leaf, and lots of freshly ground black pepper, and bring to a simmer. Reduce the heat to medium-low, and cook, uncovered, stirring occasionally, until the potatoes are tender, about 15 to 18 minutes. For a thicker soup, you can smash about a quarter of the potatoes against the bottom of your pot with your spoon.

To finish: Remove the pot from the heat, and discard the bay leaf. Stir in the cream and the reserved clams. Season well with black pepper, and salt if needed. Ladle into bowls, and garnish each bowl with bacon, croutons, and chives.

do ahead Clams and broth can be prepared 1 day ahead. Store them separately in the fridge, well sealed.

vegetables

What is a medium vegetable? Since when is a cabbage or kabocha squash small? These are all valid questions about how I've chosen to organize the next chapter, so let me explain.

Unlike, say, a piece of roasted chicken served with rice, when it comes to vegetable dishes I find the line between *Absolutely a Meal* and *No, That's a Snack* to be porous and not something everyone agrees on. I'm not interested in defining for anyone else what is and is not a meal—I will happily eat those Spiced Sweet Potato Oven Fries (page 107) as lunch—so I instead put these vegetable recipes on a continuum.

What I call Small Vegetables could be a side dish, a snack, or a light meal, depending on your mood. Big Vegetables are what I consider more substantial vegetarian mains—and many are centerpiece-worthy should you be looking for a glorious summer dish for a cookout (Tomato and Corn Cobbler, page 149), my favorite choice for a vegan dinner party (Falafel, page 143), or a vegetarian High Holiday main (Tangy Baked Eggplant and Couscous, page 157). Medium Vegetables fall somewhere in between. The Soy-Glazed Tofu with Crisped Rice (page 129) is easily a weeknight meal, but the Leek and Brie Galette (page 117), Green Angel Hair with Garlic Butter (page 125), and Toasted Ricotta Gnocchi with Pistachio Pesto (page 131) might feel more balanced with a soup or salad.

My advice? Don't overthink what is and is not a meal, and make what jumps out to you first.

small vegetables

charred brussels sprout toast with ricotta

makes 6 toasts

Olive oil

6 slices (½-inch-thick, medium-sized) sourdough or country bread

1 garlic clove, halved

Kosher salt

1 pound (455 grams) Brussels sprouts, trimmed, halved lengthwise, sliced ⅛ inch thick, or 12 ounces (340 grams) sliced Brussels sprouts

Freshly ground black pepper

1 medium lemon

1 cup (250 grams) whole-milk ricotta

Red-pepper flakes, to taste

½ cup (80 grams) hazelnuts, toasted, loose skins removed, coarsely chopped

One of my favorite recipes I learned in my early blogging years is a wildly simple sauté of shredded Brussels sprouts with lemon juice and garlic from the Union Square Cafe. It includes poppy seeds, but I never added them. You're supposed to cook the sprouts for just a few minutes, so they're just tender, still green, and somewhat crisp. But let's say, just for a random example, what if you're an easily distracted cook? You might discover that Brussels sprouts cooked to a light char—a poetic way of saying I burned them—crispy in some places, a little green in the others (the ones I had not yet burned), are fantastic. I *meant* to do that! (Hair flip, nail buff, etc.) And here, in this recipe, I really do. I take those Brussels sprouts and heap them on olive-oil-fried, garlic-rubbed toasts, add hazelnuts for crunch, ricotta for richness. Lemon juice goes on at the end, where it's the brightest. Is this dinner? Do you eat it as a snack as you stand in the kitchen? That's between you and your toasts, and I would never want to interfere.

———————

Drizzle a large pan lightly with olive oil, and add as many bread slices as fit in one layer. Turn the heat to medium, and cook until golden brown and toasted underneath, about 4 minutes. Flip, and toast the second side, about 1 minute more, then set toast aside on a plate. Repeat with the remaining bread, adding more oil as needed. Remove from heat and rub toasts with the halves of the garlic clove, and sprinkle with salt.

Increase the heat to medium/medium-high, and add enough oil to recoat the pan well. Heat the oil until hot, and add the Brussels sprouts. Season well with salt and freshly ground black pepper, and let them cook undisturbed until well browned underneath, 3 to 5 minutes. Flip, and let the second side brown well underneath, 2 to 4 minutes more. Stir once or twice, and repeat this browning-and-flipping process until the Brussels have charred spots all over. Remove from the heat, and squeeze the juice of half your lemon over the top. Taste, and season with more salt and pepper if needed.

Spread each slice of bread thickly with ricotta. Heap the ricotta with the charred Brussels sprouts. Finish with another drizzle of oil, squeeze of lemon juice, salt, and red-pepper flakes, to taste. Scatter with hazelnuts.

pea, feta, and mint fritters

makes twenty 2-inch fritters

2 cups frozen peas (10-ounce or 285-gram freezer bag)

3 large eggs, lightly beaten

Kosher salt and freshly ground black pepper

¼ teaspoon red-pepper flakes, or to taste

1 medium lemon

¼ cup (15 grams) chopped fresh mint leaves

1 cup (4 ounces, or 115 grams) crumbled feta, drained

⅔ cup (90 grams) all-purpose flour

Olive or neutral oil, for frying

¾ cup (175 grams) plain Greek-style yogurt

For absolutely no reason—they have never sneered at me, my parents didn't torment me with mushy peas—I've never been much into sweet pea-centric dishes, preferring when peas are buried in some kind of rich or heavily spiced sauce (i.e., who are we kidding, they hardly taste like peas) or are part of a medley with other vegetables. But I love challenging myself to find ways to love unfavorite foods, and what I mean by that is—stop what you're doing—these are inhalably good. We start with a bag of frozen peas, which makes me feel particularly triumphant: I turned a bag of peas into dinner! From there, we add things that taste very delicious with peas: lemon zest, mint, feta, and pepper flakes. The pancakes take approximately 7 minutes to mix, and another 10 to fry. I'll use some of the juice of a zested lemon to make a salted lemon-yogurt sauce, and then I usually leave them on a plate on the table and forget about them until I come back later for one, and they're basically gone. Children and even spouses who would sneer at a bowl of peas on the dinner table cannot walk by without taking one; the parents of kindergarteners over on a playdate text me later and ask for the recipe, and did it really have peas, because their child won't stop asking about it. I'm not trying to oversell these; I just want you to know that, from the first test, they earned their way into my forever cooking repertoire, and I hope they may do the same for you.

Defrost the peas: If your peas are still frozen, place them in a colander and rinse them under cold tap water for 1 minute.

Make the fritters: In a large bowl, whisk the eggs with ½ teaspoon salt, lots of freshly ground black pepper, red-pepper flakes, the finely grated zest of your lemon, and mint. Stir in the drained peas and feta, then flour. The batter will be thick.

Over medium-high heat, add 2 to 3 tablespoons of oil to a large frying pan (nonstick makes it easier here). Once the oil is hot and shimmering, add 2 tablespoons (or a heaped small cookie scoop) of the batter, and press gently to flatten it. Cook until it's deeply golden brown underneath, about 2 to 3 minutes, then flip and repeat until the fritter is golden on the →

second side. The peas can get a little splattery if they pop, so be careful. If the fritters are getting dark right away, reduce the heat to medium. Drain the fritters on a paper towel, and season while hot with a pinch of salt; cook off the remaining fritters, adding more oil to the pan as needed.

Make the yogurt sauce: Stir together the yogurt, the juice of half the lemon, and several pinches of salt; then taste, adding more salt and lemon if needed, to make a bright, salty sauce.

Dollop the fritters with the lemon-yogurt sauce, and eat while still warm.

do ahead Fritters keep well in the fridge for up to 3 days; they freeze well, too. You can defrost and retoast them on a baking sheet in a 350°F (175°C) oven.

charred salt and vinegar cabbage

2 pounds (905 grams, or roughly 1 medium) green cabbage, halved, cored, then cut into 1-to-2-inch chunks

2 tablespoons (25 grams) olive oil

1 teaspoon (3 grams) kosher salt

½ teaspoon freshly ground black pepper

2 tablespoons (30 grams) unsalted butter

4 garlic cloves, lightly smashed

⅓ cup (80 grams) vegetable broth

⅓ cup (80 grams) white vinegar

Sea salt, to finish

note Delightfully (to me and perhaps to you, too), this works best with green cabbage, that inexpensive, sturdy workhorse you can find everywhere and often even in the back of my fridge, neglected.

The origin of this recipe is, as you might have guessed, the god-like invention known as salt-and-vinegar potato chips. I used this method to imbue thick potato slices with vinegar and salt, and then, later, on a whim, I added chunks of cabbage, just to see if they, too, appreciated a vinegar roast/braise, and what happened next was that we neglected all of the potatoes to eat the cabbage.

I, too, was flabbergasted. The potatoes were good! But the cabbage was better, way better. It stole the show. So I made it again with just cabbage, and, look, I am not going to try to convince you that you're going to like chunks of charred-edged cabbage with some chiplike flakes braised in vinegar with soft cloves of garlic and pats of butter, if you are skeptical about these things. I know it's not for everyone. But if it's for you, and I bet you know already whether it is, you are in for my new favorite way to roast cabbage. It's going to seem too charred, too vinegary, too vegetal when you first pull it from the oven, but the pan will not make it to the table intact.

———————

Heat the oven to 475°F (245°C).

On a rimmed 9-by-13-inch baking sheet, toss the cabbage with the olive oil, salt, and pepper to coat evenly, but leaving any chunks intact—that is, there's no need to separate the leafy layers. Dot the butter over the top—it will melt in the oven. Roast for 15 minutes, until the cabbage is black in spots. Use a spatula to turn the cabbage over and scatter the garlic cloves in the pan.

Return to the oven and roast for another 15 minutes, until the cabbage looks worrisomely charred (but it will be perfect, I promise). Pour the broth and vinegar carefully into the pan, and return it to the oven a final time, to roast for yet another 15 minutes, or until the garlic cloves are tender and the liquids have been reduced to a thin (or nonexistent) puddle. Finish with a sprinkling of sea salt, and good luck not eating the crunchy bits right from the pan.

skillet white beans "caesar"

serves 1 or 2

Olive oil

½ cup (30 grams) panko-style plain or coarse breadcrumbs

Kosher salt

2 garlic cloves

3 anchovy fillets

1 tablespoon drained capers

Red-pepper flakes

Grated zest and juice of ½ lemon

One 15.5-ounce (440-gram) can white beans (cannellini, navy, or other), drained and rinsed

¼ teaspoon smooth Dijon mustard

1 tablespoon grated Parmesan

1 tablespoon chopped fresh flat-leaf parsley (optional)

note Despite its cooking-for-one vibe, this is also very nicely doubled as a more substantial side dish.

Sometimes I daydream about writing a cookbook entirely devoted to ways you can doctor up a can of beans. It's usually during lunch on a weekday, which on all of the days when I'm not working on a wildly successful, ready-by-1:00-p.m. recipe that I don't need to save for dinner—that would be just about all of the days—is highly likely to be a peanut-butter-and-jelly sandwich. When I do make time for experimentation, canned beans are one of my favorite muses. My two favorite things to do with them are to treat them as you would pasta—warming them in some tomato sauce with Parmesan, or an aglio olio, or a basil pesto—or to apply a favorite salad dressing to them and scoop them onto toast. This version is a little of both. To a quadfecta of ingredients—olive oil, garlic, anchovies, and lemon—that could make a crumpled piece of paper taste good (note: not fact-checked), I add a smidge of Dijon mustard and a small amount of capers (they're so good here; please, try them), and warm a can of beans in it. They're finished with some fried breadcrumbs reminiscent of the croutons essential to all good Caesar salads, and Parmesan, and then you're supposed to slide them onto a bowl or plate—but nobody is going to know if you eat them straight from the pan.

In a medium-sized skillet, warm 1 to 2 tablespoons of olive oil over medium heat; then add the breadcrumbs. Season with salt, and cook, stirring, until they're crisp and evenly golden brown, about 5 minutes. Scrape them into a bowl and set aside.

On a cutting board, mince together the garlic, anchovies, and capers. Heat another 2 tablespoons of olive oil in the skillet over medium-high heat. Add the garlic-caper mixture, pepper flakes, and zest, and cook until the garlic is lightly golden at the edges. Add the beans, and cook until they're warmed through, 2 to 3 minutes. Stir in the Dijon mustard, and cook with the beans for 30 seconds. The beans will look a little creamy; add 1 table-spoon water if they don't. Season with salt to taste. Turn the heat off, and finish with a squeeze of lemon juice. Transfer to a bowl or plate, and finish with crumbs, Parmesan, and parsley, if using. Eat right away.

spiced sweet potato oven fries

serves 4, as a side dish

1½ pounds (680 grams) sweet potatoes, unpeeled, cut into ½-inch sticks

2 tablespoons (25 grams) olive oil

1¼ teaspoons (4 grams) kosher salt, plus ½ teaspoon for sauce

Heaped ¼ teaspoon garlic powder

¾ teaspoon ground coriander

¾ teaspoon ground cumin

¼ teaspoon ground cayenne, or adjusted to taste

Scant ¼ teaspoon ground cardamom or cinnamon

¾ cup (175 grams) plain Greek-style yogurt

1 tablespoon (15 grams) white vinegar

2 garlic cloves, minced

1 tablespoon harissa, or adjusted to taste

note The yogurt sauce makes a bit more than what you'll need, but it's so good, we like to put it on everything, from sandwiches to a dip for whatever other roasted vegetables you might make.

My extremely controversial opinion (okay, this opinion is neither extreme nor particularly controversial) on sweet potato fries is that they're not worth frying, because they lose their exterior crisp—the key value-add of a plunge into boiling oil—very soon after they emerge. Sweet potatoes are tender and moist, and I think we are all happiest in the kitchen when we do not fight the nature of our ingredients. However, I'm always impressed with the crisp and char I can get on sweet potato fries in the oven, which has the added benefit of hands-off ease. I love them with a roll in intense spices—here, inspired by spit-fired shawarma—that offset the sweetness of the potatoes, and a dip into a garlicky white sauce swirled with harissa. I could eat these for dinner at least once a week all winter, and probably would if left to my own devices. Don't fret if you don't have all of the spices called for. Use as many as you have—the fries will forgive.

Make the potatoes: Heat the oven to 400°F (205°C), and line a baking sheet with parchment paper. Toss the potatoes with 2 tablespoons olive oil. Add 1¼ teaspoons kosher salt, garlic powder, coriander, cumin, cayenne, and cardamom, and toss to coat evenly. Spread the potatoes on the prepared baking sheet, trying not to leave any spices behind in the bowl and separating the fries as much as possible, and roast until they're brown underneath, 15 minutes. Flip the fries, and roast for another 10 minutes, so they get brown on another side, and then return to the oven for a final 5 minutes, until they're nicely brown and blistered all over.

Make the yogurt sauce: Meanwhile, combine the yogurt, vinegar, remaining ½ teaspoon kosher salt, and garlic cloves. Dollop the harissa on top, and use a knife to marble it in. When the fries are ready, serve immediately with the yogurt sauce.

broccoli rabe with broken burrata

serves 2 very enthusiastic rabe-
eaters, or 4, as a side dish

**1 bundle (12 ounces,
or 340 grams) broccoli rabe**

Olive oil

**3 garlic cloves, minced,
or more to taste**

Grated zest and juice of ½ lemon

Red-pepper flakes

Kosher salt

**8-ounce (225-gram) ball burrata,
drained, patted dry, and brought
to room temperature**

I married a guy who could eat a mountain of bitter greens and never tire of them. I used to find this baffling, but now I've fallen in love with them, too, and the essential contrast they provide against rich or heavy foods. What I'm saying is: I make a *lot* of broccoli rabe, as would most people if their life partner's favorite vegetable took fewer than 10 minutes to cook. (Alas, mine is artichokes, and they take forever to steam.) This means I also have a lot of opinions on the best way to prepare broccoli rabe, and the first one is that there's no reason to blanche it to mute the bitterness (especially galling if, for you, too, the bitterness is the point). However, I love to add a splash of water near the end, which adds a little tenderness and brightens the greens. Broccoli rabe is always wonderful sautéed in olive oil, pepper flakes, and as much garlic as you have the patience to chop that day; some people consider a squeeze of lemon juice at the end optional, but it is not. Technically, this is all you *need,* but if you have burrata, just you wait. Atop warm, bitter vegetables, burrata acts the way a poached egg might elsewhere, breaking open and spilling out, enriching everything around it. It will make you question why you'd ever limit your burrata intake to tomato season again.

Cut the stems and leaves of the broccoli rabe into 1-to-2-inch segments. In a large frying pan, heat 2 tablespoons olive oil, garlic, lemon zest, and pinches of red-pepper flakes (to taste; ¼ teaspoon will give the greens a nice heat) together over medium-high heat. Cook, stirring, until the garlic just begins to take on color, about 2 minutes. Add the rabe and ½ teaspoon salt, and cook until it's wilted, about 2 minutes. Add 2 table-spoons water, and cook with a lid on the pan for 2 minutes. Remove the lid, and cook, stirring everything, for 1 more minute, just to make sure it's not watery.

Transfer the greens to a low bowl, and squeeze lemon juice over the top. Make a nest in the center of the greens, and add the burrata. Use a knife to tear it open and to spill the center out a bit. Drizzle the burrata with a little more olive oil, and sprinkle with more salt and pepper flakes.

braised winter squash wedges

serves 4

2¼ to 2½ pounds
(1 to 1.15 kilograms) winter
squash (about ½ kabocha
or red kuri squash)

2 tablespoons (30 grams)
unsalted butter

2 tablespoons (25 grams) olive
oil, divided

Leaves from 6 sprigs fresh thyme

Kosher salt and freshly ground
black pepper

6 garlic cloves, smashed

1 cup (235 grams) vegetable
broth

¼ cup (60 grams) apple-cider
vinegar

1 cup (230 grams) plain
Greek-style yogurt

2 cups (55 grams) baby arugula
leaves

note If you can find it—you
can often buy squash in halves
or quarters from a farmers'
market, which is great, because
it runs large—kabocha is my
favorite here, followed by red
kuri squash. Butternut and acorn
squash work, too. The peel of
winter squash is fully edible, so
no need to trim it away.

This is my favorite way to cook winter squash. It takes a cue from fondant, or melting, potatoes, a technique in which thick slices of potato are roasted on both sides before they finish cooking braised in a puddle of broth. From the oven, they're crisp and somewhat glazed outside, creamy inside, and booming with more flavor than it seems possible to lock inside a potato. Clearly, I'm a fan—but I had no idea that when I applied this technique to big wedges of winter squash I'd never want to cook it another way again.

I add to the pan everything I like with winter squash—thyme, garlic, and cider vinegar, which gets sweet/tangy when cooked and really helps cut through the sweetness of squash—and then I put the whole thing on a plate of tart yogurt and peppery baby arugula. Any slightly syrupy broth left in the pan is poured over everything, and it's all so good together, you might wonder why you'd ever consider squash a side dish again. This is centerpiece squash, and it wants you to know it.

———————

Heat the oven to 425°F (220°C).

Cut the squash in half and scoop out the seeds and pulp, then slice the halves into 1½-inch wedges. Add butter and 1 tablespoon of the oil to a 10-by-15-inch baking sheet, and place in the oven until the butter melts, about 2 minutes. Remove the tray from the oven, and roll the butter around so that it evenly coats the pan. Arrange the squash wedges in one layer, and sprinkle with thyme, ½ teaspoon salt, and lots of freshly ground black pepper. Roast for 15 minutes, or until deeply browned underneath. Flip the slices, and season the second side on top with another ½ teaspoon salt and more pepper. Scatter the garlic cloves in the pan, and return the pan to the oven to roast for another 12 to 15 minutes, until the wedges are browned on the second side. Don't worry if the squash isn't fully cooked yet. Carefully pour the broth and vinegar into the pan, and roast for another 10 to 15 minutes, until the squash is tender and the liquid is somewhat cooked off. →

braised winter squash wedges *(continued)*

To serve the squash: Use the back of a spoon to swirl plain yogurt onto a serving platter into a thin layer. Toss the arugula with the remaining table-spoon olive oil and a pinch of salt and pepper, and scatter over the yogurt. Arrange the squash wedges on top, scrape out every bit of pan juice that's left, and pour it over the squash.

spinach spiral bread

makes 8 to 10 slices

dough

¾ cup (175 grams) warm water
(about 110°F to 116°F, or 43°C
to 46°C)

1¾ teaspoons instant yeast

2 cups plus 2 tablespoons
(275 grams) all-purpose or
bread flour

2½ teaspoons (about 7 grams)
kosher salt

Olive oil, for coating the bowl

filling

2 tablespoons (30 grams)
red-wine vinegar

¼ cup (35 grams) raisins or
dried currants

2 tablespoons (25 grams)
olive oil

1 small/medium yellow onion,
halved, very thinly sliced

2 garlic cloves, minced

5 ounces (140 grams) baby
spinach leaves

Kosher salt and freshly ground
black pepper

¼ teaspoon red-pepper flakes

½ cup (55 grams) chopped
walnuts, toasted

assembly

1 large egg, beaten with
1 teaspoon water (optional)

8 ounces (225 grams) feta
cheese, crumbled, at room
temperature

¼ cup (60 grams) sour cream,
plain yogurt, or mascarpone

This loaf fills an extremely specific gap in my repertoire, one for a savory, vegetable-full bread that might accompany a soup or be added to a brunch or join a picnic spread. Wanting it to be as easy to make as possible—or else, as you might imagine, it will not get made—I channeled stromboli, a Philadelphia-born rolled sandwich often made with pizza dough and filled with sliced meat and cheese. However, this filling has neither, going its own way with a mix of sautéed spinach, onion, and garlic, and accents from raisins or dried currants (just trust that they're excellent here) and chopped walnuts. It tastes so much more balanced and nuanced than your average cooked greens, almost Sicilian-style. Finally—and this is especially welcome if you're bringing it to a picnic or a party—we're going to make an easy whipped feta spread to be served on the side. The sharp, salty fluffiness is the perfect complement here, but it's also delightfully optional, should you wish to keep this bread dairy-free.

Make the dough: Turn your oven on to warm (200°F or 95°C), let it stay at that temperature for 5 minutes, and turn it off. Combine the water and yeast in a large mixing bowl, and let it rest for 5 minutes. Add the flour, then the salt, and mix with a wooden spoon until a rough, craggy mass forms. Turn the dough and any loose bits out onto a lightly floured counter, and knead for a few minutes, or until you have a smooth, elastic dough. Coat the inside of the mixing bowl with olive oil, return the dough to the bowl, and cover with plastic wrap. Place the bowl in the previously warmed oven, and let it sit for 30 minutes, or until doubled. Remove the dough from the oven.

Make the spinach filling: Pour the vinegar over the raisins, and set them aside. Heat the oil in a large frying pan over medium heat. Cook the onion until softened, about 8 to 10 minutes. Add the garlic, and cook for another minute. Pour in any vinegar not absorbed by the raisins, and cook for 1 minute. Tear the spinach into slightly smaller pieces as you add it to the pan, along with 1 teaspoon salt, red-pepper flakes, and grinds of black pepper. Cook the spinach until soft. Stir in the raisins and walnuts, and let the mixture cool until needed. →

notes

- The dough recipe here yields just about 1 pound of pizza dough; feel free to swap in a prepared dough instead.

- The amount of salt in the dough will seem high, but it makes a balanced final bread.

- I'll keep leftovers of this bread, unsliced, for the first day at room temperature, and, after that in the fridge for 3 or 4 days. It's great at room temperature, but if it's chilled, it's better rewarmed in a low oven. The slices are nice toasted when the bread gets to the staler end of its lifespan.

Heat the oven to 400°F (205°C), and line a large baking sheet with parchment paper.

Assemble the bread: Roll out the dough on a floured counter to a large, thin, and slightly wide rectangle. (There's truly no wrong shape for this.) Scatter the spinach evenly over the center of the dough, leaving a 1-inch border clear. Roll the dough into a log, and pinch it closed along the seam. Transfer to the prepared baking sheet, seam side down, and let it rest for 15 minutes at room temperature before baking.

For more shine, brush the log with the egg wash. Cut a few ½-inch-deep slits in the loaf on a diagonal.

Bake the bread: Bake the loaf for 20 to 25 minutes. Note that there will be some range, depending on how thick or thin your dough has been rolled. Look for a loaf that is nicely browned on top and underneath, with an internal temperature of 200°F (95°C).

Make the feta dip: While the bread bakes, if you are making the whipped feta, add the feta and sour cream to a blender or food processor and blend at high speed, scraping down the bowl as needed, until it is evenly mixed and lightened in texture.

To serve: The bread is good warm from the oven or at room temperature. Serve in slices alongside the feta dip with a knife for spreading.

medium vegetables

leek and brie galette

serves 6 to 8 as an appetizer

1 medium lemon

¾ cup (100 grams) all-purpose flour

½ cup (65 grams) rye or whole-wheat flour

Kosher salt

½ cup (4 ounces, or 115 grams) unsalted butter, chilled

¼ cup (60 grams) plain yogurt or sour cream

¼ cup (60 grams) cold water

2 to 3 large leeks (but see note)

2 tablespoons (25 grams) olive oil

Freshly ground black pepper

1 large garlic clove, minced or finely grated

1 tablespoon (15 grams) smooth Dijon mustard

4 ounces (115 grams) brie, cold, sliced ¼ inch thick

1 egg, lightly beaten (optional, for shine)

I thought it would be easy, silly me, but the truth is that I made a lot, I mean *a lot,* of leek galettes on the way to this one. There were a few with potatoes (so heavy), a few with leeks that had been caramelized on the stove (so much work), one with a garlicky Parmesan béchamel underneath (even more work), one with leeks boiled until meltingly tender, closer to classic leeks vinaigrette (but too sapped of flavor), one with salt-wilted leeks (that tasted grassy when baked). So I hope you know that when I tell you this is the one leek galette you should make, I don't say it lightly.

My goal was a galette to show off the gorgeousness (those fanned yellow-to-green ombré layers) and flavor (one part mild onion, one part green vegetable) of leeks without being a horror to prepare or eat. Long ribbons of leeks are awfully pretty, but they're a pain to cut neatly once cooked, so, here, segments of leeks bake (hands off!) in an easy puddle of olive oil, lemon zest, salt, and pepper until they're tender and sweet, and then they're arranged on a layer of brie, which rests on top of a dead-simple crust that comes out so flaky and rich, few will believe you didn't use puff pastry. What emerges from the oven is luxurious, a dream of a holiday appetizer or a show-stealing potluck contribution. Listen, I'm going to be a total embarrassment here, an absolute mom-staying-too-long-on-the-first-day-of-school, but I'm getting a little verklempt at imagining all the places you might take it. I hope you have fun together.

Heat the oven to 375°F (190°C). Finely grate the zest of your lemon into a 9-by-13-inch or 3-quart baking dish, and set aside. (We zest before juicing to avoid bad moods.)

Make the crust: Whisk the flours and ½ teaspoon salt in a large bowl. Cut the butter into small pieces, and sprinkle them over the flour. Use a pastry blender or your fingertips to squash the butter into the flour until the mixture resembles coarse meal, with the biggest pieces of butter the size of tiny peas. Add the yogurt, water, and 2 teaspoons lemon juice (from half the zested lemon), and stir this into the butter-flour mixture →

note Leeks' sizes range *tremendously,* even from week to week in the same store or market stand. Plus, some have a larger dark-green portion, which we won't use here, and some only have a little, so weight is little guidance to how much usable leek you'll get from each one. Instead, if they look small either in width (1-inch-thick stalks) or usability (i.e., the white/light-green portion looks very squat, only a small proportion of the stalk), just grab an extra bundle.

until a large mass forms, with no unmixed pockets of yogurt. Wrap it with a large piece of parchment paper—we will use the paper again—and chill for 1 hour, or up to 2 days.

Prepare the leeks: Fill a large bowl with cold water. Lop off the darkest-green parts of the leeks; we will use the white through medium-green parts for this galette. Halve the usable leek parts lengthwise, and fan them open under water, letting any dirt and debris fall to the bottom of the bowl. Shake off the excess water, and cut them into 2-inch diagonal segments.

Bake the leeks: Add olive oil, 1 teaspoon salt, many grinds of pepper, and garlic to the zest in the baking dish, and mix. Arrange the leek segments, cut side down, in the dish, and cover with a lid or tightly with foil. Bake for 25 minutes, or until the tip of a knife can be easily inserted without meeting rubbery resistance. Transfer the baking pan to a cooling rack, carefully remove the foil, and set it aside to cool to lukewarm while the crust finishes chilling.

Increase the oven temperature to 400°F (205°C) degrees.

Assemble the galette: Unwrap the chilled dough, and flatten the parchment paper that wrapped it on a large baking sheet. On a floured counter, roll the dough out into a large roundish shape, about 14 inches across. Gently transfer it to the parchment paper. Spread Dijon mustard thinly on the dough, leaving a 2-to-3-inch border clear. Arrange the brie slices over the mustard, then season the brie with salt and pepper. Use a thin spatula to lift the leek segments from the baking dish, and arrange each, cut side up, over the brie. Scrape any juices left in the pan over the leeks. Season with more black pepper, then fold the edges of the dough in pleats over the filling, leaving the center open. For a darker, glossier crust, beat an egg with 1 teaspoon of water, and brush it over the crust.

Bake the galette: Bake for 30 minutes, until the crust and leeks are a shade darker and the brie is melted. Finish with a squeeze of juice from the remaining lemon half, cut the galette into wedges, and serve it warm.

do ahead This galette keeps in the fridge for 3 days. Rewarm on a baking sheet in a 350°F (175°C) oven for 10 to 15 minutes.

carrot tarte tatin

serves 6 as an appetizer

1 pound (455 grams) trimmed slim carrots, multicolored if you can find them, scrubbed

3 tablespoons (45 grams) unsalted butter

2 tablespoons (40 grams) honey

1½ teaspoons (4 grams) kosher salt

Lots of freshly ground black pepper

1 teaspoon fresh thyme leaves, plus more for garnish

3 tablespoons (45 grams) balsamic vinegar

1 sheet puff pastry (see note), defrosted in fridge overnight

2 ounces (55 grams) goat cheese from a log, thinly sliced

Flaky sea salt

notes

• For aesthetics, I use rainbow carrots, and am grateful they've become so readily available in the last few years, but of course single-color carrots work here, too, just as well. The carrot bundles can range a lot in size, since they're often weighed with giant fronds attached. You might need two or even three bundles. Use any leftover carrots for the Sesame Asparagus and Carrot Chop (page 46). →

For a very long time, tartes Tatin were my nemesis, especially when made with apples. It took me years—and finally calling in help from an expert—to make one that wasn't too thin, sparse, pale, over- or under-cooked. Buoyed by this triumph, no longer fazed by upside-down tarts, I suddenly didn't want to stop making them, and, strangely, it wasn't the pineapple or peach that became my favorite but this, a savory version, with carrots.

Wait, come back. I know it sounds finicky. If you're picturing melting sugar on the stove until it reaches an exact temperature, stop right there. This one is as easy as sautéing carrots in all of the things that make sautéed carrots delicious—butter, salt, pepper, thyme, balsamic vinegar, and a little honey. They'll be good enough to eat right from the pan. But covering them with a little goat cheese and a round of prepared puff pastry and popping this into the oven to cook the pastry, and then flipping it back over, is such a flex, such a stunner, it turns cooked carrots into something magnificent, and I think we deserve magnificence, whether it's for a light Tuesday night dinner or as a contribution to a Thanksgiving table.

———————

Heat the oven to 400°F (205°C). Line a 9-inch round cake pan with a circle of parchment paper.

Prepare the carrots: If your carrots are very thin (½ inch or less across at the top), cut them in half lengthwise. If they're slightly thicker (more than ½ inch), quarter them lengthwise.

In a large sauté pan, heat the butter and honey together over medium-high heat until the butter is melted and the mixture is bubbly. Add the carrots, salt, pepper, and thyme, and toss to coat. Cover with a lid, reduce the heat to medium, and cook for 12 to 15 minutes, or until the carrots are mostly cooked through. Insert the tip of a knife into the thick end of a few carrots; you're looking for a little tightness/resistance, but no crunch. While you're cooking the carrots, occasionally lift the lid to stir and ensure they're cooking evenly. If they're browning in the pan, reduce the heat a little. →

- If you are feeding anyone who doesn't like goat cheese—something I'm familiar with—leave it out of the tart, and serve it on the side for those who like it to add on top.

- Most puff pastry comes as a single sheet in either 12- or 14-ounce (340- or 400-gram) packages. Some comes in a larger package (17.3-ounce) but will include two sheets; you only need one here. If you can find one that's all-butter, you will taste the difference.

carrot tarte tatin *(continued)*

With the lid off, increase the heat, allowing most of the liquid to cook off. Add the vinegar, and cook for about 2 more minutes, turning the carrots over in the sauce as carefully as you can without breaking them, until a small syrupy puddle remains. Tip the carrots and all the pan juices into the prepared cake pan. Nudge them around so they evenly cover the bottom.

Assemble the tart: On a floured counter, roll out the puff pastry to a 10-inch round. Scatter goat-cheese slices over the carrots in the pan. Top the carrots with the pastry, tuck in the dough edges all around, and cut a vent in the center of the dough. Bake for 25 to 30 minutes, or until the pastry is a deep golden brown. (I find a deep color essential for puff pastry that won't fully flatten once flipped.)

Remove the tart from the oven and let it rest for 10 minutes; then run a knife around the edges and flip it out onto a plate. Remove the parchment paper if it's stuck to the carrots, and scrape any juices left in the pan over the tart. Nudge any wayward carrots back into place. Garnish the tart with additional thyme leaves and flaky salt. Cut into wedges with a serrated knife, and serve.

do ahead This tart is best warm. If you're making it in advance, leave it in the baking pan and gently rewarm it in the oven before flipping it onto a plate.

skillet piperade eggs

serves 2 to 4;
can double easily to feed more

¼ cup (50 grams) olive oil, plus more for drizzling

1 medium yellow onion, halved, thinly sliced

4 garlic cloves, minced

1 large (about 7 ounces, or 200 grams) green bell pepper, stemmed, seeded, thinly sliced

1 large (about 7 ounces, or 200 grams) red bell pepper, stemmed, seeded, thinly sliced

1½ teaspoons (4 grams) kosher salt, plus more for the eggs

One 14.5-ounce can (410 grams) diced or crushed tomatoes, or 1¾ cups small-diced fresh tomatoes

½ teaspoon granulated sugar

½ teaspoon piment d'Espelette or hot smoked paprika

4 large eggs

Freshly ground black pepper

Cooked rice or grilled bread, for serving (optional)

I was always ambivalent about green bell peppers. I didn't refuse them or anything, but I always felt that, if we were reading their school report cards, it would say that more could be done for them to reach their potential—like, perhaps, leaving them on the vine until they turned red. (It's a thing, I swear!)

Enter: piperade or piperrada. Green peppers star in this classic Basque dish, and they're cooked in olive oil with tomatoes, onion, garlic, and hot pepper (usually piment d'Espelette) until everything is tender and rich and absolutely impossible not to eat right from the pan, even if it burns your tongue. And it turns out, the green peppers are perfect here. This dish is impossibly good; savory, saucy, sweet, and so flavorful. You could stop right here, or serve it with a side of rice, or as a side dish to fish or grilled meat. But my favorite thing to do with it is to nest a few eggs in the pan and cook them until they're perfect, the whites set and the centers still a little runny. Serve with grilled bread or rice and, if you're me, probably get way too excited about finding a way to love something you once thought you didn't.

———

In a large, deep skillet over medium-high heat, heat the oil until it is hot but not smoking. Add the onion, garlic, peppers, and 1 teaspoon kosher salt, and sauté, stirring frequently, until the onions are translucent and the peppers have softened, about 10 minutes. Add the tomatoes, sugar, more salt (½ teaspoon), and the piment d'Espelette, and reduce the heat to medium. Cook the pepper mixture for 5 minutes, stirring occasionally, until the tomatoes look saucy. If the sauce looks dry or is sticking to the pan, add ¼ cup water and cook for another minute.

You can use this pan to cook the eggs, but, to allow for deeper wells, I often transfer the peppers to a 3-quart saucepan at this point. If you do so, bring the mixture back to a simmer in its new pan.

Make wells for the eggs, and break an egg into each one. Sprinkle each egg with a pinch of salt and black pepper, and cover the pan with a lid. Simmer for 6 to 10 minutes (see note), until the whites are set but the →

yolks are runny, then scoop peppers and eggs onto plates and serve with rice or grilled bread.

note The trickiest part of any baked-egg dish, even when prepared on the stovetop, is getting the eggs exactly right, neither undercooked nor hard-boiled. I vote for checking them as often as needed, and occasionally rotating the pan for even cooking. Most important, ask yourself: Am I eating this the second it comes off the stove or ten minutes later? If the latter, take them off the heat while the egg whites are still wobbly, because they'll continue to cook in the sauce as the pan rests.

green angel hair with garlic butter

serves 4

½ cup (4 ounces, or 115 grams) salted or unsalted butter, sliced into a few pieces

Kosher salt

1 large head garlic, halved crosswise

1 pound (455 grams) thin spaghetti, such as angel hair or capellini

5 ounces (140 grams) baby spinach

Freshly ground black pepper and/or red-pepper flakes

Pecorino Romano, to finish

In the 1990s heyday of roasted garlic, it was in restaurants everywhere: whole heads of garlic roasted until the cloves were soft and slightly sweet, easily squeezed from their skins and spread across breads, dropped in salads, and mashed into potatoes. Then, as will always happen post-ubiquity, the pendulum swung the other way and roasted garlic heads seemingly went into hiding. But if overalls and bucket hats can make a comeback, why not this? A few New Year's Eves ago, I set out to make my case for its return, except, instead of roasting the garlic with a drizzle of olive oil, I used a stick of butter ("Whoops!"), roasted it for the better part of an hour, and blended it smooth, and we smeared it on pieces of bread and, did you know, I also made a *cheese soufflé* that night? And *beef Wellington*? (The theme was old-school decadence.) Neither of those dishes made the impression that the roasted garlic butter did.

This headnote should stop here. But what if you want weekday garlic butter confit in your life? And your life doesn't have crostini and sparkly cocktails on a Tuesday, much as that needs correction? Well, then, you should take this garlic butter and blend it with spinach until the garlic butter is brilliantly green, and toss it with spaghetti finished with black pepper and sharp Pecorino cheese for—please don't tell the other ninety-nine recipes in this book—what might be the best thing I have ever made for dinner.

Heat the oven to 375°F (190°C).

Arrange the butter slices across the bottom of a small (2-cup) baking dish. Sprinkle with salt: ¼ teaspoon if using salted butter, and ½ teaspoon if unsalted. Place the garlic halves, cut side down, over the butter and salt. Cover the dish tightly with foil, and bake for 35 to 45 minutes, until the garlic is absolutely soft when poked with a knife and golden brown along the cut side. Carefully remove the foil. Empty the garlic cloves into the melted butter. I do this by lifting the peels out of the butter with tongs, allowing most cloves to fall out, and using the tip of a knife to free the cloves that don't. Scrape any browned bits from the sides of the baking vessel into the butter. $\rightarrow$

Meanwhile, cook your pasta in well-salted water until 1 to 2 minutes shy of done. Before you drain it, ladle 1 cup pasta water into a cup, and set it aside. Hang on to the pot you cooked the pasta in.

Place the spinach in a blender or food-processor bowl, and pour the garlic butter over it, scraping out any butter left behind. Add another ¾ teaspoon salt and several grinds of black pepper, and/or a couple pinches of red-pepper flakes, and blend the mixture until totally smooth. If it's not blending, add 1 to 2 tablespoons of reserved pasta water to help it along. Taste for seasoning, and add more if needed.

Pour the spinach sauce into the empty spaghetti pot, and add the drained pasta and a splash of pasta water. Cook over medium-high heat, tossing constantly, for 2 minutes, until the sauce thickens and coats the spaghetti. If the pasta sticks to the bottom of the pot, add more reserved pasta water in splashes to get it moving. Tip the pasta into a serving bowl, finish with more salt and pepper and freshly grated cheese, and hurry—it disappears fast.

notes

- I know you're going to balk over the angel hair, a most unpopular pasta shape, and though it's not required here, it's made for this—a thin sauce that clings easily to fine strands.
- You can replace half the butter (4 tablespoons, or 55 grams) with olive oil, if you wish. You can bump up the greens to 8 ounces if you like it even greener, but make sure the dish is seasoned extra well to adjust.

soy-glazed tofu with crisped rice

serves 3

One 14-ounce (397-gram) package extra-firm tofu

1 pound (455 grams) fresh, crunchy vegetables, cut into thin matchsticks

2 to 4 tablespoons (30 to 60 grams) unseasoned rice vinegar, divided, plus more to taste

2 teaspoons toasted sesame oil, plus more to taste

3 scallions, thinly sliced, divided

Kosher salt and freshly ground black pepper

Vegetable oil

2½ cups (425 grams) cooked rice, cooled

1½ tablespoons cornstarch

1 tablespoon minced garlic

1 tablespoon minced fresh ginger

2 tablespoons (30 grams) black vinegar or unseasoned rice vinegar

3 tablespoons (45 grams) tamari, or light or low-sodium soy sauce

2 tablespoons (25 grams) packed dark-brown sugar

Toasted sesame seeds, to finish

Crispy chili oil or sriracha, to serve

This is my favorite preparation for main-course tofu. I love eating tofu and want it to be the center of my plate more often than my family agrees to—or agreed to, until this recipe. Browning the tofu well gives it a firmer edge, and reducing the soy sauce and rice vinegar with garlic, ginger, and brown sugar in the pan gives you an intense, deliciously lacquered glaze to pour over the tofu. It will not stay crisp for long once you've added the sauce, but I hardly mind, because I love the softness of the tofu against a pile of crisped rice. From there, I will grab any crunchy vegetable I need to use up in my fridge—I've used Napa or savoy cabbage, rainbow-colored peppers, carrots, cucumbers, and even celery—to make a quick salad to serve with this, delighted to rise to the nonexistent challenge nobody posed to me, calling, "Can I slaw this? I bet I can!" Matchstick vegetables tossed with a light, toasty dressing, glossy tofu, and crispy rice are so good together, I think we should make this once a week forever, don't you?

Prepare the tofu: Drain the tofu, and cut it into six even slices, the short way. Arrange the slices on a few layers of paper towels, and then cover with more paper towels; set aside for 5 minutes, or until the rice is done (see below).

Make the slaw: In a large bowl, toss the sliced vegetables with 2 tablespoons (30 grams) of the unseasoned rice vinegar, sesame oil, and two-thirds of the scallions; season well with salt and pepper. Add more oil or vinegar to taste. Set aside for serving.

Crisp your rice: Heat a large frying pan—nonstick makes things easier here—over medium-high heat. Add 2 tablespoons vegetable oil and warm it a full minute; scatter your precooked rice in the pan, season it lightly with salt, and press it gently into one layer. Cook the rice undisturbed, except nudging a spot to check for color, until the underside is golden brown and crisp, about 5 minutes. Use a spatula to flip the rice in sections then continue to cook it, undisturbed, on the other side until that is also crisp. Divide the rice between three plates, and wipe out the pan so you can use it again. →

notes

- If salt is a concern, replace 1 tablespoon of the soy sauce with water. Just note that the color won't be as dark. The black vinegar also helps give this glaze a dark, lacquered appearance, although either kind of rice vinegar will taste good here. (See note to Ginger Garlic Chicken Noodle Soup, page 72.)

- My favorite rice to crisp here is leftover short-grain brown or white rice.

- The yield here is low, because I wanted to align the recipe with common tofu package sizes. You could double it to make more servings, or add another vegetable, such as sautéed greens, on the side to stretch it further.

soy-glazed tofu with crisped rice *(continued)*

Cook the tofu: Sprinkle a large plate with cornstarch, and roll each piece of tofu in it. Reheat your large frying pan over medium-high heat. Add 2 tablespoons vegetable oil. Once the oil is hot, brown the tofu well on both sides, about 8 to 10 minutes total. Transfer two slices to each plate, with the crisped rice.

Add more oil to the pan, if needed, and cook the garlic and ginger, stirring, for 1 minute. Add 2 tablespoons unseasoned rice vinegar, plus 2 tablespoons black vinegar if you have it, or simply 4 tablespoons unseasoned in total, plus the soy sauce and sugar, and cook, stirring, until it's reduced and thickened, about 5 minutes.

To serve: Pour the glaze over the tofu slices on the plates, and don't worry if it doesn't look like a lot; a little goes a long way. Heap some slaw on the side. Sprinkle with the remaining scallions and the sesame seeds, and eat right away, preferably with some chili crisp.

toasted ricotta gnocchi with pistachio pesto

serves 2 to 4

gnocchi

2 cups (from one 1-pound or 454-gram container) whole-milk ricotta

1 large egg

½ cup (50 grams) finely grated Parmesan, plus more for serving

1½ teaspoons (4 grams) kosher salt

1 cup (130 grams) all-purpose flour

Olive oil

pesto

½ cup (70 grams) shelled pistachios, salted or unsalted

1 large or 2 small garlic cloves

1 teaspoon (3 grams) kosher salt

Freshly ground pepper and/or red-pepper flakes, to taste

1½ cups (45 grams, or 1½ ounces) arugula leaves

½ cup (105 grams) olive oil

I f you've ever sworn off gnocchi-making forever after bombing at it, I'm here to tell you what a reader once told me: Psst, you should try ricotta gnocchi. I'm so glad she did, because ricotta gnocchi is much, much harder to fail at, and believe me, I try all of the time. It requires none of the baking or ricing potatoes or persnickety kneading—oh no, that was too much kneading, and now they're a gluey mess heading for the trash can!—of potato gnocchi. You can go from a tub of store-bought ricotta to golden, crisp-edged, cheesy nuggets in under 45 minutes.

Why nuggets? I personally find ricotta gnocchi that's been boiled a bit too fluffy and soft. But I've always loved the potato gnocchi at Barbuto, a restaurant in the West Village, where fresh gnocchi are browned in butter and oil instead of boiling, for gorgeous color and texture. I started doing this with ricotta gnocchi and have never looked back.

This recipe makes what looks like two servings, but I'm telling you, it's closer to four. Ricotta gnocchi are rich, and I've yet to meet anyone who could eat a heap of them. I add a quick, sharp, crunchy pesto here for even more contrast. In the summer, we love this with a simple tomato salad (oil, vinegar, flaky salt) on the side.

Prepare the ricotta: Lightly dust a large baking sheet with flour. On your counter, stack two squares of paper towels, and scoop the ricotta on top, flattening out the cheese to mostly cover the towels. Cover with another two squares of paper towel, pat it on top, and set it aside for 15 minutes.

Form the gnocchi: In a large bowl, beat together the egg, Parmesan, and salt to combine. Add the drained ricotta, and mix it thoroughly. Add the flour, and mix only until it disappears.

Flour your counter well, and scoop the ricotta mixture onto it. Divide the ricotta in half. Using floured hands and a gentle touch, roll the first half into a ¾-inch-thick rope about 25 to 28 inches long. (If this is a challenge on your counter space, you can roll it into four 12-to-14-inch ropes.) Cut the rope into ¾-inch segments, and scatter them on the prepared baking sheet. Repeat with the second half of the ricotta dough. →

Freeze the gnocchi on the tray for 10 to 15 minutes, until cool and lightly firmed to the touch but not frozen through. (Firming them up makes them easier to brown in the pan, but if you have utter confidence in your frying skills, you can skip this step.)

Meanwhile, make the pesto: Blend the nuts, garlic, salt, and a couple pinches of pepper in a food processor until roughly chopped. Add the arugula, and let the machine roughly chop it, too. In a thin stream, add the olive oil, running the machine the whole time. Taste the pesto, and add more salt or pepper to taste.

Cook the gnocchi: In a large nonstick pan, heat 3 tablespoons olive oil over medium heat. Add half of the gnocchi—try to space them apart a tiny bit, but don't go crazy with it—and let them cook, undisturbed, until they are a deep golden brown underneath, about 2 to 3 minutes. Now that the gnocchi have set a little, you can flip and toss them a few times until they're browned on more sides, about 5 to 7 minutes total cooking time. I find them much easier to move around with a fork than a spatula, but of course be careful of your pan's finish. Use a slotted spoon to transfer gnocchi to a serving bowl. Repeat with the second half of the gnocchi, adding more olive oil if needed; leave them in the pan when they're done. (The second batch always goes faster, because the pan is hotter.)

Assemble the gnocchi to serve: Return the first half of toasted gnocchi to the pan, and add 2 tablespoons water. Cook, stirring the gnocchi, for 1 minute; this will help the pesto to coat them smoothly. Remove from the heat, and add half of the arugula pesto, gently stirring, and then add more to taste. Pour the gnocchi into the serving bowl, and garnish with Parmesan.

pecorino polenta with garlicky kale

serves 4

Kosher salt

1 cup (140 grams) dried polenta

2 bunches Tuscan or lacinato kale (about 1 pound, or 450 grams), leaves stripped from ribs and torn into 1½-inch pieces

¼ cup (50 grams) olive oil, plus more to finish

4 garlic cloves, thinly sliced

¼ teaspoon red-pepper flakes

1 teaspoon freshly ground black pepper, plus more for serving

2 tablespoons (30 grams) unsalted butter

1 cup (100 grams) grated Pecorino cheese, divided

note Although I love greens and polenta alone as a meal, I'd be remiss not to mention how amazing this dish is with the meatballs from the Perfect Meatballs and Spaghetti (page 209) on top.

A technique I've become enamored with over the last few years is something I'm calling Everything in the Oven Right Now. (Apologies if you were expecting something more cheffy.) Many things that I used to make on a stove because I thought I needed to start them there (see Slumped Parmesan Frittata, page 15), either by sautéing them (see the leeks in the Leek and Brie Galette, page 117), or boiling them (see lasagna noodles, page 163; the orzo, page 155; the couscous, page 157) before adding them to a dish that would then need more cooking time—and leave me with more dishes to do—I simply don't do anymore, or certainly not when I can avoid it. I have nothing against the stove, especially for quicker preparations; it's just that cooking over a gas flame demands a level of attention that an oven does not.

Polenta is absolutely something I thought I could only make on the stove, because of the stirring. Watch any Italian cooking channel on YouTube (what, you don't do this?) and you will see someone getting tsk-tsked by a lovely nonna whom I wouldn't dare cross, either, about the lumps that will form if they do not stir, stir, stir. Yet there are no lumps in this polenta, and I only stir it for a moment at the beginning and the end. Plus, it tastes a bit like cacio e pepe. And since I have one pan in the oven while making dinner, I go ahead and add a second, here the garlicky greens I love most of all with a rich bowl of polenta. You can then finish the dish with a dollop of something rich, like mascarpone or ricotta, or a fried or poached egg, or you can just eat it straight.

———————

Heat the oven to 375°F (190°C).

Prepare the polenta: Combine 4⅓ cups room-temperature water and 2 teaspoons salt in an ovenproof baking dish (3 to 4 quarts), and gradually whisk in the dried polenta. It will sink; don't worry about that. Cover tightly with foil or a lid, and bake for 30 to 40 minutes. The polenta is done when it looks a little watery but thickened.

Meanwhile, prepare the kale: In a second ovenproof baking dish, combine the kale leaves with the olive oil, garlic, ½ teaspoon salt, pepper →

pecorino polenta with garlicky kale *(continued)*

flakes, and 1 tablespoon water. Cover the dish tightly with foil or a lid, and bake it above or next to the polenta for 20 minutes, or until the kale is softened. Carefully remove the foil or lid, and give the kale a stir. Return it to the oven and cook for 10 more minutes, until there's a little color at the edge of some leaves. Remove it from the oven, stir again, and taste for seasoning.

To finish the polenta: Remove the lid, add 1 teaspoon black pepper, and whisk for 1 minute; it will thicken and take on a more cohesive texture, but if it's thicker than you'd like, or thickens too much as it rests, you can add 2 more tablespoons of water. Whisk in the butter so that it melts, then add ¾ cup of the Pecorino. Add more salt and black pepper to taste. Leave it covered until you're ready to eat.

To serve: Add a big scoop of polenta and a slightly smaller scoop of the greens to each bowl. Finish with 1 tablespoon of the reserved Pecorino and more black pepper, to taste.

cauliflower cheese baked potato

serves 4 as a main dish,
8 as a side

4 baking potatoes, russet or
Idaho (each about 8 ounces,
or 225 grams)

Olive oil

1 large (2½-to-3-pound, or 1130-
to-1360-gram) head cauliflower,
cut into medium florets

Kosher salt, and freshly ground
pepper or ground cayenne

4 tablespoons (55 grams,
or 2 ounces) unsalted butter

1 medium leek, white and light-
green parts, halved lengthwise,
cleaned, thinly sliced

4 tablespoons (35 grams,
or 1 ounce) all-purpose flour

2 teaspoons mustard powder,
or ¾ teaspoon smooth Dijon
mustard

Ground cayenne pepper (optional)

2 cups (475 grams) milk, whole
or low-fat

1¼ cups plus 2 tablespoons
(about 155 grams, or 5½ ounces,
total) grated sharp cheddar

2 tablespoons minced fresh
chives, for garnish (optional)

Sour cream

I think it is criminal that cauliflower cheese—cauliflower florets draped with a sharp cheddar cheese sauce spiked with a bit of cayenne, then baked in the oven until bronzed and bubbly—is not as much of a thing, or really a thing at all, in the United States.

I first encountered this delicacy in the U.K. many years ago and have been doing my best PR for it since then—with only moderate success, judging from restaurant menus. (I even tried to make the argument that it was low-carb mac-and-cheese, but few were enchanted.) While we're at it, can we start calling baked potatoes "jacket potatoes"? It sounds much more dapper, doesn't it?

Here we snug these two very hearty and cozy things tightly in a baking dish for the kind of dead-of-winter comfort food some days require. Don't even look at this recipe in July—so rich, so monochrome—but it makes absolute sense the first day the puddles freeze.

Bake the potatoes: Heat the oven to 450°F (230°C). Pierce the potatoes all over with a fork, and rub them with 1 tablespoon olive oil. Place the potatoes on the oven rack, and bake for 1 hour, or until tender in the center when pierced with a skewer.

While the potatoes bake, prepare the cauliflower: Coat a baking sheet with 2 tablespoons olive oil. Add the cauliflower florets, and toss to coat. Season well with salt and pepper. Roast for 25 to 30 minutes total, tossing once, until nicely browned at the edges. Let the cauliflower cool while the potatoes finish.

Meanwhile, make the sauce: In a medium saucepan, melt the butter over medium heat. Add the sliced leek, and cook until softened, about 8 to 10 minutes. Add the flour, and whisk to combine; cook for 1 minute to ensure you get rid of the floury taste. Add the mustard powder and a pinch of cayenne or few grinds of black pepper, and stir to combine. Drizzle in the milk in a thin, steady stream, whisking the whole time so that no lumps form. Season with salt, and bring the mixture to a simmer, stirring with a spoon; the sauce should begin to thicken. Remove from the heat, and stir →

cauliflower cheese baked potato *(continued)*

in 1¼ cups grated cheddar, a handful at a time, letting each handful melt before adding the next. Taste the sauce, and adjust seasonings if needed. Add the roasted cauliflower, and stir until it's coated with sauce.

Assemble potatoes: Once the potatoes are ready, slice them in half lengthwise, and, using a pot holder, arrange them snugly, cut side up, in a 9-by-13-inch baking dish. Season the cut sides with salt and pepper, and use the tip of a knife to score them in a grid, cutting ½ to 1 inch into the potato. Spoon the cauliflower cheese sauce over each potato. Sprinkle them with the remaining cheddar, and return them to the oven to cook until the cauliflower topping is browned, 5 to 10 minutes.

To serve: Scatter with chives, if desired. Serve with sour cream.

big vegetables

portobello hoagie

makes 2 large sandwiches

2 tablespoons (25 grams) olive oil

4 portobello mushroom caps (about 12 ounces, or 340 grams), thinly sliced

3 garlic cloves, minced

Kosher salt and freshly ground black pepper

1 tablespoon (15 grams) Worcestershire sauce

1 tablespoon (15 grams) soy sauce

2 tablespoons (30 grams) unsalted butter

1 large onion, thinly sliced

1 tablespoon dry Marsala wine or sherry vinegar, to deglaze

Two 8-inch seeded hoagie or other oblong sandwich rolls

4 to 6 slices Swiss cheese

note If you'd like to skip the cheese, this is also great with a little mashed avocado or mayo on the bun for contrast.

I love mushrooms, and I love hearty vegetable sandwiches, but I never liked grilled whole portobello sandwiches—I find them hard to season throughout and quick to get rubbery. Not this one. Here, we thinly slice the mushrooms and cook them with garlic, a bit of Worcestershire, and soy sauce and . . . Oof, I so dislike the word "meaty" applied to vegetables, as if their highest calling would be to approximate a steak, whereas I think it should be the other way around (shots fired!), but here the flavor is abundant. Then we brown an onion, perk it up with a little vinegar, heap everything on a bun with Swiss cheese, and cook it in the oven until the cheese melts and . . . I'm sorry, how are you still reading this? Go, go make these. You'll be so glad you did.

———

Heat the oven to 400°F (205°C).

Make the mushrooms: In a large pan, heat the olive oil over medium-high heat until it's very hot; then add the mushrooms. Don't disturb them until they have a little color underneath, in 2 to 4 minutes; then cook, stirring, until they begin to soften. Add the garlic, salt, and freshly ground black pepper, and cook until the juices are released from the mushrooms. Add the Worcestershire and soy sauce, and cook until little liquid is left in the pan. Adjust the seasoning to taste, and transfer the mushrooms to a bowl.

Cook the onion: Melt butter in the same pan over medium-high heat, and add the onion and a couple pinches of salt. Cook the onion until the slices are wilted and browned, about 12 to 14 minutes. Add the Marsala or vinegar, and cook until it disappears, less than 1 minute.

Split your rolls in half, keeping one side attached. Divide the mushrooms between the two rolls, then the onions. Arrange the cheese slices on top, and close the sandwiches. Wrap them tightly in foil, and bake them on a tray in the oven until the cheese is melted and the sandwiches are hot throughout, about 8 to 10 minutes. The foil will help them stay warm until you're ready to eat.

falafel

makes 19 small pieces of falafel

½ pound (1¼ cups or
225 grams) dried chickpeas

Kosher salt

½ large onion, roughly chopped,
or 1 cup chopped scallions

3 to 4 garlic cloves, peeled

¼ cup finely chopped fresh
parsley, if you're measuring,
or a big handful

¼ cup finely chopped fresh
cilantro, if you're measuring,
or a big handful

½ to 1 teaspoon hot red-pepper
flakes or mild ones, such as
Urfa biber or Aleppo

1 teaspoon ground cumin

Peanut or vegetable oil, for frying

to serve

Pitas, tahini sauce (see page
144), tomato-cucumber salad,
harissa or another hot sauce
(such as zhoug), and any pickled
vegetables you wish, such as
cucumbers, red onion, or mango
(amba)

Until recently, if you'd asked me if I ever wanted to make falafel at home, I'd have said "sure, one day," but what I would mean was "nah, why bother?" I was certain that falafel was fussy to make and had a long ingredient list. It was probably related in some way to a fritter, meaning that it was bound with eggs and flour, and probably had breading on it, too, all pesky steps, and this is before you get to the peskiest of all: deep-frying them. But this isn't the whole truth. The fact is that below 14th Street, there are two locations each of Taïm and Mamoun's, and every time I even distantly considered whether I needed a homemade falafel recipe in my life, I knew I could get a perfectly executed sandwich in my hands before I even wrote out a grocery list.

Had I spent less time rationalizing the reasons why I didn't need to make it at home and more reading a few recipes, I'd have learned many extremely cool things about falafel—such as the fact that while you *do* need to start with dried chickpeas (come back!), you don't even have to cook them, or at least not in the classic long-simmered way. You soak them overnight in cold water, grind them up with seasonings and herbs, pack them into spoonfuls, fry them in less than an inch of oil in merely a few minutes, and that is it. There's no egg. There's no breading. It's vegan, it's gluten-free, and it's easy, I mean criminally easy, to make. And I had to do it immediately.

The night before: Place chickpeas in a large bowl with ½ teaspoon kosher salt and enough water to cover them by a few inches. Let the chickpeas soak overnight.

An hour or so before you'd like to eat falafel: Drain the chickpeas well. In the bowl of a food processor or a really strong blender, place the onion, garlic, and herbs and pulse the machine until they're coarsely chopped. Add the drained chickpeas, salt, red-pepper flakes, and cumin, and process until blended to a fine chop but not puréed. You're looking for a texture like cooked couscous with some slightly larger bits throughout. You should be able to pinch it together into a shape that holds. →

falafel (*continued*)

- I know many of us dread frying foods, but for whatever it's worth, making falafel involves none of the headaches that other fried foods do. You don't need a lot of oil (¾-inch depth is fine.) You don't need to stress over anything burning on the outside while still being unsafe to eat in the middle. You don't need to use an entire roll of paper towels and every counter in your home to drain the falafel, because they don't pick up much oil at all.

- This makes nineteen pieces of falafel, each about 1½ inches in diameter, using a 1½-tablespoon cookie scoop to measure. I estimate 3 to 4 for each medium-large pita sandwich portion. This recipe scales easily; I'd recommend doubling it for a crowd or even just to stock your freezer for a future falafel night.

Transfer the chickpea mixture to a bowl, cover with plastic, and place it in the refrigerator—for a few hours, if you have the time, but I find even 30 minutes helps the mixture to thicken and hold a shape better. (This is when I like to get everything else ready.)

To shape the falafel: Form the chickpea mixture into walnut-sized balls with a tablespoon measure, or even a small cookie scoop (as I do). If the mixture seems very wet, you can press out most of the excess liquid as you compress the ingredients in the spoon, and then gently roll the mixture in the palms of your hands to form a ball. Repeat with the remaining chickpea mixture; go ahead and form these all now so you can focus as you fry them. Don't worry if they feel fragile; they will set up when frying.

To cook the falafel: Heat ¾ to 1 inch of oil in a medium-large frying pan to 375°F (190°C). Fry about six falafel fritters at a time, turning them over once they're a nice toasty brown underneath, and removing them once the other side has the same color. This takes about 3 minutes per batch. Drain on paper towels and repeat with the remaining fritters.

(Don't have a thermometer? Well, 375°F is very, very hot. It takes my frying pan of oil on high heat about 5 minutes to reach this temperature. You can also test a small ball; if it cooks in about 3 minutes, the oil's probably the right temperature.)

To serve: I like to split open a pita and start with a little tahini sauce (below) and a spoonful of tomato-cucumber salad at the bottom before adding 3 or 4 falafel fritters. Stuff and finish with a more generous scoop of tomato-cucumber salad, more tahini sauce, the hot sauce of your choice, and pickles, if you want them.

tahini sauce

Whisk together ½ cup well-stirred tahini; 1 clove garlic, minced or finely grated; juice of ½ lemon, plus more lemon juice to taste; salt, to taste; and water, as needed, to thin the tahini into a sauce. It's not strange to need at least as much water as you do tahini to keep it loose and spoonable, but I add it a tablespoon at a time, whisking to combine, tasting along the way.

deepest dish broccoli cheddar quiche

serves 12

crust

2 cups (260 grams) all-purpose flour

1 teaspoon (3 grams) kosher salt

1 cup (225 grams, 8 ounces, or 16 tablespoons) unsalted butter, chilled

½ cup (120 grams) very cold water

filling

1¾ pounds (800 grams) broccoli

4 tablespoons (55 grams, or 2 ounces) unsalted butter

1 large or 2 small white or yellow onions, finely chopped

3 garlic cloves, minced

3 teaspoons (8 grams) kosher salt, divided

1 teaspoon freshly ground black pepper, divided

6 large eggs

2¼ cups (535 grams) milk (whole is ideal)

¾ cup (175 grams) heavy cream

8 ounces (230 grams) sharp white cheddar cheese, coarsely grated (about 3 cups), divided

1 heaped tablespoon (15 grams) smooth Dijon mustard

My cooking style when having people over is less "lots of little things" and more "a few epic things." Since I'll only find out whether this is due to space limitations or cooking style when some sort of windfall allows me to buy a sprawling New York City apartment big enough that I can even consider putting out a dozen dishes at once—i.e., hold that thought, maybe forever—I enjoy finding a solution when the things I want to cook don't feed the number of people I want to pack around the table.

Quiche, for example, has always posed a problem, which is a bummer, because I am always really excited when someone serves a quiche for brunch or lunch. In a pie or tart pan, it serves "eight"—sure, but those are slim little wedges that require a salad and sometimes another dish, and there's little room for seconds. What's a quiche lover to do? Well, I doorstopped it.

Inspired by the towering version in Thomas Keller's *Bouchon,* I love both the drama and the yield of springformed quiches. This one channels the broccoli-cheddar soup on my website that's heavy on the broccoli— I like my quiches with as much vegetable as custard—but is still uncompromised in decadence. Whether we make it for ten people crammed around a table or a third as many, aspiring for leftovers, this recipe understands that the only thing better than an astoundingly delicious quiche is a quiche that nobody has to skimp on enjoying.

Make the dough: Place the flour and salt in a large bowl, and whisk to combine. Cut the butter into small cubes, and add them into the flour mixture. Toss them around so that they're coated, and use your fingers to work the butter into the flour mixture until it looks like coarse cornmeal. (You could also use a pastry blender, stand mixer, or food processor for this step.) Pour the water over the butter-flour mixture, and use a flexible silicone spatula or scraper to bring it all together into a dough that will seem too wet and sticky but will be just fine. Scrape the dough onto a large piece of plastic or parchment paper, pat into a flat packet shape, and wrap tightly. Chill for 2 hours, or until completely firm; it can stay chilled for up to 4 days.

Prepare the crust: Lightly coat a 9-inch springform pan with 3-inch sides with butter or nonstick spray. For added security against leaks, →

- We keep a 1-inch overhang on the crust over the sides of the springform; it's not for decoration, but to keep everything in place over the long baking time. It will be trimmed away before serving.

- Store leftover quiche in the fridge for up to 5 days.

you can tightly seal a piece of foil around the outside bottom and sides of the pan. Place the pan on a rimmed baking sheet until needed.

Roll the dough on a floured surface to a 16-inch round. Gently fold the dough (don't crease it) in quarters and transfer it to the prepared pan, then gently unfold it, allowing the slack of the dough to drape into and fill out the center. Press it against the sides, trim the overhang to 1 inch (see note), and use the scraps to patch any tears or holes; be as watchful as you can here, because tears or holes = leaks. Let the crust chill in the fridge while you prepare the filling.

Heat the oven to 350°F (175°C).

Make the filling: Prepare the broccoli by peeling the thickest stems (removing tough outer skin and knobs) and cutting them into a medium (½-inch) dice. Cut the florets into 1-inch pieces. You'll have a total of about 8 cups chopped.

Melt the butter in a large, deep skillet over medium-high heat. Add the onion and garlic, and cook until they're translucent, about 5 minutes. Stir in the broccoli, 2 teaspoons kosher salt, and ½ teaspoon freshly ground black pepper, and cook with onion and garlic for 8 minutes, until the broccoli is slightly softened. It should be bright, tender-crisp, and a bit salty; adjust seasoning if it's not. Transfer to a large plate or bowl, and cool for 10 minutes.

Meanwhile, whisk the eggs, milk, cream, remaining 1 teaspoon salt and ½ teaspoon pepper. Add three-quarters of the grated cheese, and stir to combine. Remove the springform with the dough from the fridge, and place on a foil-lined baking sheet. Brush or spread the Dijon over the bottom of the crust. Add the broccoli-onion mixture to the crust. Pour the custard over the mixture, and finish with the remaining cheese.

Bake the quiche: This quiche needs a long baking time. Bake it for 1½ to 1¾ hours, until it's nicely bronzed on top and the custard is just set. I insert a knife into the center of the custard and turn it slightly; you should see no liquid custard pouring into the crevice created when it's done. Let it cool in the pan for 10 to 15 minutes.

To serve: When ready to serve, carefully cut away any part of the crust's 1-inch border that has stuck to the outside of the springform ring, then loosen the clamp of the ring and remove it. Slide the quiche onto a serving plate, and serve in wedges with a green salad.

tomato and corn cobbler

serves 6 as a main,
8 as part of a spread

filling

2 to 2½ pounds
(about 1 to 1.3 kilograms)
beefsteak tomatoes

1 teaspoon (3 grams) kosher salt

Freshly ground black pepper

3 cups (420 grams) fresh corn
(from 3 to 4 ears)

1½ cups (6 ounces,
or 170 grams) grated sharp
white cheddar cheese

⅓ cup (70 grams) mayonnaise

2 tablespoons (30 grams)
fresh lemon juice

2 scallions, finely chopped,
divided

2 tablespoons finely chopped
fresh basil

biscuits

2 cups (260 grams) all-purpose
flour

2¼ teaspoons baking powder

¾ teaspoon baking soda

2 teaspoons granulated sugar

1 teaspoon (3 grams) kosher salt

6 tablespoons (85 grams)
unsalted butter, chilled,
cut into cubes

¼ cup (50 grams) mayonnaise

½ cup (115 grams) buttermilk

One of my forever favorite recipes from the late *Gourmet* magazine is a Southern-style Tomato and Corn Pie adapted from James Beard and Laurie Colwin. It tastes like the epitome of summer—sweet corn, ripe tomatoes, scallions, basil, chives, and cheddar, baked in a tender butter crust. It also includes mayonnaise, but few ever detect it, so no need to bring it up if you're among skeptics. (The mayo just makes everything better—more tangy and rich.) But I've always struggled with the juiciness of peak-season tomatoes sogging the crust, no matter how much I blotted them, so, a few years ago, I ditched that recipe and turned it into a biscuit-topped cobbler, and, yes, I worked some mayo in, too. I love serving this to friends and family, because nobody knows what it is at first. I love the polite faces people make when they want to be hopeful, to be supportive, but they're just not so sure about this one, Deb. And then they tepidly try it, and then much less tepidly, and soon the whole pan is gone. It manages to taste like nothing you've ever had before but it's instantly familiar, like everything good about summer in one casserole dish.

———————

Heat the oven to 400°F (205°C).

Cut the tomatoes into ¼-inch-thick slices, and blot lightly with a paper towel. Arrange half of the tomatoes in a 9-by-13-inch baking dish, and sprinkle with ½ teaspoon kosher salt and many grinds of pepper. Combine the corn, cheddar, ⅓ cup mayonnaise, lemon juice, half the scallions, and all of the basil in a bowl. Spoon half of the corn mixture over the tomatoes in dollops. Repeat with a second layer, using the remaining tomatoes, salt, pepper, and corn mixture.

Parbake the tomatoes and corn for 30 to 35 minutes, until the tomato juices are bubbling.

Meanwhile, make the biscuits: Whisk the flour, baking powder, baking soda, sugar, and salt together in a large bowl. Add the butter, and use your fingertips or a pastry blender to work it into the flour until it's in small bits. Add ¼ cup mayonnaise, buttermilk, and remaining scallions, and stir to combine. The mixture should begin to form a larger mass →

tomato and corn cobbler *(continued)*

with floury bits around; knead it a few times in the bowl so it's in one mass.

On a floured counter, pat or roll the biscuit dough out ½ inch thick, and cut into 2-to-3-inch circles. Arrange, with space between them, over the tomatoes and corn, and return the dish to the oven to bake for 15 to 17 minutes, until the biscuits are golden on top.

Let the cobbler rest for 5 minutes before serving. This dish is also good cooled to lukewarm.

do ahead The entire dish can be rewarmed, but the biscuits do absorb more juices from underneath the longer they sit. If you'd like to get prep out of the way but bake it right before serving, I would assemble the tomatoes and corn in a pan, ready to parbake, and shape the biscuits, leaving them on a lined baking sheet in the fridge until you're ready to begin the baking process.

creamy coconut rice with chili-lime vegetables

serves 4

risotto

Kosher salt

One 13.5-ounce (400-gram) can low- or full-fat coconut milk, well shaken

1 cup (200 grams) uncooked jasmine rice

2 garlic cloves, minced

1 tablespoon minced fresh ginger

½ teaspoon ground turmeric

vegetables

3 cups chopped fresh cauliflower (small head, 1½ pounds, or 680 grams)

2 cups chopped sweet potato or winter squash (about 1 pound, or 460 grams)

2 garlic cloves, minced

2 tablespoons (30 grams) neutral oil or coconut oil

¾ teaspoon kosher salt

Freshly ground black pepper

finish

1 fresh red chili pepper, thinly sliced

1 to 2 tablespoons white vinegar

Grated zest and juice from ½ lime

Fresh cilantro leaves, roughly chopped

This coconut rice is inspired loosely by risotto. I'd been taught that, like polenta, risotto is something that could only be made on the stove. The broth, warmed in a separate saucepan, needed to be added a ladleful at a time, and you needed to stir constantly. When I realized I could make risotto in the oven, virtually hands-free, and just as delicious, I tried (unsuccessfully) to get a refund on all the stirring time I'd squandered. I also started making creamy baked-rice dishes a lot; I find it useful in convincing kids (not naming names) who believe that pasta is the only acceptable carb.

My flavor inspiration here is the coconut-vegetable curry I always order at Thai restaurants—but instead of serving saucy vegetables with regular rice, I've inverted the textures so that the rice is creamy. I cook the vegetables on a separate tray where they get browned and crisped before I finish them with lime juice, cilantro, and marinated red chilis. The rice is rich and cozy, and the vegetables are blistered and bright, and I hope this becomes a staple for you, too.

———

Heat the oven to 375°F (190°C).

In a 9-by-13-inch or 3-quart baking dish, combine 2½ cups water, 2 teaspoons kosher salt, and the remaining risotto ingredients. Seal it tightly with foil, and bake until the rice is tender, about 40 to 45 minutes.

Meanwhile, on a rimmed baking sheet, combine the vegetables with garlic, oil, ¾ teaspoon salt, and pepper. Roast alongside the risotto for 20 to 22 minutes, then flip and roast for another 15, until tender and browned.

While the risotto and vegetables cook, combine the chili pepper and vinegar in a small bowl, and set aside. When the vegetables are finished, sprinkle the lime zest and juice, the cilantro, and the chili on top, and toss to combine. →

creamy coconut rice with chili-lime vegetables *(continued)*

note I'm using cauliflower and sweet potato or winter squash here, but you can and should use whatever vegetables you'd enjoy that roast well, such as broccoli or broccolini, carrots, or green beans.

To finish the risotto, transfer the baking dish with the rice to a trivet or cooling rack on your counter. Carefully remove the foil and stir for (just!) 2 minutes, or until the rice looks creamy and more risotto-like. Taste, and adjust the seasonings.

To serve: Spoon the risotto into bowls, and add the roasted vegetables on top.

baked orzo and artichokes

serves 4

2 tablespoons (25 grams) olive oil

1 tablespoon (15 grams) unsalted butter

4 scallions, thinly sliced, white and green parts separated

1 medium onion, thinly sliced into half-moons

3 garlic cloves, minced

Two 14-ounce (400-gram) cans artichoke hearts in water, drained, roughly chopped

Finely grated zest and juice of 1 lemon

Kosher salt and freshly ground black pepper

Red-pepper flakes

8 ounces (225 grams) uncooked orzo

3 tablespoons minced fresh parsley

3 tablespoons minced fresh mint

2 tablespoons minced fresh chives

4 ounces (115 grams) mozzarella, cut into small cubes

½ cup (50 grams) grated Parmesan

1½ cups (355 grams) vegetable broth

Way back in the Smitten Kitchen archives is a baked-orzo dish inspired by Yotam Ottolenghi that manages to be absolutely jammed with vegetables, luxurious (cheese *sssstretches* from every forkful) but unheavy, devoid of milk, cream, or even a marinara sauce. It's perfect for late summer. But this is the version I make for spring, lemony, herby, and artichoke-rich. Despite being a devout artichoke-lover, I've struggled with canned artichokes, because they can have a flattened, tinny flavor. But here they're triumphant. Sautéed onion, scallions, garlic, lemon zest, and pepper flakes even them out; lemon juice, three herbs, and Parmesan wake up their dynamic flavor. The orzo cooks right in the pan and the recipe comes together quickly. You could have this as a side dish for a bigger spring feast, but I often just make a salad and call it a delicious day. The flavors are bright and warm; you could even take a bite, close your eyes, and beam spring to you all the way from January.

———————

Heat the oven to 350°F (175°C).

Heat a large sauté pan (ideally one that can go into the oven) over medium heat. Once it's hot, add the oil and butter; when the butter is melted, add the scallion whites, onion, and garlic. Cook for 3 to 4 minutes, until softened. Add the artichokes, zest, 1 teaspoon kosher salt, many grinds of black pepper, plus red-pepper flakes, to taste, and cook for another 3 to 4 minutes. Remove from the heat. Add the lemon juice, and stir to scrape up any stuck bits. Stir in the orzo, scallion greens, and herbs, then mozzarella and half of the Parmesan.

If your pan isn't oven-safe, transfer everything to a 2-to-2½-quart baking dish, which often measures 8 by 11 inches. Pour the broth over the top, giving it a light stir to distribute it, and then add the remaining Parmesan on top. Cover tightly with foil, bake for 20 minutes, remove the foil, and bake for another 20 to 25 minutes, or until the orzo on top is crisp and the orzo below the top layer is cooked through. Serve warm. →

baked orzo and artichokes *(continued)*

notes

- You'll have a bit over 1 pound, or 3 cups, of artichokes, once they're drained and chopped. You can replace half, if you wish, with frozen peas or another spring vegetable, such as asparagus.
- If you want to skip the cheese, I'd suggest doubling the onion and the olive oil for richness.
- You could easily double everything for more servings.
- Leftovers will keep for 5 days in the fridge and reheat well.

tangy baked eggplant and couscous

serves 4

Olive oil

Kosher salt and freshly ground black pepper

1½ pounds (680 grams) eggplant (globe and fairy-tale both work here), cut into ½-inch slices

1 medium-large onion, halved, thinly sliced

2 garlic cloves, thinly sliced

½ cup (130 grams) tomato paste

1 tablespoon (15 grams) granulated sugar

¼ teaspoon red-pepper flakes

Juice of ½ lemon

2½ cups (590 grams) water

1 cup (150 grams) uncooked pearl couscous

This is the kind of dish I start thinking about every September, when late-summer produce is still booming but the weather has cooled off slightly. Roasted eggplant is shingled in a tangy tomato sauce and baked with couscous, a perfect weeknight meal that we've also welcomed on our High Holiday table. I don't think I've ever met an intersection of eggplant and tomato that I didn't like, especially when there's a lot of garlic and a heavy hand of seasoning involved (although, technically, this describes most of them, caponata to eggplant caviar to imam bayildi), but there's something particularly homey to me when the sauce is a little sweet-and-sour. I couldn't put my finger on why, so I reached out to the cookbook author and Jewish food expert Leah Koenig, who provided me with some context. She said that sweet-sour preparations are popular in the Middle East and other places where Jewish immigrants from all over have settled, but that doesn't necessarily mean the combination originated there. In fact, a sweet-sour eggplant dish is equally likely to be Romanian or Balkan and have originated in Turkey. My conclusion? I would really like to go on an eggplant-and-tomato world tour. For now, it starts here.

Heat the oven to 425°F (220°C).

Coat a half-sheet pan with 3 tablespoons of olive oil, and sprinkle the oil with ¾ teaspoon salt and several grinds of black pepper. Arrange the eggplant slices in one layer. Drizzle them with 2 more tablespoons oil, another ¾ teaspoon kosher salt, and more black pepper. Roast until nicely browned underneath, 20 minutes. Use a thin spatula to turn the eggplant slices over, and roast until browned on the second side, another 10 minutes. We are aiming here for good browning, but don't worry if the eggplant isn't fully cooked through yet; we are not done with it. Reduce the heat to 350°F (175°C).

If you have a large ovenproof skillet or a shallow Dutch oven (3 to 4 quarts), use it here. If not, use a large frying pan for the sauce, and have a 3-to-4-quart baking dish nearby to transfer the sauce into once it's ready. →

note The eggplant and couscous will continue to absorb the sauce as they rest, so I will sometimes add another couple tablespoons of water, stirring it in as carefully as possible, before rewarming the dish.

Warm the pan over medium-high heat. Once it's hot, add 2 tablespoons olive oil. Once the oil is hot, add the onion, and cook until soft and beginning to brown at the edges, 8 to 10 minutes. Add the garlic, and cook for 1 to 2 minutes more. Add the tomato paste, sugar, 2 teaspoons kosher salt, red-pepper flakes, and many grinds of black pepper, and cook, stirring, for 3 to 4 minutes, until the tomato paste is one shade darker. Add the lemon juice and water, and bring the liquid to a simmer. Stir in the couscous, and remove from heat.

If you're baking in this skillet or frying pan, nestle your roasted eggplant slices into it, overlapping them slightly, and cover with a lid or foil. If you're using a baking dish, transfer the tomato mixture, couscous, and all of the liquid to the baking dish. Nestle in your roasted eggplant slices, as above, overlapping them slightly, and cover with a lid or foil.

Bake for 40 to 50 minutes, until the couscous is cooked through and the eggplant is very tender. Remove from the oven, and let rest 5 minutes before serving.

swiss chard enchiladas

serves 4

filling

1-pound bundle Swiss chard

1 large red onion

Kosher salt and freshly ground black pepper

Olive oil

4 garlic cloves, thinly sliced

1 cup (140 grams) corn kernels, fresh or frozen

One 15.5-ounce can (1¾ cups, or 440 grams) black or small red beans, drained and rinsed

1 cup (3.5 ounces, or 100 grams) crumbled Cotija cheese

sauce

One 14.5-ounce can (1½ cups, or 410 grams) crushed or fire-roasted tomatoes

1 tablespoon ground chili powder, or 1 tablespoon chipotle purée from a can, plus more to taste

½ teaspoon granulated sugar

¾ teaspoon ground cumin

1 teaspoon dried oregano

assembly and finish

Eight 8-inch (20-centimeter) flour tortillas

1 cup (4 ounces, or 115 grams) coarsely grated Monterey Jack or cheddar cheese

Handful of fresh cilantro, roughly chopped

1 firm-ripe avocado, thinly sliced

½ cup (120 grams) sour cream

This recipe is adapted from the wonderful chard enchiladas in Lukas Volger's *Start Simple* cookbook, a vegetarian cookbook brimming with clever, doable recipes. I enjoy chicken and steak enchiladas, but never enough to make them regularly at home. Then something about stuffing tortillas with a heap of greens called to me and wouldn't let up. The result was so good, this recipe has since become my vegetable enchilada muse. We add black beans, corn, and lots of sharp Cotija cheese inside, plus meltier cheese on top, but never skimp on the greens. I've found that if I leave the edges of the tortillas just a little bare of sauce, they become simultaneously crisp and tender, reminiscent of the corner pieces of baked ziti I always snatch first from the pan. I bet they'll be your favorite part, too.

Heat the oven to 400°F (205°C).

Strip leaves from chard stems and cut into ½-inch ribbons, and set aside. Cut stems into ¼-inch segments. Cut red onion in half, and one of the halves in half again. Thinly slice one of these quarters, season it with a pinch of salt, and set it aside for garnish. Finely chop the remaining three-quarters of the onion.

Heat a large frying pan over medium-high heat. Add 2 tablespoons olive oil, and once it is hot, add the chard stems, chopped onion, and garlic, and season with salt and pepper. Cook until the stems soften slightly and the onion is browned at the edges, 5 to 7 minutes. Add the greens and more salt and pepper, and cook until the chard is wilted down and tender, 5 to 8 minutes. Add the corn, and cook for 2 minutes. Transfer to a bowl, and add the black beans and crumbled Cotija. Taste the filling, and make sure the seasoning is as you'd like it.

In a blender, combine the tomatoes, 3 tablespoons olive oil, chili powder, sugar, ground cumin, and oregano until the mixture is absolutely smooth. Season well with salt—I use ¾ to 1 teaspoon here. This will make about 1¾ cups enchilada sauce.

Coat a 9-by-13-inch baking dish lightly with oil or nonstick spray, and pour in ½ cup of enchilada sauce; spread it evenly across the bottom. →

If your tortillas are going to crack or tear when they bend, wrap them in foil and warm them on the oven rack for 5 minutes before assembling.

Grab your first tortilla, and spread 1 tablespoon sauce on it. Scoop one-eighth of the filling (6 to 7 tablespoons, but please just eyeball it for your own sanity) onto the sauce, and roll the tortilla into a cigar shape. Arrange it, seam side down, at one short end of the baking dish. Repeat with the remaining seven tortillas and filling, using up all the filling. Pour the remaining enchilada sauce over the tortillas, but—this is just my preference—leave the last ½ inch of tortilla on each side exposed, so it gets crispy. Sprinkle with grated cheese, and bake for 20 minutes, until the cheese is melted, the sauce is bubbling, and any exposed parts of the tortilla are browned.

Scatter with reserved red onion, cilantro, and avocado, and dollop with sour cream. Eat right away.

do ahead Once these are assembled, you can freeze them before or after the baking step; enchiladas rewarm well in a 350°F (175°C) oven for 25 to 30 minutes. Save the toppings for when you serve it.

zucchini and pesto lasagna

serves 6 to 8

Olive oil

3 garlic cloves, 2 thinly sliced, 1 minced

2½ pounds (1.15 kilograms) zucchini (about 5 medium) or other slim summer squash, halved and thinly sliced (about 10 cups)

Kosher salt, red-pepper flakes, and freshly ground black pepper

1 pound (455 grams) dried lasagna noodles (not the no-boil type)

½ cup (115 grams, or 8 tablespoons) unsalted butter

½ cup (65 grams) all-purpose flour

3½ cups (830 grams) milk, whole or low-fat milk

1 cup (250 grams) whole-milk ricotta

½ cup (120 grams) prepared or homemade basil pesto/pesto Genovese

1¼ cups (4½ ounces, or 125 grams) finely grated Parmesan

I know that zucchini season and turn-your-oven-on-long-enough-to-make-lasagna season rarely overlap, so I carried this vision of what I'd consider the perfect midsummer green lasagna for what felt like years, until we were home on an unusually cold and rainy Saturday in July that should have made us grumpy, but did not because it ended in this. It was worth the wait. I like vegetable lasagnas in which the vegetables are central, and here a great mountain of thinly sliced zucchini is cooked in olive oil and garlic until it almost collapses into the pan; this, to me, is when zucchini becomes the most flavorful. I prefer dried noodles over the no-boil kind, but I still don't boil them, just soak them in hot tap water for 10 to 15 minutes before assembling the lasagna. They come out of the oven perfect, and never soggy. Finally, I like very tall lasagnas; we will use the whole pound of noodles. We'll bake this on a tray, just in case our hubris trips us up and it bubbles over. When it's done, it's sky-high, the top layer crackly with bronzed melted cheese, and you might even find yourself looking forward to the next rainy summer day.

———————

Prepare the zucchini: Heat a large skillet or sauté pan over medium heat. Once the pan is hot, add ¼ cup oil. When the oil is hot, add the sliced garlic, and cook, stirring, until it's just golden at the edges, about 1 minute. Add the zucchini, 1½ teaspoons kosher salt, and red-pepper flakes to taste, and increase the heat to medium-high. Cook, turning over occasionally, until the zucchini becomes soft and starts to break down, about 5 minutes. Reduce the heat to medium, and cook 15 to 20 minutes more, at which point the zucchini will be jammy and very tender and soft. Taste for seasoning, adding more salt or heat if needed. Let it cool slightly while you soak the noodles and make the sauce.

Heat the oven to 375°F (190°C).

Prepare the noodles: Place the lasagna noodles in a large, wide bowl or deep 9-by-13-inch baking dish, and cover with the hottest tap water you can get. Soak for 10 to 15 minutes, or until the noodles are pliable, while you prepare the sauce. →

Make the sauce: Melt the butter in a large saucepan (or the wiped-out pot that you used for the zucchini filling, if it can hold 2 quarts) over medium-high heat. Once it's melted, add the flour all at once, and whisk it until smooth. Add the milk, a small glug at a time, whisking constantly so that no lumps form. When the flour mixture has reached a batterlike consistency, you can begin adding the milk in larger pours, whisking the whole time. Once you've added all the milk, then add the minced garlic, 1½ teaspoons salt, and many grinds of black pepper, and bring the sauce to a boil, stirring frequently. The sauce will immediately begin to thicken once it boils. Reduce the heat to medium, and simmer for 2 to 3 minutes. Stir in the ricotta, and remove from the heat.

Assemble the lasagna: Spread ½ cup of ricotta sauce in the bottom of a deep 9-by-13-inch baking dish. Shake the water off the noodles, and arrange your first layer of noodles, slightly overlapping their edges. Spread 1 cup of sauce over the noodles. Scatter a quarter of the zucchini on top of the sauce, followed by 1½ tablespoons pesto, and ¼ cup Parmesan. Repeat three times, then arrange the final noodles on top. Coat the noodles with the last ½ cup of ricotta sauce and remaining ¼ cup Parmesan.

Bake the lasagna: Cover tightly with foil, and bake on a tray (just in case it drips) for 30 minutes, or until the pasta is tender—a knife should easily pierce the noodles. Remove the foil carefully, and bake for another 20 minutes, until the lasagna is golden on top and bubbling like crazy. Keep it in the oven for another 5 minutes if the color on top isn't as dark as you wish.

Wait, then serve: The best lasagna has time to settle before you eat it. When it comes out of the oven, it might seem a bit wet, but 15 minutes later, it will be glorious—the excess wetness absorbed into the noodles and filling, ready for a relatively clean slice. Cut into generous squares, and dig in.

do ahead Leftovers should stay in the pan. I like to reheat lasagna in a 350°F (175°C) oven with the foil off, because I prefer it when the top gets very dark. To freeze for future use, allow it to cool completely and wrap it two or three times in plastic wrap before freezing.

meat
and one perfect plate of shrimp

crispy chili garlic butter shrimp

serves 4 as a fancy snack or
meal accompaniment, but double
it if friends are coming over,
if they're nice

**1 to 1½ pounds (455 to
680 grams) jumbo shrimp in
their shells, heads on or off
(see note)**

**3 tablespoons (45 grams) dry
white wine**

**Kosher salt and freshly ground
black pepper**

**6 tablespoons (85 grams)
unsalted butter, in a few slices**

4 garlic cloves, minced

**¼ teaspoon red-pepper flakes,
or ½ teaspoon hot smoked
paprika, or more to taste**

Juice of ½ lemon

**2 tablespoons chopped fresh
flat-leaf parsley**

Crusty bread, for serving

note If you can buy shrimp
already deveined but with the
shell on, grab them. If you'd like
to remove the vein—this
is totally personal preference,
it's not dangerous to eat—
use kitchen shears to cut along
the length of the back of each
shrimp just deep enough to
expose the vein; then remove
and discard it.

In the time since my last book, I've been lucky enough to visit Spain twice, although it generally only takes a single trip to fall in love, as I did, with gambas al ajillo, one of the most classic Spanish tapas. The shrimp are so sweet and tender, and the puddle of oil, garlic, wine, and chili pepper around them is so good, you'll be grateful for the nearby bread to swipe it up, or you'll otherwise drink it straight.

They're not always served in the shell, but I prefer this way, because shell-on shrimp is to shell-off shrimp what crisp-skinned, juicy roasted chicken is to chicken breast cutlets: it changes everything for the better. The cooking time is more forgiving; if they go a minute over, they don't immediately turn to rubber. I'm convinced the meat inside is sweeter and more tender because it's not exposed directly to a pan or grill. The shell collects whatever wonderful things you pour over the shrimp, rather than letting them run off into the pan or under the grill grates. And if all goes well, the shells get crispy, and weirdos like me don't peel them at all, just chomp away with them on. (But you can. The shells come off cleanly and neatly when the shrimp are perfectly cooked.)

That said, I don't actually make tapas shrimp here; I cook them on the grill in the summer, and in a pan on the stove in the winter. I use butter instead of olive oil (surprising nobody) for peak decadence. Once crackly-shelled and cooked through, they're tossed immediately in more chili-garlic butter, then finished with lemon juice, parsley, and more salt and pepper, and we eat them piping hot, standing up, as messy and happy as food like this should be.

———————

On a grill: Prepare your grill for medium-high heat.

Toss the shrimp in a large bowl with wine, and season well with salt and freshly ground black pepper. In a large saucepan, add the butter, garlic, ½ teaspoon salt, and pepper flakes or paprika, and heat over medium-high heat until the butter is melted and the garlic begins to sizzle in the butter. Turn the heat off, pour all but 1 generous tablespoon of this chili garlic butter over the shrimp, and toss to evenly coat. Reserve the generous tablespoon for later. →

crispy chili garlic butter shrimp *(continued)*

Grill the shrimp, turning them over once or twice as needed for even color, until the shells are a deep shade of coral and the insides are cooked through (the exposed parts of the shrimp will turn from translucent to opaque), about 5 minutes. Place the cooked shrimp in the saucepan with the remaining chili garlic butter, add the lemon juice, parsley, and a little more salt and black pepper, and toss to coat. Transfer to a serving plate (remember to put an empty bowl on the table for those who discard the shells), and eat right away.

On the stove: Toss the shrimp in a large bowl with wine, and season well with salt and freshly ground black pepper. In a large sauté pan, add the butter, garlic, ½ teaspoon salt, and pepper flakes, and heat over medium-high heat until the butter is melted and the garlic begins to sizzle in the butter. Add the shrimp, and toss to coat evenly in the butter. Cook, shaking the pan for even cooking, for 5 minutes, or until the shells are a deep shade of coral and the insides are cooked through (the exposed parts of the shrimp will turn from translucent to opaque). Turn the heat off, squeeze some lemon juice and drizzle it over the top, season with more salt and pepper, and finish with parsley. Transfer to a serving plate, leaving absolutely no chili garlic butter behind in the pan, and eat right away, using the bread to sop up any butter left on the plate.

the angry grandma (pizza)

makes 2 large pizzas, or 16 slices total

dough

2 cups (475 grams) lukewarm water (not hotter than 116°F or 47°C)

2 teaspoons (6 grams) kosher salt

2 teaspoons (5 grams) instant yeast

1 tablespoon (15 grams) olive oil

4 cups (520 grams) all-purpose flour

assembly

Olive oil

¾ to 1 cup (170 to 230 grams) prepared tomato sauce

½ teaspoon red-pepper flakes

12 ounces (340 grams) mozzarella, torn or diced into bite-sized pieces

½ small red onion, thinly sliced

2 to 3 tablespoons pitted, chopped black olives

4 ounces (115 grams) pepperoni, or hot or sweet soppressata, thinly sliced

½ small (95 grams) fennel bulb, trimmed, very thinly sliced, or 4 canned or marinated artichoke hearts, drained, thinly sliced

2 Calabrian chilis from a jar, thinly sliced, or more red-pepper flakes, both to taste

½ cup (2 ounces, or 55 grams) grated Pecorino Romano

If you've ever struggled with making pizza in your home oven, if you've been frustrated that it didn't get ripping-hot enough to emulate a pizzeria and instead turned your thin-crust efforts into overcooked crackers with none of the blistered, chewy charm of a Neapolitan pie, come, sit down. Grandma wants to talk.

Grandma pies are what your nonna would make at home if you had one. No special ovens, no pizza stones, and no intense rules, the grandma pie is *just pizza,* baked in a rectangular pan. The oven isn't as hot, the pizza is less likely to burn, and oiling the pan leads to a golden, crunchy crust that reminds me of the pan pizzas we'd beg for as kids. I make my grandma pizzas slightly on the thicker, more Sicilian side, with a looser dough I've adapted from Alexandra Stafford's incredible *Bread Toast Crumbs* cookbook. That's impossible to mess up. I can fit two rectangular pans of pizza in the oven at once—one for today and one for tomorrow (or two days from now)—and the leftovers reheat perfectly. Everything about grandma-style pizza is incredibly chill, the exact energy I was missing in our at-home pizza nights.

So how does one pivot from "chill energy" to "angry grandma"? The Angry Grandma is a delightfully named item on the menu of a slice shop we sometimes go to at the Jersey Shore. It uses a spicy arrabbiata (which translates as "angry") sauce and loads up the toppings—fennel and onion and pepperoni and sometimes artichokes and sweet peppers, all of my husband's and son's favorites. At home, our slightly thicker grandma-style pies take well to these extras—never sogging the way thin-crust pizza can—and it's so good, your pizza night is going to be a real rager (sorry).

Make the dough: Whisk the water, salt, yeast, and oil together in a large bowl. Add the flour, and use a spoon to bring it together, stirring it a few times. Cover the bowl with plastic or a dishcloth, and let the dough rise until doubled and jiggly, from 1½ to 2 hours at room temperature, or you can move it to the fridge right before it's fully doubled—for this, plastic wrap is best—and let it finish there overnight. $\rightarrow$

the angry grandma (pizza) *(continued)*

To assemble: Heat the oven to 450°F (230°C). Coat two 9-by-13-inch pans (or two 12-inch or 30-centimeter round skillets) each with 2 tablespoons olive oil. Use two forks to divide the dough in half; then I use them like salad tongs to lift each dough half out of the bowl and into its pan. Turn the dough over in the oil so it's now coated all over. Oil your fingers, and use them to dimple each dough out to the edges of its pan as best as you can; it's normal for it to not reach the edges yet. Wait 20 to 25 minutes, and repeat the process; at this point, it should fight back a little less. While waiting, combine your tomato sauce and pepper flakes.

Divide the toppings and cheese between the pizzas, and scatter them all over the dough. For grandma-style pizzas, you put the sauce on last, and you soon will be converted, too. Once you've added the toppings, dot the smaller amount of sauce around it and also to the edges. Add the remaining sauce if it looks like your pizzas need more; I usually use all of a thicker sauce and less of a thinner one. Don't worry if things spill over the edge of the dough into the pan; your pans are well oiled, and those crispy parts are bliss.

Bake the pizzas: Bake for 20 to 30 minutes. Check them at the 20-minute mark because ovens and pans will vary, but I almost always go for the full 30—you want a good deep golden brown color and crunchy edges on your pizzas; the well-oiled dough underneath is at little risk for burning.

To serve: You can serve your pizzas in their pans, but I prefer to run a knife around each to loosen it, then shimmy it onto a cutting board, where I cut it into eight rectangles or wedges. Eat right away. Leftovers, should any survive, reheat fantastically on a baking sheet in a 350°F (175°C) oven.

"russian" blt

pickled iceberg

½ cup (120 grams) water

½ cup (120 grams) white vinegar

2 teaspoons (6 grams) kosher salt

1 teaspoon granulated sugar

1 large garlic clove, minced

1 tablespoon chopped fresh dill

½ medium (about 12-ounce or 340-gram) head iceberg lettuce, cut into ½-inch ribbons

spread

⅓ cup (70 grams) mayonnaise

1 tablespoon (15 grams) minced cornichons or prepared sweet pickle relish

1 tablespoon (15 grams) ketchup

1 tablespoon (15 grams) lemon juice

¼ teaspoon kosher salt

Hot sauce, to taste

assembly

8 slices white sandwich, Pullman, or sourdough bread (½ inch or 1½ centimeters thick), toasted

1 pound (455 grams) bacon, fried, baked, or grilled until crisp

2 medium beefsteak tomatoes, cut into thick slices

Freshly ground black pepper

BLTs are perfect, especially when you can tell from the first bite that the person making the sandwiches loves them, or you, enough to prepare them with the utmost attention to detail: the bread is toasted and warm, the bacon is crisp, the tomatoes are at peak ripeness, there's just enough mayo, and the iceberg is very cold. But, to be absolutely honest, I always long for something more vinegary and bright inside. I've been working up the courage to tell you about my favorite extra for three books, and have decided it's now or never, so here goes:

Your BLT needs pickled iceberg—wait, come back. This is something my Russian mother-in-law makes, and it's amazing and delicious, and you need it in your life. Fresh iceberg that's been soaked in a garlicky, dill-flecked vinegar bath is vibrant and dynamic, and I have yet to find a sandwich not improved by the addition of a small pile—most especially a BLT. If you make nothing else, make this element. You'll find yourself putting it on everything.

But why be a little "Russian" if you can be a lot? Okay, okay, I know that there is absolutely nothing Russian about Russian dressing, but the Russian I am married to thinks it's perfect on a hearty, heavy sandwich like a Reuben, and my pared-down, hot-sauce-spiked version is pretty great here, too.

Pickle the iceberg: Combine the water, vinegar, salt, sugar, and garlic in a large bowl, and whisk until the sugar and salt dissolve. Add the dill and iceberg, and turn to coat the lettuce evenly. It will not be fully submerged in the vinegar mixture yet. Set it aside for 30 minutes, turning the pieces once or twice. In 30 minutes, the lettuce will become halfway softened and pickle-flavored. You can use it now; or you can cover and chill it for up to 1 week.

Meanwhile, make the spread: Combine all of the ingredients in a small bowl, adding the hot sauce to taste.

Assemble your sandwiches: Spread eight slices of toast with a slick of the dressing, and arrange the bacon and tomatoes on top of half the slices. Grab a tongful of iceberg, shaking off the extra vinegar, and pile it on each of the sandwiches. Close your sandwiches with the remaining slices of bread. Cut in half and eat right away.

chicken with rice, chorizo, and tomatoes

2 to 2¼ pounds
(about 1 kilogram) bone-in,
skin-on chicken thighs (4 or 5)

Kosher salt and freshly ground
black pepper

3 tablespoons (40 grams) olive
oil, divided

4 ounces (115 grams) cured
Spanish chorizo, diced

1 medium onion, thinly sliced

2 garlic cloves, chopped

½ teaspoon ground cumin

1 teaspoon smoked paprika
(sweet or hot)

¼ cup (60 grams) white wine,
or 2 tablespoons (30 grams)
white-wine vinegar

One 14.5-ounce can (410 grams)
diced or crushed tomatoes,
or 1¾ cups diced fresh tomatoes

1½ cups (250 grams) uncooked
white rice, any variety

2 cups (475 grams) chicken broth

This is one of my family's favorite dinners, and it's the absolutely coziest, while also feeling like a triumph, in that way that one-pan meals do. There's tender, almost-falling-apart chicken thighs, chorizo, tomato, a little smoky heat, and broth-soaked crispy-bottomed rice, and I have never, not even once, suggested we have it for dinner and been turned down. It started as a distant cousin to an arroz con pollo, but it's also a tiny bit paella, and tiny bit Basque chicken—but it's absolutely none of these accurately in the end. Pared down in a pandemic kitchen, this dish turned out to be about what we reliably had around. It's forgiving of swaps, but cured chorizo is my favorite here, because it infuses everything with an inky red oil, and it keeps longer than either bacon or pancetta in the fridge.

I come from a long line of home cooks who cannot make rice without burning it (rice nights meant a pot soaking in the sink until morning), but here we're trying to turn shortcomings into an asset. The rice shouldn't be burned, of course, but cranking up the heat at the end and moving the pan around the burner gives it an intentional crust. These chewy and crunchy caramelized bits at the bottom steal the show.

If there are leftovers, I use a fork to separate the chicken from the bones, nestle it in the rice, and heat it up the next day in the microwave for the least sad work-lunch ever.

Prep the chicken: Spread the chicken thighs on a plate, and season on both sides with salt and pepper. Heat a large sauté pan (it should hold 3 to 4 quarts and have a lid) over medium-high heat, and add 2 tablespoons of the oil. Brown the chicken on both sides—it takes about 4 to 5 minutes on the first side, 3 to 4 minutes on the second. Transfer it to a plate.

Cook the chorizo and rice: If the pan looks dry, warm the last tablespoon olive oil in it. Otherwise, just add the chorizo, and cook for 2 to 3 minutes, until it's beginning to crisp. Add the onion and garlic, and cook, stirring, until softened, about 5 minutes. Add the cumin and paprika, and cook for 1 minute. Add the wine, and cook until it's almost all $\longrightarrow$

chicken with rice, chorizo, and tomatoes *(continued)*

reduced, 1 to 2 minutes. Add the tomatoes plus 2 teaspoons salt. If they're fresh, cook for 5 minutes, until they begin to lose their shape and look a little saucy; this may happen 1 to 2 minutes sooner with canned tomatoes. Add the rice, and cook for 1 to 2 minutes in the tomatoes and spices. Nestle the chicken thighs back into the pan, including any juices that collected on the plate. Pour in the broth, and bring to a simmer. Reduce the heat to the lowest possible simmer, and cover the pan. Cook for 20 to 25 minutes, until the rice has absorbed the liquid and is tender, and the chicken is cooked through.

(If your rice is undercooked, add ¼ cup water and cook for another 5 minutes.)

To get the rice crispy: With the lid on the pan, increase the heat to medium-high. Cook, moving the pan around every minute or so, allowing the bottom to color evenly, until the rice is dark and crispy underneath. You'll hear it crackling in the pan. Remove it from the heat, and let it rest with the lid on for 10 minutes. The steam that collects helps it to loosen.

Serve the chicken with the rice, scraping up stuck bits from the pan with a thin spatula.

cabbage and kielbasa with rye croutons

serves 4

Olive oil

Kosher salt and freshly ground black pepper

1 medium (1¾ to 2 pounds, or 795 to 905 grams) head savoy cabbage

About 2 cups (4 ounces, or 115 grams) rye or another crusty bread torn into 1-inch pieces

½ pound (225 grams) kielbasa, diced medium (½-inch or 1¼-centimeter pieces)

2 tablespoons (15 grams) finely chopped shallot

2 tablespoons (30 grams) white- or red-wine vinegar

1 teaspoon spicy brown mustard

I am lucky to live near the East Village Meat Market, a butcher shop that's been smoking fresh kielbasa in its kitchen since 1970, and this garlicky Polish sausage makes its way onto our dinner plates in various formats many times a year. Kielbasa is wonderful grilled—if you make little notches or score a grid onto it, the edges get crunchy, so, yes, we always do that—but it's also wonderful indoor food. Still, I don't think anyone has quite used it like this before, so please don't run before you hear me out. First, we're going to roast savoy cabbage on a sheet pan, and if you haven't done this, you're about to be converted. Savoy is lacier and less heavy than white or red cabbage, a perfect starter cabbage for those who are cabbage-suspect. The outer leaves get crispy in the pan (we fight over them), and when you spoon on a sizzling mustardy kielbasa dressing the whole thing is incredibly seasoned and perfumed, like a warm, robust salad for cold weather. I'm always tempted to add more things to the pan—diced potatoes, sliced peppers, or thin wedges of red onion—but when I added torn pieces of leftover rye bread, which are kind enough to brown and crisp at the same time and temperature as cabbage, I knew I had found the absolute winner. Let's make it for dinner tonight.

––––––––––

Heat the oven to 475°F (245°C). Coat a large baking sheet with 2 tablespoons olive oil, and sprinkle it with ½ teaspoon kosher salt and lots of freshly ground black pepper. Cut the cabbage into eight wedges, and arrange them in a single layer on the pan, pushing them as close as necessary to fit. Scatter the torn rye bread around it. Drizzle everything with 2 to 3 more tablespoons of olive oil (don't miss the croutons!), another ½ teaspoon salt, and freshly ground black pepper. Roast for 8 to 10 minutes, until the cabbage is charred underneath (don't panic if you see a few thin black edges; they're going to taste amazing). Use a spatula to flip each cabbage wedge over, and rearrange the croutons around it. Roast another 5 to 7 minutes, until the edges of the cabbage and croutons are dark brown. →

cabbage and kielbasa with rye croutons *(continued)*

While the cabbage finishes in the oven, place a heavy skillet on the stove and heat 3 tablespoons of olive oil over medium-high heat until hot; then add the diced kielbasa. Cook, stirring occasionally, until the sausage is crispy and browned at the edges, about 7 to 9 minutes. Add the shallot, and cook, stirring, for 1 minute. Add the vinegar, and simmer for 5 seconds. Whisk in the mustard, and immediately pour the hot dressing over the cabbage and croutons on the baking sheet. You can transfer it to a platter, but we never bother.

weeknight lemon chicken wings

serves 3 or 4

3 tablespoons (45 grams) unsalted butter, melted

1½ teaspoons smooth Dijon mustard

3 garlic cloves, minced

2 teaspoons (6 grams) kosher salt, plus more to finish

1 teaspoon freshly ground black pepper

2 lemons (1 whole, for zesting, and 1 thinly sliced)

2 pounds (905 grams) chicken wings, cut in half at the joint (wing tips saved for stock), or 1½ pounds (680 grams) wingettes, already jointed and wing-tip-free (sometimes sold as "party wings")

These are not bar chicken wings. They're not fried until crisp, bathed in butter and hot sauce, and served with blue-cheese dressing, although you can deliver those here any day and we will not leave a single one behind. These are weeknight wings, which, if they're not a thing yet, I think should be, because, at some point after having kids, I discovered that oven-roasted wings deserved more credit in the Weeknight Greatness category. They're perfectly sized for small hands. They take on the flavor of whatever you pour over them without requiring brining or an overnight marinade. They're often done in 35 minutes, but they have enough natural fat in them so they're forgiving if you distractedly leave them in almost twice as long—they just get more browned and crisp. I love them as lemony as possible, and here, I add the lemon in three ways: in zest, in slices that caramelize in the pan (even the almost black, crispy lemon slices are wildly good here), and in juice at the end. Dijon mustard adds more punch, as do garlic and a lot of black pepper. The sticky juices that collect on the foil are my favorite part. We find these inhalable.

Heat the oven to 450°F (230°C). Coat a 9-by-13-inch baking sheet with nonstick spray. Combine the butter, Dijon mustard, garlic, salt, and pepper. Finely grate the zest of the whole lemon, and add it to the butter mixture. Add the chicken and lemon slices and toss to coat; then spread them evenly in the prepared pan. Season with additional salt and pepper, and roast for 35 minutes, flipping the wings and lemon slices once, at the 20-minute mark, and then back to the first side for the last 5 minutes, or until the wings are a deep golden brown and some of the lemon slices look worrisomely dark. (Do not worry. They are not burned.) You can move the pieces around a bit as you flip them if the edge pieces are picking up color much faster than those in the center.

To serve: Slice the zested lemon in half, and squeeze the juice of one half over the tray; cut the second half into wedges for serving. Eat right away.

steak and corn tacos

serves 4

½ small red onion, thinly sliced

2 tablespoons (30 grams) red-wine vinegar

Kosher salt

Pinch of granulated sugar

⅓ cup (80 grams) sour cream

⅓ cup (70 grams) mayonnaise

3 ounces (heaped ½ cup, or 85 grams) crumbled Cotija cheese

Olive oil

3 medium ears corn, shucked

1 lime, halved

Freshly ground black pepper

Handful of fresh cilantro leaves, chopped

1½ pounds (680 grams) skirt or flank steak

Twelve 5-inch (13-centimeter) flour or corn tortillas

Tajín seasoning, chili powder, or hot sauce

note Tajín is a powdered condiment of chilis, lime, and salt, though you can also use chili powder or hot sauce in its place.

While pulled-pork sandwiches (page 199) are my favorite special-occasion meal for a summer crowd, this is my favorite summer special-occasion meal just for us. Except that the concept of a special occasion is pretty vaguely defined. More often than not, I like picking a week that feels blah and trying to end it with something that feels special, and for the last few summers, this has deliciously fit the bill. Tacos are my preferred application for steak at home, because I like the way it stretches a small piece into many servings. Here we cook almost everything on the grill and pile it on something of a deconstructed esquites, the off-the-cob version of elotes, a Mexican dish in which grilled corn is slathered with mayonnaise, Cotija, lime, and chili powder. Simple as the components are, there are a few steps involved, but the final tacos are such an incredible mix of flavors and textures—the creamy, salty Cotija mixture at the bottom; followed by the warm, thinly sliced steak; sweet, crunchy grilled corn dressed with lime juice and cilantro; topped with lightly pickled red onions and Tajín—that I have never once regretted the effort.

Place the sliced red onion in a small bowl, and douse it with the red-wine vinegar, 1 tablespoon water, two pinches of kosher salt, and one pinch sugar. Stir, and set aside while you prepare the rest of the tacos—at least 20 minutes, or up to 1 day in the fridge.

Combine the sour cream, mayo, and Cotija cheese in a small bowl.

Heat your grill to medium-high. Lightly oil the grill grates, and place the corn cobs directly on them. Cook the corn until it's charred in spots all over, turning as often as needed. Leave the grill on, and transfer the cobs to a cutting board to cool slightly. Cut the corn from the cobs with a sharp knife, and toss the kernels in a bowl with 1 tablespoon olive oil, the juice of half the lime, plus salt and pepper to taste. Stir in the cilantro. Cut the second half of the lime into wedges for serving.

Season the steak generously on both sides with salt and pepper. Grill the steaks for about 4 to 5 minutes on each side for medium-rare. →

steak and corn tacos *(continued)*

Let the meat rest for 10 minutes before slicing it into thin pieces. While the steak rests, wrap your stack of tortillas in foil, and place the packet on the (now cooling off) grill; keep them there until you're ready to assemble, to warm them.

You can serve everything like this and let everyone assemble their own tacos, but, because this is the rare dish that we all agree on, I go ahead and put them together for all of us. I like to shmear each tortilla with 1 tablespoon of the Cotija mixture, add a few slices of steak, spoon on some corn, and finish with red onions. Shake some Tajín, chili powder, or hot sauce over the toppings, to taste. Serve with extra lime wedges, and eat right away.

skillet chicken parmesan

serves 4

1¾ to 2 pounds
(800 to 900 grams) boneless,
skinless chicken thighs

Kosher salt and freshly ground
black pepper

2 large eggs

2 cups (120 grams) panko-style
breadcrumbs

1 cup (100 grams) finely grated
Parmesan, divided

Vegetable or canola oil, for frying

Olive oil

2 garlic cloves, minced

1 teaspoon dried oregano

Red-pepper flakes, to taste

One 28-ounce (795-gram) can
crushed tomatoes

8 ounces (225 grams)
mozzarella, torn into bite-sized
pieces

2 tablespoons chopped fresh
parsley or basil

A few years ago, when my kids still looked at me with wide-eyed wonder, we went to an old-school Italian restaurant at the Jersey Shore and ordered what everyone else already seemed to know about: the chicken Parmesan that's about the size of the platter it's served on. My kids squealed "Pizza chicken!" with far more fervor than they ever had about Pizza Beans (sigh), and then asked if I knew how to make it. They think I know how to make everything, and since I (and you, capisce?) will not tell them otherwise, I put it on my cooking docket that week.

I think we can all agree that golden, crunchy chicken cutlets burrowed in tomato sauce, covered in cheese, and broiled until bronzed on top are a thing of glory. I love it, but it always saddens me to do so much work pounding, seasoning, three-part dredging, frying, draining, seasoning again, just to smother those cutlets in crisp-eradicating sauce. So I decided to make it right, once and for all. "For the kids," you know?

The first thing I did was eliminate the pounding (but you can pound them, if you wish) by using chicken thighs, which arrive pretty flat and (bonus) rarely dry out when cooking. The second was eliminating the flour component of the classic three-part breading. This is my mother-in-law's method, and the result is so much lighter and crispier. Plus, since they're less work, I actually make them more often. Finally, I make a simple tomato sauce in a wide skillet, but we don't drown the chicken in it. We leave the edges of the chicken exposed, so they arrive at the table in a glorious balance of crispy/crunchy and gooey/rich, and everyone is happy.

———

Prepare the chicken: Pat the chicken dry. If you'd like thinner cutlets (but I rarely bother), you can pound them flatter between two pieces of plastic wrap with a flat-sided mallet or even the back of a heavy frying pan—I've done it all. Arrange the chicken on a large tray, and season well on both sides with salt and pepper.

Coat the chicken: In one wide, shallow bowl, beat the eggs with a fork until loose. Fill a second wide, shallow bowl with breadcrumbs and ½ cup of the Parmesan. Dip each piece of chicken into the egg, let all excess drip →

do ahead

- You can cover breaded but not yet fried cutlets loosely with plastic wrap and store them in the fridge overnight.

- Fried cutlets are at their peak for 1 to 2 days, also stored in the fridge, if you'd like to make the sauce and finish the dish at the last minute.

- Rewarm the chicken before assembling, because you won't be broiling the assembled dish long enough to warm it thoroughly otherwise. I feel like I don't need to tell you that leftover chicken Parm, even when it's not as crispy, is a god-level dish. Rewarm in a 350°F (175°C) oven, and practice your "Leftover chicken Parm? I don't know her" shrug if anyone asks where it went.

off, and then dip the chicken into the crumbs, pressing carefully so that the crumbs stay on. Return each coated chicken thigh to the tray where you seasoned the chicken, and repeat with the remaining pieces.

Fry the cutlets: Pour just about ½ inch of vegetable oil into an 11-to-12-inch frying pan, and heat over medium-high heat until a droplet of water flicked into the pan hisses dramatically, or until the temperature is 350°F (175°C). Place your first few breaded cutlets in the oil—but don't crowd them, or it will lower the temperature a lot, leading to heavier and greasier chicken. Cook the chicken, flipping once, until it's deep golden brown on both sides, about 4 to 5 minutes on the first side and 3 to 4 on the second. Remove the chicken from the oil, letting the excess oil drip off for 10 to 20 seconds, and drain it on paper towels or paper bags. Season right away, while still sizzling hot, with salt. Repeat with the remaining cutlets.

Make the sauce: Drain (and safely discard) the vegetable oil, and wipe out the pan. Heat 2 tablespoons olive oil over medium heat. Add the minced garlic, oregano, and some pepper flakes, and let sizzle until the garlic is golden, 30 seconds to 1 minute. Add the tomatoes (beware the splatter!), and season with 1 teaspoon salt. Let the mixture simmer over low heat for 8 to 10 minutes, stirring occasionally, until it's a little thicker and saucier. You should have about 3 cups of sauce.

Heat your oven: Heat your oven's broiler, or if there's no broiler, heat your oven to its top temperature.

Assemble the dish: Remove about half of the tomato sauce (a generous 1½ cups) from the pan, and set it aside. Arrange the chicken cutlets in the sauce in the pan, slightly overlapped. Spoon ½ to 1 cup of the reserved sauce on top, leaving some edges of the chicken exposed. Sprinkle with remaining ½ cup Parmesan and all of the mozzarella.

Finish and serve: Transfer the pan to the oven and cook until bubbly and golden on top, 5 to 10 minutes. Finish with fresh herbs, and serve with the remaining sauce on the side.

slow-roasted chicken with schmaltzy croutons

serves 4

for the chicken

1½ pounds (680 grams) bread (sourdough, miche, or sturdy country loaf)

Olive oil

6 medium garlic cloves, but who's counting, unpeeled

Kosher salt and freshly ground black pepper

4-pound (1.8-kilogram) whole chicken

1 lemon

A few sprigs fresh thyme

for the salad

Juice of 1 lemon

1 teaspoon smooth Dijon mustard

4 tablespoons (50 grams) olive oil

¼ cup (125 grams) roughly chopped green olives

1 small fennel bulb, sliced very thin

4 ounces (115 grams) firm, leafy lettuce, such as escarole

I always thought that the rules for achieving perfectly juicy, bronzed, and crisp-skinned roast chicken were simple: pat it very dry, and blast it in a very hot oven. It's the only way . . . right? Yet it seems out of step with so many other kinds of roasts that benefit from longer, lower-temperature cooking times. Curious, I gave it a try on a cold, lazy weekend afternoon, and what emerged from the oven a couple hours later defied all of my expectations. Not only did it have deeply bronzed and very crisp skin, it was also the most succulent, juicy chicken I have ever eaten. My pickiest child couldn't stop eating it. The pickiest adult (that's me, and I prefer the term "skeptical," thank you) couldn't, either. This is now the method I wish everyone would try, because nobody can make a bad roasted chicken this way.

I've put all sorts of things under and around my chicken over the years—potatoes, mixed vegetables, just onions, and even cabbage—but croutons cooked slowly in salty drippings until they're part burnished and crisp, part tender, rich, and schmaltzy, was the one that got me a "Don't you dare use anything else, ever again." If you've ever had the Zuni Café roast chicken, you'll know that the best thing to eat with chicken, and chickeny croutons, is a bright salad. The one you make here is both bright and crunchy, balancing the richness. If you come over for dinner this fall, you know what we're eating.

Heat the oven to 325°F (165°C) degrees.

For the croutons: Cut the bread into 1-inch-thick slices. Coat a 9-by-13-inch roasting pan or baking dish with olive oil. Arrange the bread snug in the bottom, cutting the slices into small pieces as needed. (Tetris-heads, this is our time to shine.) Nestle the garlic cloves between the bread pieces throughout the pan. Drizzle the bread with 2 tablespoons olive oil, ½ teaspoon kosher salt, and lots of freshly ground black pepper.

For the chicken: Sprinkle the chicken with 2 teaspoons kosher salt, black pepper, finely grated zest from the lemon, and the leaves from a couple $\rightarrow$

thyme sprigs. Cut the lemon in half, and toss it, and any additional thyme sprigs, into the bird's cavity. Place the chicken on top of the bread, and—this is essential to keep the bread from drying out until the chicken releases any juices—sprinkle the exposed pieces of bread around the chicken with ½ cup water. Roast for about 2 hours to 2 hours 20 minutes, or until a thermometer inserted into the thickest part of the breast reads 155°F, or 165°F for the thigh.

Finish the croutons: Transfer the chicken to a cutting board, but before you do, take a look at the croutons. If they're very dry, tilt the bird over them, drizzling juices that have collected inside the bird over the bread to moisten it. If they are not yet dried out, you can skip this. In all cases, use a spatula to flip the croutons, and return them to the oven to cook for about 15 to 20 minutes, or until they're largely crisp and golden brown, while the chicken rests. The amount of time this takes depends on how dried out they were going in; they sometimes need longer.

Meanwhile, prepare your salad: Combine the lemon juice and Dijon mustard in a large bowl, and whisk in the olive oil in a thin stream. Season well with black pepper and more salt. Add the olives and fennel, and toss to combine. Set aside until right before serving; then add the salad greens, and toss to coat them. Season salad with additional salt and pepper.

To serve: Remove the pan with the croutons from the oven, and transfer them to a serving platter. Shmear the garlic cloves over the toasts, discarding the peels. Heap the salad on top. Carve the chicken, and arrange the pieces on top of the salad and croutons. Pour any juices from the cutting board over the chicken, and serve immediately.

turkey meatloaf for skeptics

serves 4

meatloaf

1 medium yellow onion, roughly chopped

1 garlic clove, smashed

1 slim carrot, roughly chopped

Olive oil

Kosher salt and freshly ground black pepper

½ cup (30 grams) panko-style breadcrumbs

¼ cup (60 grams) chicken broth

½ tablespoon tomato paste

1 teaspoon Dijon mustard

1 tablespoon (15 grams) Worcestershire sauce

2 tablespoons chopped fresh flat-leaf parsley

1 large egg

1 pound (455 grams) ground turkey, preferably a mix of dark and light meat, or just dark

glaze

1 heaped (20 grams) tablespoon ketchup

1 tablespoon molasses

1 tablespoon (15 grams) apple-cider vinegar

1 teaspoon hot sauce of your choice (optional)

1 teaspoon Worcestershire sauce

Kosher salt and freshly ground black pepper, to taste

Meatloaf has a PR problem. It took me a while to come around to it; I didn't grow up eating it, and certainly nothing about the name—a *loaf,* a loaf of *meat*—convinced me I was missing a thing. But, slowly, I have tiptoed into the light, and now I get it. It's not cute, but it's objectively delicious. Imagine if we only ate things that were camera-ready—it would be a world without gravy, mushroom soup, and lopsided made-with-love frosted cakes. We absolutely must not stand for that.

But I'd only made meatloaves with either ground beef or ground pork, never turkey. Turkey, which I suspected would be too dry or bland for any recipe to overcome, was the final frontier, and I tried it a whole bunch of ways before realizing that what I wanted most on top was not strips of bacon or a thick layer of ketchup, but a simple barbecue-type sauce. In the oven, it gets glossy and dark, and it goes really well with Crushed Ranch-y Potatoes (recipe follows). Unlike their mashed counterpart, crushed potatoes are full of contrasts: big and small chunks, some parts puddled with cream, some parts saltier—and that slight chaos of forkfuls plays well off the reliable, steady slices of meatloaf.

———

Heat the oven to 350°F (175°C).

Prepare the meatloaf: Lightly coat a 9-by-13-inch baking dish or small sheet pan with nonstick spray. Very finely dice the onion, garlic, and carrot in a food processor, or by hand on a cutting board. Heat a large skillet over medium heat. Once the skillet is hot, coat the bottom with olive oil, and heat it for a minute; then add the vegetables. Season with salt and pepper, and cook, stirring frequently, until they begin to brown, about 7 to 10 minutes; transfer them to a large bowl. Add the breadcrumbs, broth, tomato paste, mustard, Worcestershire, parsley, 1 teaspoon salt, and ½ teaspoon pepper, and stir to combine. Add the egg by beating it directly into the vegetable mixture (I like to use a fork). Add the turkey, and combine just until the vegetable-egg mixture is dispersed through the meat. Pat the turkey mixture into about a 4-by-8-inch shape in your prepared pan. $\rightarrow$

Make the glaze: In a small bowl, combine the glaze ingredients. Brush or spoon the glaze over the meatloaf.

Bake: Bake the meatloaf for 30 to 35 minutes, until the internal temperature is 160°F (70°C). If you don't have a thermometer, you can insert a knife into the center and hold it there for 10 seconds. You should feel no resistance, and when you pull it out, the blade should feel hot.

Let the meatloaf rest for 5 minutes, then cut it into 1-inch slices to serve with crushed potatoes.

note This is a small-sized meatloaf, and it works for my family of four. It doubles easily, either as two small loaves (baking time the same) or one larger, freeform loaf that will take between 60 and 70 minutes in the oven.

crushed ranch-y potatoes

serves 4

Kosher salt

1½ pounds (680 grams) small red or Yukon Gold potatoes

¼ cup (60 grams) heavy cream

1 garlic clove, minced

3 tablespoons (45 grams) unsalted butter, cut into pieces

2 scallions, finely minced (white and green parts)

⅓ cup (80 grams) sour cream

2 teaspoons white vinegar

Freshly ground black pepper

2 tablespoons minced fresh flat-leaf parsley (or 1 tablespoon each parsley and dill)

In a large saucepan, cover the potatoes with cold salted water, and bring to a simmer. Cook, simmering, until the potatoes are fork-tender, about 20 minutes. Drain. You can keep the potatoes warm until they're needed by letting them rest in the empty pot off the heat, covered with a lid, then transfer to a bowl when you're ready to finish them.

In your emptied saucepan, heat the cream and garlic together until simmering. Keep a close eye on it to make sure it doesn't boil over. Remove the pan from the heat, and whisk in the butter until it melts. Stir in the scallions, sour cream, and vinegar. Season well with salt (I use up to 1 teaspoon kosher salt here) and black pepper.

In a large bowl, use a fork or potato masher to smash each potato once or twice, but leave them mostly in craggy chunks. Pour the cream-garlic mixture over them, add the herbs, then season again with salt and several grinds of black pepper, and combine everything with two big folded stirs. I like these best with some pockets of the garlic cream not mixed in. Serve hot, with the meatloaf.

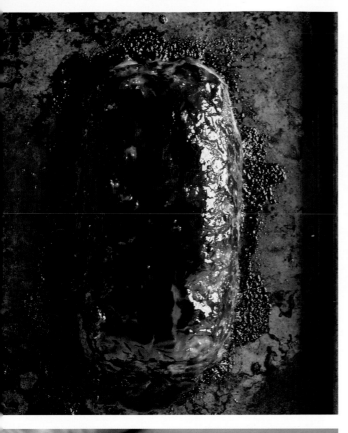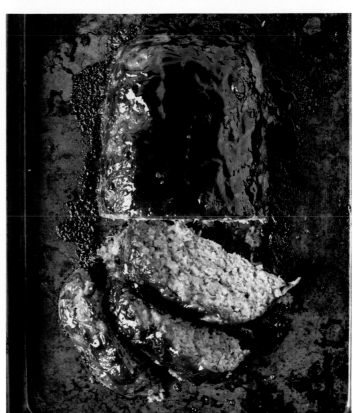

oven-braised beef with harissa

serves 6 to 8

3-to-3½-pound
(1.3-to-1.6-kilogram) boneless
beef chuck roast, tied with a
string

Kosher salt and freshly ground
black pepper

One 28-ounce (795-gram) can
whole tomatoes

2 tablespoons prepared harissa,
or more to taste (see note)

1 tablespoon ground cumin

1 tablespoon ground coriander

1 medium head garlic, halved
crosswise

1 cup sliced carrots
(6 ounces or 170 grams)

1 large (about 7 ounces, or
200 grams) red bell pepper,
stemmed, seeded, sliced

to finish

3 cups (115 grams) mixed fresh
herbs (parsley, cilantro, mint)

2 garlic cloves

1 tablespoon minced fresh lemon
peel and pulp, seeds removed

6 tablespoons (75 grams) olive
oil, plus more if needed

note If you're looking for heat-
level guidance, I've tested this
harissa amount with a milder
brand and a spicier one, and in
both cases, no skeptical child
detected the spiciness. If you're
still worried, use less; you can
always add more at the table for
those who want it.

There is a 2001 *Gourmet* magazine recipe for Oven-Braised Beef with Tomato Sauce and Garlic that's a cult favorite across the web, including here at the Smitten Kitchen. I know we food writers always say, "It couldn't be simpler!," and we're only sometimes telling the truth, but here, hand on a stack of Dr. Seuss books (okay, someone left them next to the sofa), I want you to know I really mean it. Who doesn't want to throw a chuck roast into a pot with a big can of tomatoes and a head of garlic and, 3 to 4 hours later, pull out something rich, cozy, and fall-apart tender? Few dishes match this simplicity and ease. Readers call it a perfect set-it-and-forget-it dish; they love to have it waiting for them on Christmas Eve, or in the background on snow days. And it's turned a lot of people who thought they weren't pot-roast people, who thought pot roasts were watery and undynamic (okay, these "people" are "me"), into full converts.

I loved it so much that it became a core recipe that I tweaked to fit my mood. But the first time I made it like this, that was it; I'll never want it another way. Two big spoonfuls of harissa—a flavorful, spicy North African chili paste—and a spoonful each of ground cumin and coriander join the tomatoes, which I chop right in the can with kitchen shears, and I mix the sauce there, too. I leave the head of garlic intact, but halved, so it's easier to fish out at the end; all the garlic cloves that haven't deposited themselves in the pan can be easily freed with the tip of a knife. You can stop right here, but if you like a bright, herby contrast above all else, you can make this with herbs, garlic, and minced lemon. This is the kind of dish that is going to make your home smell eat-the-air good while it cooks, and, honestly, I hope it's your new favorite thing to have waiting for you when you get home.

Heat the oven to 300°F (150°C). Place the beef in an ovenproof 4-to-5-quart heavy pot or a casserole dish with a lid. Sprinkle it with 2 teaspoons kosher salt and many, many grinds of black pepper. Turn the beef over, and season the second side. Open your can of tomatoes, and use kitchen shears or very clean scissors to chop them roughly right inside the →

can. Add the harissa, cumin, coriander, and 2 teaspoons salt to the can, and give it a quick, careful stir. Pour the tomato-harissa mixture over and around the beef. Place the garlic-head halves on either side, and cover with the lid.

Braise the beef in the middle of the oven for a total of 3 to 4 hours. At the 2½-hour mark, carefully remove the pot from the oven and add the vegetables, cover again with the lid, and return to the oven for 30 to 90 minutes longer, or until the beef is very tender.

Meanwhile, in a food processor, combine the herbs, 2 garlic cloves, and minced lemon until well chopped. Add the oil in a drizzle, running the machine the whole time, and scraping down the sides as needed. Season with salt and pepper to taste. Spoon into a bowl, and set aside for serving.

When the beef is tender, remove the garlic halves from the braise, freeing any stuck cloves with the tip of a knife and discarding the paper skins. Cut and discard the string around the meat. Let the roast rest 10 to 15 minutes before slicing and serving with the accompanying herb sauce.

note One of my favorite ways to tweak this into an even fuller meal is to add 1 cup (200 grams) uncooked basmati or another long-grain rice to the pot, as shown in the photo on page 196. There's usually a lot of delicious cooking liquid in pot roasts, and the rice is happy to drink it up. But this method comes with two things to watch out for:

1. **Timing:** Figuring out the exact right moment to add the rice so that it doesn't overcook is tricky. I often do it an hour before the pot roast is done, or at the 2½-hour mark with the vegetables, but if your pot roast takes the full 4 hours to tenderize, the rice might become mushy. If you've made this a few times without rice, you might be better at assessing the ideal window for when to add it.

2. **Liquid level:** While there's usually a lot of liquid in the pot, occasionally a pot roast produces less. If so, you might want to add up to 2 cups of water or beef broth along with the uncooked rice to ensure it softens without drying out the meat. You also might need a little water or broth to keep the mixture saucy once the rice is cooked, should the rice drink up all the liquid in the pot while it cooks, or if you'd like to rest it for a while before serving.

Because of difficulties pinning down the extra variables adding rice creates, I'm leaving it as merely an option here, but do know that we always find it worth the trouble.

crispy oven pulled pork

serves 10 to 12

3 tablespoons (25 grams)
kosher salt, plus more for slaw

6 tablespoons (80 grams) packed
brown sugar, divided

1½ tablespoons sweet or
smoked paprika

1 to 1½ teaspoons ground
cayenne or chipotle powder

1 boneless pork shoulder
(sometimes called Boston butt),
about 3¾ pounds (1.7 kilograms)

1 cup (235 grams) apple-cider
vinegar

¼ cup (70 grams) ketchup

1 teaspoon freshly ground black
pepper, plus more for slaw

1 small (1½-pound,
or 680-gram) head green
cabbage

¼ cup (50 grams) mayonnaise,
plus more to taste

12 sandwich rolls

I was first introduced to oven-crisped pork roasts via David Chang's famous Bo Ssam: a spectacularly low-effort, high-reward way to feed a crowd. The masterful thing about this slow roast is that the exterior takes on a dark, glossy, crisp edge that collapses easily under the tines of a fork, revealing pale, perfectly cooked pulls of pork within, and that you did almost nothing to make this happen—the ingredients are essentially sugar and salt. But one of the ways I use the recipe the most these days is like this, adapted for barbecue-style sandwiches.

I make a slew of adjustments. I prefer a boneless pork shoulder over a bone-in one; it's smaller, cooks faster, and has a more dramatic collapse. Instead of a simple salt-and-white-sugar rub, I channel barbecue flavors, keeping the salt but swapping in brown sugar, paprika (smoked is wonderful here), and cayenne. I enlist a thin marinade known as a mop throughout the process—initially to baste the roast, then to flavor the slaw, to dress the final roast as you pull it apart, keeping it moist, and then to add at the table. You won't need a barbecue sauce.

My favorite part of this dish is that the entire thing has only ten ingredients. I used to make ribs for summer holidays. With this almost completely hands-off recipe, those days might be over.

The night before, prepare the roast: Combine 3 tablespoons kosher salt, 4 tablespoons of the brown sugar, all of the paprika, and 1 teaspoon cayenne in a small bowl. It should taste saltier than sweet, and have as much kick as you like, so add more seasonings if you wish.

If the pork shoulder has a thick fatty layer on one side, scoring can help prevent it from tightening the meat below as it shrinks. To score the fat, make shallow (⅛-inch-deep) diagonal cuts in two directions a little under an inch apart, forming a diamond pattern.

Use your hands to pat the rub onto all sides; it's going to be very thickly coated, but don't leave any rub behind. Place the roast in a bowl or, if it fits in your fridge, the pan you'd like to roast it in tomorrow, cover with plastic wrap, and refrigerate for at least 6 hours or overnight. →

crispy oven pulled pork *(continued)*

Make the mop: Combine remaining 2 tablespoons brown sugar, all of the cider vinegar, ketchup, black pepper, and ⅓ cup water in a bowl, and whisk until the sugar dissolves. You want the mop to be pleasantly sharp (the fatty meat will cut right through any overpowering vinegar vibe) but not quite sour. I don't find that I need salt, but you can add some if you wish. You'll have a little over 1⅔ cups of mop.

Cook the pork: The next day, heat the oven to 300°F (150°C). Remove the plastic wrap from the pork, and discard any juices in the dish. If your pork is not in a roasting dish, transfer it to one now. Cook pork for approximately 5 hours, or until it collapses, yielding easily when pulled back with a fork. After the first hour, add ¼ cup mop to the juices in the pan, and baste the meat with it. Continue to baste once an hour with the juices that collect.

Make your slaw: Quarter, core, and thinly slice your cabbage. If the slices are long, I cut them into 1-to-2-inch lengths, so the slaw doesn't end up too cumbersome to pile on a sandwich. Place the cabbage in a large bowl, add ⅓ cup of the mop, and toss to combine. Add the mayonnaise, and mix well. Season with salt and pepper, if you wish, taste, and add more mop or mayo if needed. Refrigerate the slaw until you're ready to eat.

To finish and serve: Once the meat is cooked, you can leave it at room temperature for up to 1½ hours. Rewarm briefly in a 450°F (230°C) oven. Shred the pork into bite-sized pieces, discarding any larger chunks of fat; pour up to ½ cup of the reserved mop over it as needed, to season and keep the meat moist.

Serve the pulled pork on buns with the slaw, seasoning with a splash of the remaining mop and/or a barbecue sauce of your choice.

fettuccine with white ragù

serves 4

2 tablespoons (25 grams) olive oil

1 small onion, finely chopped

½ cup (70 grams) finely chopped carrot

½ cup (70 grams) finely chopped celery

2 garlic cloves, minced

Kosher salt, freshly ground black pepper, and red-pepper flakes

1 pound (455 grams) ground pork

¼ cup (60 grams) dry white wine

1 cup (235 grams) chicken broth

½ cup (120 grams) milk

1 bay leaf

Water, as needed

¼ cup (60 grams) heavy cream

½ pound (225 grams) dried fettuccine, or 1 pound (455 grams) fresh

½ cup (50 grams) finely grated Parmesan, to serve

2 tablespoons minced fresh parsley (purely for aesthetics)

A couple of Octobers ago, we spent a leaf-crunching weekend in Kingston, New York, stopping the first night at Lola Pizza. I know the excellent pizza is the star, but we also ordered a pasta with pork—and, I was assured, very little else—that I have not stopped thinking about since. I went home, consumed with trying to re-create it, but I couldn't suspend my disbelief that a dish with such cozy abundance could have no secret ingredients up its sleeve.

Still, since I'd already, ambitiously, bought some ground pork, I decided to see what would happen if I cooked it with a minimalist amount of onion, carrot, celery, and garlic and a single bay leaf for a couple hours, and the answer is, we were swept off our feet by the aroma alone. I could not get over how good the apartment smelled, and how dynamic, from so few ingredients. It is impossible not to sneak tastes while it cooks. I could hardly believe it really worked, so I set about tinkering with the recipe. Maybe it needed some added mushrooms (they added nothing). Maybe I should start with sausage meat (but it doesn't need it). Maybe it needs more wine or something; doesn't a sauce need an angle besides *pork cooked for a long time with some cream*? It doesn't. Maybe I need to ask my editor, who was politely skeptical, to make this and tell me what's wrong with it? She loved it, too.

Friends, I don't know what to tell you; this dish has depleted me of words. I know it looks beige. I know it sounds like something that shouldn't work. I never for a moment thought that what was missing in my pasta-eating life was a pancetta-and-tomato-free ragù, but here we are—sort of. I'm actually in the kitchen, already on my second bowl.

Build the sauce: Heat a medium-to-large heavy pot or Dutch oven (4 to 5 quarts) over medium-high heat. Add 2 tablespoons olive oil, and once it is warm, add the onion, carrot, celery, and garlic; season well with salt and black pepper and/or pepper flakes, to taste. Cook, stirring occasionally, for 10 minutes, until the vegetables are lightly browned all over. Don't worry if anything sticks. Add the pork, season it generously with salt and pepper, and cook it until it has browned, about 8 to 10 minutes. Add the wine, and scrape up any stuck bits; cook until the wine disappears, 1 to 2 minutes. →

Add the broth, milk, and bay leaf, and bring to a simmer; then reduce the heat to the lowest simmer, leaving the lid off. Congratulations, you've now reached the "walk away" portion of the recipe.

Cook the ragù: Here's how the next 1 to 1½ hours will go: Keep a glass of water by the stove. Check in on the sauce from time to time, adding more water if needed to keep it loose, but not enough to submerge the meat (which would boil, not braise—*shudder*). Taste it from time to time, and add more seasoning if needed. The sauce is done when the meat tastes tender, buttery, and rich; this takes 60 to 90 minutes. There's little harm in going a little longer (up to 2 hours) if real life is more interesting. Do a final taste for seasoning, and cook any remaining liquid down to a saucy puddle. Remove from heat; discard the bay leaf. Add the cream, and stir to combine.

To finish: Cook your pasta 1 to 2 minutes shy of done in well-salted water. Before you drain it, ladle a cup of the pasta water into the glass by the stove. Drain the pasta, and add it directly to the ragù, along with a quarter to a half of the reserved water. Cook the pasta and sauce together for 2 minutes, adding more pasta water if needed to keep it moving. Serve in wide bowls, finished with Parmesan and parsley (if you wish).

lamb skewers with crackly vinegar glaze

serves 4

glaze

½ cup (120 grams) sherry vinegar

¼ cup (85 grams) honey

1½ teaspoons fennel seeds, lightly crushed

1½ teaspoons coriander seeds, lightly crushed

½ teaspoon freshly ground black pepper

1½ teaspoons ground Aleppo or another kind of mild chili flakes

mint-yogurt sauce

1 cup (230 grams) plain Greek-style yogurt

3 tablespoons chopped fresh mint

1 garlic clove, minced

Grated zest and juice from ½ lemon

½ teaspoon kosher salt

Freshly ground black pepper

lamb

2 pounds (905 grams) boneless lamb shoulder, trimmed, cut into 1-to-1½-inch pieces

Kosher salt and freshly ground black pepper

8 to 10 wooden or metal skewers

This is a love letter to the lamb ribs we used to order, along with very cold beer, from the snack menu at the late DBGB restaurant on Bowery. Those tiny, crispy, fatty, and impossibly delicious ribs came from the lamb breast, and though you can special-order them from some butchers, when I've done so I've found both the price tag and the volume lost in trimming (I truly wasn't kidding about the fattiness) a little devastating, so they're a rare treat. In trying to rework these flavors so we could enjoy them more often and scale them up for when friends come over, I turned to lamb skewers. I love the surprise on people's faces when they're expecting lemon and garlic—that perfect, classic lamb pairing—and, instead, they get this: tender nuggets of lamb, crackly with heat and a sweet-salty sherry-vinegar glaze with the cooling contrast of a minted garlic yogurt.

Make the glaze: Combine the vinegar and honey in a small saucepan over moderate heat. Add the fennel, coriander, black pepper, and chili flakes, and bring to a light simmer. Lower the heat, and allow the mixture to reduce by half, about 10 minutes.

Make the mint-yogurt sauce: Combine the yogurt, mint, garlic, lemon zest and juice, kosher salt, and many grinds of black pepper. Taste, and adjust seasoning.

Prepare your grill: For a charcoal grill, heat the grill until the coals are at their hottest. For a gas grill, turn all burners to high, cover, and heat the grill until it's hot, about 10 minutes. For both, lightly oil the cooking grates.

Prepare the skewers: Pat the lamb dry with paper towels, and sprinkle with 1½ teaspoons salt and a lot of freshly ground black pepper. Tightly thread the lamb onto the skewers, leaving the top 2 to 3 inches of each skewer exposed. Using a brush, coat the lamb with most of the glaze. →

Grill, turning frequently, until the meat is well browned on all sides, approximately 5 to 7 minutes total. As they cook, brush them with the remaining glaze, one or two more times.

Serve the lamb with the yogurt sauce and more fresh mint.

note We love serving these skewers on a bed of purple napa cabbage leaves, which are both visually stunning and provide a crisp contrast. We also serve the skewers with grilled pita wedges and thinly sliced cucumbers.

perfect meatballs and spaghetti

serves 4

3 teaspoons (8 grams) kosher salt, divided, plus more for the pot

1 pound (455 grams) ground meat (see note)

½ cup (30 grams) panko-style breadcrumbs

⅓ cup (80 grams) milk, any kind (nondairy will work, too)

2 tablespoons finely chopped fresh parsley, plus more to serve

2 tablespoons (15 grams) finely grated Parmesan or Pecorino Romano, plus more to serve

Red-pepper flakes and/or freshly ground black pepper

½ teaspoon onion powder

2 large eggs

4 garlic cloves, minced, divided

1 pound (455 grams) dried spaghetti

2 tablespoons (25 grams) olive oil

One 28-ounce (795-gram) can crushed tomatoes

One 14.5-ounce (410-gram) can whole or diced tomatoes

I am going to go out on a limb here and say that it's probably been too long since you've made spaghetti and meatballs, and even longer since you invited friends over to join you in eating it for dinner. This recipe has a single goal: to fix that. I realized a while back that the only way I was going to be able to have dinner with friends—especially on Fridays, when nobody wants to try to find the right restaurant to seat eight people, some young and fidgety, at the last minute—was if I took all of the "dinner party" gloss off it. Entertaining doesn't need to be showy. Truly, is there anything less comforting than someone showing off to you, even with the warmest of intentions? Most of us aren't getting treated to impeccable meatballs and spaghetti at home on a regular basis, so this is a welcome treat and one of my favorite things to cook for friends.

This is my forever recipe: a moderate yield, easily scaled, and a simple homemade sauce. Eager to avoid the mess of frying meatballs, I tucked them into the oven for a quick bake one day, and this led to my biggest aha moment: not only did my stove stay clean, but, since I could build the sauce and boil the pasta while the meatballs cooked, this whole dish could be done in 40 minutes (I've timed it!), which means we get these even more often.

Get ready: Bring a large pot of very well-salted water to a boil, and heat your oven to 425°F (220°C).

Prepare the meatballs: Line a large baking sheet with foil for easy cleanup, and coat it lightly with a nonstick spray. Place the meat, crumbs, milk, parsley, cheese, 1 teaspoon of the salt, the pepper, onion powder, eggs, and one-third of your minced garlic in a large bowl, and mash everything together with a fork or potato masher until it's evenly mixed. Using wet hands if needed, form the mixture into 2-inch meatballs (a 3-tablespoon scoop will make eight or nine large meatballs), and arrange them on the prepared tray. Roast for 12 minutes, until they're cooked through (you can cut one in half to check). $\rightarrow$

note I've made these meatballs entirely with ground turkey (a mix with dark meat in it is much better), and those are a little softer (you could use a tablespoon less milk) but taste delicious. You could skip the Parmesan and replace the milk with water if you wanted to make it dairy-free. Finally, you can make your own breadcrumbs from any old piece of bread. Grind it up and use ⅔ cup instead of ½.

Cook the spaghetti: Once the water is boiling, cook the spaghetti until 1 minute shy of tender. Set aside 1 cup of the cooking water before draining the pasta.

Make the sauce: In a deep sauté pan or a wide saucepan, heat 2 tablespoons olive oil over medium heat. Add the remaining minced cloves of garlic and a pinch or two of pepper flakes, and let the garlic sizzle until it's golden, 30 seconds to 1 minute. Add the tomatoes (beware the spatter!), and season with the remaining 2 teaspoons salt. Let the mixture simmer for about 5 minutes, stirring occasionally, although longer will do it no harm if your meatballs aren't ready yet.

When the meatballs come out of the oven, add them to the sauce, and gently spoon the sauce over them so they are coated. Reduce the heat to a low simmer, put a lid on the pot, and simmer the meatballs in the sauce for 10 minutes. At this point, should you not be eating them right away, you can remove them from the heat and set them aside.

To finish and serve: Return the spaghetti to its empty cooking pot. Push the meatballs aside, grab a few ladles of the sauce, and pour it over the spaghetti. Add half of the reserved pasta water, and cook the spaghetti and sauce over high heat for 1 minute, tossing the whole time. Use additional pasta water as needed to loosen the sauce. Use tongs to transfer the spaghetti into a large, wide serving bowl. (If you give the bowl a little spin as you lower the spaghetti into it, you can make cute little piles.) Add the meatballs and their sauce on top. Garnish with parsley and additional grated cheese. Eat right now; do not wait.

raclette tartiflette

serves 8, with salad

2 small garlic cloves

1 tablespoon (15 grams) unsalted butter

Kosher salt

3 pounds (1.4 kilograms) Yukon Gold potatoes

½ pound (225 grams) thick-cut bacon, cut into ¼-inch lardons or matchsticks

2 medium yellow onions, halved, thinly sliced

Freshly ground black pepper

⅓ cup (80 grams) dry white wine

½ cup (120 grams) crème fraîche or heavy cream

1 pound (455 grams) Raclette with rind, kept chilled so it's easier to slice

notes

- Raclette is a cheese from the Swiss Alps, and, just to be confusing, also the name of the dish it was created for, in which the cheese is warmed and scraped over boiled potatoes. Chablochon, an imported Reblochon, can be used, too, but I don't see it very often.

- I've made this without bacon, too, adding in mushrooms that I'd thinly sliced and sautéed in butter, seasoning them well.

I have never been to the Alps, and I barely know how to ski, but I don't see why that should keep me from harnessing my favorite holiday energy in my kitchen each winter to make things I imagine you'd eat on a ski vacation in the mountains of France, Switzerland, and Italy. Like Kaiserschmarrn (chopped fluffy pancakes with plum compote). Like cured meats, rich cheeses, breads, and thick soups with cabbage and cream. And like tartiflette.

Tartiflette is a dish from Savoy, in the French Alps, made with boiled potatoes, Reblochon cheese, lardons, onions, white wine, and thick cream. I have an obsessive history with this dish—my friend Julie (she of the Punked Strawberry Tart in *Smitten Kitchen Every Day*) made it for us more than a decade ago, an unparalleled decadence she called a "simple student meal"—but I've never made it, because Reblochon is difficult to get in the United States and also quite expensive. Unwilling to live without this decadence any longer, I began making it with the far more accessible and accessibly priced Raclette cheese, and it became my immediate and forever favorite New Year's Eve tradition.

Here's how it goes: This recipe makes one tartiflette. But it really wants to join a party, so we're going to scale the recipe to assemble as many pans of these tartiflettes as required, and prep a ton of lettuce, because a big green salad isn't just good with tartiflette, it's essential. We will chill a lot of white wine, and also some bubbly. If you're feeling posh or someone else is paying, get your friends to work with some oysters, knives, and cut-resistant gloves while you bake these tartiflettes until the cheese melts and the rinds brown and all your guests are about to fight each other (gently! with holiday cheer!) for the portions of the lid that have the crunchiest cheese corners in them. Toss the salad, and cut each tartiflette into eight seemingly excessive but actually perfect squares, and I hope you'll agree from the very first forkful that there's no better grand finale for a year.

_____

Prepare the dish: Halve one garlic clove, and rub the cut side of one half around the inside bottom and sides of a 9-by-13-inch or 3-quart baking dish. Butter the dish generously. Mince the second half and the remaining whole clove of garlic and set aside. $\rightarrow$

Parcook the potatoes: Cover the potatoes with cold salted water, and bring it to a boil. Cook the potatoes until you can insert a skewer into them without hitting a crunchy center but they're still fairly firm (they'll get more cooking time in the oven); smaller potatoes will take 12 to 15 minutes, larger ones 15 to 20. Drain the potatoes and set them aside.

Heat the oven to 425°F (220°C).

Meanwhile: Add the bacon to a cool, dry large sauté pan, and turn the heat to medium-high. Cook the bacon, stirring occasionally, until it's darker and crisp. Scoop it out with a slotted spoon, and set it aside. Pour off all but 2 tablespoons bacon fat, saving the rest for another use.

Add the onions and the minced garlic to the pan, season with salt and pepper, and cook until the onions are soft and translucent, about 6 to 8 minutes. Add the wine carefully—it will splatter. Scrape up any stuck bits with the wine, and continue cooking until the wine is almost completely cooked off. Remove the pan from heat, and stir in the crème fraîche and reserved bacon.

Assemble the tartiflette: Cut the potatoes into scant ½-inch-thick slices. Arrange half of them in a single layer in the prepared dish. Season with salt and many grinds of black pepper. Spoon half of the bacon-cream-onion mixture over the potato slices. (This is not a gratin; don't fret if the potatoes are far from submerged in cream.) Arrange the second half of the potato slices on top. Season with more salt and pepper, and spoon the remaining onion mixture over them.

Cut the Raclette into ¼-inch-thick slices, including the rind. (The rind is edible, and delicious once baked.) Tile the cheese slices over the filling; it should almost fully cover the top.

Bake the tartiflette: Bake for 25 minutes, until the cheese is melted. For a deeper color on top, broil for a few minutes at the end.

Cut into eight portions and serve with a big green salad (see page 65).

sweets

cookies

chocolate peanut butter cup cookies

makes 22 to 24 cookies

filling

⅔ cup (170 grams) creamy peanut butter

⅔ cup (80 grams) confectioners' sugar

Two pinches of flaky sea salt

cookie

½ cup (115 grams, or 4 ounces) unsalted butter (at room temperature for a mixer; cold is fine for a food processor)

½ cup (100 grams) granulated sugar, plus more to coat cookies

½ cup (110 grams) packed dark-brown sugar

¼ cup (65 grams) creamy peanut butter

1 large egg

1 teaspoon vanilla extract

½ teaspoon kosher salt

⅔ cup (55 grams) Dutch-process cocoa powder (see note)

2 teaspoons baking powder

1⅓ cups (175 grams) all-purpose flour

notes

• This filling works best with a smooth, processed nut or seed butter. →

I'd seen recipes for various peanut-butter-stuffed chocolate cookies around the internet for years before I tried my hand at one, and immediately, as you can guess, kicked myself for waiting so long. I will try not to make you wait much longer. I've tweaked mine so that the chocolate here is really dark and intense, the peanut butter a little salty, and—if you can find a warm-spirited work-holiday cookie-baking contest that will allow you to bake with peanut butter (or sunflower-seed butter, my favorite swap here)—these brownielike and slightly pillowy cookies are practically shoo-ins. (This has been fact-checked!) But first they will need to make it out of your kitchen. Mine simply never have. We're looking into the matter and will get to the bottom of it soon, I'm sure.

———

Heat the oven to 375°F (190°C).

Make the filling: Line a small tray or plate with parchment paper. In a medium bowl, mix the peanut butter, confectioners' sugar, and salt with a fork; it's a little messy, but it will come together. Once it's evenly mixed, use a teaspoon measure to scoop heaped teaspoons of filling into little balls. Spread them out on the prepared tray. Once you've used all the filling, put the tray in the freezer, and leave it there while you make the cookie dough.

To make the cookie dough with a hand or stand mixer: Beat the softened butter with the sugars and peanut butter until they're creamed together. Add the egg, vanilla, and salt, and beat until everything is combined. Sift in the cocoa and baking powder, beat to combine everything, add the flour, and mix until the flour disappears.

To make the cookie dough in a food processor: Pulse the flour, cocoa, baking powder, salt, and sugars in the food processor until mixed. Cut the cold butter (softened works fine here, too) into chunks, and add it to the bowl. Run the machine until everything is fully blended. Add the peanut butter, egg, and vanilla, and run the machine until the mixture is blended, scraping the sides down as needed, and then keep running until the dough balls together. →

chocolate peanut butter cup cookies *(continued)*

- If you don't have Dutch-process cocoa and want to use natural (i.e., any American brand, such as Hershey's, or one labeled as natural), you can do so here and use the more standard ½ teaspoon baking soda instead of 2 teaspoons baking powder; it simply makes a lighter-colored cookie.

Assemble the cookies: Place 1 to 2 tablespoons of additional granulated sugar in a small bowl. Line a large baking sheet with parchment paper. Take a scoop of cookie dough that's just shy of 2 tablespoons (a #40 scoop holds 1¾ tablespoons and is perfect for this), and place it in the palm of your hand. Flatten it with your fingers. Take a ball of peanut-butter filling from the freezer, place it in the center of the dough, wrap the chocolate dough around it, and roll it in your palms until it's smooth. Roll it in the granulated sugar to coat, place it on your prepared baking sheet, and gently flatten the cookie, just slightly, with your fingers. Repeat with the remaining dough and filling.

Bake the cookies for 8 to 10 minutes. This is going to seem like very little time, and the cookies are definitely going to look underbaked, but remember that we are just baking a thin outer shell of a cookie (the center doesn't need to be baked), and this does not take long. Let the cookies rest and set up on the baking sheet for 5 minutes before transferring them to the cooling rack to cool to room temperature.

To store: These cookies will keep at room temperature in an airtight container for 1 week.

thick molasses spice cookies

makes 22 to 24 cookies

2⅓ cups (305 grams)
all-purpose flour

2 teaspoons ground ginger

¾ teaspoon ground cinnamon

¼ teaspoon ground cloves

¼ teaspoon ground allspice

½ teaspoon baking soda

1 teaspoon (3 grams) kosher salt

¼ teaspoon ground black pepper

¾ cup (12 tablespoons,
6 ounces, or 170 grams) unsalted
butter, melted, cooled slightly

½ cup (150 grams) molasses
(see note)

⅔ cup (145 grams) packed
dark-brown sugar

1 large egg yolk

3 tablespoons (45 grams) finely
chopped crystallized ginger

6 tablespoons (75 grams)
granulated or turbinado sugar,
for rolling

These cookies are my winter obsession. I had been on the hunt for a thick, soft-but-not-too cakey, deeply spiced, and a little kicky dark-molasses cookie for as long as I could remember. I tried dozens over the years, but none were exactly right. Over the pandemic winter that left us devoid of parties and all the usual holiday cheer, I decided that I would at least get this one perfect. (I also ran my local store out of molasses and ground ginger, and begged my friends to swing by so I could fling samples off the balcony down to them—don't worry, we're not high up—because we were, at one point, blockaded by cookies.) Do you know what it's like for your apartment to smell like a gingerbread house blew up in it every day for the whole month of December? It was, despite the larger circumstances, a very good time, and at the end, I had these: my forever molasses cookies, and soon, perhaps, yours, too.

Heat the oven to 350°F (175°C). Line a large baking sheet with parchment paper.

Whisk the flour, spices, baking soda, salt, and pepper in a large bowl until fully mixed. Make a well in the center of the dry ingredients. Pour in the melted butter, molasses, brown sugar, yolk, and candied ginger. Whisk these together in the center a couple times (until the egg yolk is dispersed); then switch to a spoon or rubber spatula to continue mixing. The dough will be very thick!

Scoop the dough into balls—I either use a medium cookie scoop (1½ tablespoons) or take just shy of 2 tablespoons of dough for each. Roll each in your hands briefly to shape it into a ball, then into the granulated or turbinado sugar for coating.

Space the cookies evenly on the parchment-lined baking sheet (they barely spread), and bake for 10 to 12 minutes. You want what looks like a *quite* underbaked cookie. It will feel totally soft on top; you will be sure it's raw. But if you lift a cookie, you'll see that it's one shade darker underneath. They're done. Remove the pan from the oven, and let the cookies →

note   You can use either unsulphured or blackstrap molasses here; I've tested it with both. If you can't get molasses where you are, use treacle. As for the egg yolk, I tested this recipe several times with a whole egg and with just a yolk and vastly prefer the yolk-only version: it's less crunchy and better holds the pillowy shape that I like in a molasses cookie.

cool for 5 minutes before transferring them to a cooling rack. The cookies set as they cool. If you cut into one in the first 15 minutes, you'll yell, "Deb! These are *raw* in the middle! How could you?" But after that, you will have a more cookielike, perfect texture—crisp outside and tender inside.

do ahead   You can chill the dough in the fridge for an hour or even several days before baking it, but let it warm up a bit at room temperature before scooping (trust me, I broke two cookie scoops learning this the hard way). Store the cookies in an airtight container to retain their softness. They keep for up to 2 weeks at room temperature, but their texture is best in the first week.

oatmeal date shortbread

makes 30 to 32 cookies

1½ cups (195 grams) all-purpose flour

6 tablespoons (80 grams) packed light-brown sugar

¼ cup (50 grams) granulated sugar

1 teaspoon (3 grams) kosher salt

1 teaspoon vanilla extract

1 cup (8 ounces or 225 grams) unsalted butter, cold for food processor or stand mixer, room temperature for hand mixer

1⅓ cups (130 grams) old-fashioned rolled oats

1 cup (140 grams) chopped, pitted dates

About ½ teaspoon (but, please, just eyeball it) finely grated orange zest

This combines two of my favorite types of cookies: classic tender, buttery, perfect-every-time shortbread cookies, and oatmeal raisin cookies. Honestly, I was just playing around, trying to see how many oats I could stuff into a slice-and-bake shortbread and still keep the cookies delicate and somewhat melting in your mouth. But they came out so good, and disappeared so fast, I had to make them again, and then again. They're making a good case for becoming our new House Cookie, the kind of moderately sweet, not-too-heavy treat I might even make on a weekday, if asked nicely. They're easy; you don't have to plan a whole lot or buy any special ingredients. I used dates when I ran out of raisins, and found that I vastly prefer them here; they're tender and even more harmonious with butter, brown sugar, and vanilla.

In a food processor or stand mixer: Combine the flour, sugars, and salt. Add the vanilla and cold butter in chunks, and blend (in a food processor) until the mixture is sandy and no chunks remain; or beat (in a stand mixer) until the butter is fully blended into the flour. Add the oats, dates, and orange zest, and mix until everything is combined and the dough looks a little clumpy.

With a hand mixer: Beat room-temperature butter, sugars, and salt together in a medium-to-large bowl until light and smooth. Add vanilla, flour, oats, dates, and orange zest and beat until combined; the mixture will seem crumbly.

Divide the dough in half, and transfer each to a 9-by-13-inch piece of parchment paper. Draw up the sides of the paper over one half of the dough, press the dough from the outside of the paper into a tight log, and then roll the extra paper up around it. Repeat with the second half of the dough, forming another log. Chill the logs until they're firm, about 1 hour in the fridge or 20 minutes in the freezer.

Heat the oven to 350°F (175°C). Unwrap each cookie log, and use the parchment to line a large baking sheet. →

- You can make a variation like this: Oatmeal, Date, and White Chocolate Shortbread: Reduce the dates to ⅔ cup, and add 1 cup (6 ounces, or 170 grams) chopped white chocolate when you add the dates. This is our second-favorite way to make the cookies—delicious, but sweeter and slightly less delicate.

- For a prettier cookie, beat 1 egg until it's blended and brush it over the cooled cookie log, then roll the log in coarse or turbinado sugar before slicing.

oatmeal date shortbread *(continued)*

Carefully cut each log with a sharp serrated knife into ½-inch slices. If the slices break apart, just squeeze them back together. Arrange them on the prepared baking sheet(s). The cookies will barely spread.

Bake them for 12 to 14 minutes, or until the edges are just beginning to get golden brown. Let them cool slightly before transferring the cookies you don't eat immediately to wire racks to cool.

do ahead The dough log can be made ahead and stored, wrapped in plastic, for 1 week in the fridge, or 1 month in the freezer. Baked cookies keep in an airtight container for 5 days, or so I've heard.

chocolate chip cookies with salted walnut brittle

makes 16 large cookies

1 cup (200 grams) granulated sugar, divided

1 cup (115 grams) chopped walnuts

1 teaspoon flaky salt, divided

8 tablespoons (115 grams) unsalted butter

½ cup (110 grams) packed light-brown sugar

1 large egg

1 teaspoon vanilla extract

¾ teaspoon baking soda

½ teaspoon baking powder

1⅔ cups (220 grams) all-purpose flour

8 ounces (1⅓ cups) semi- or bittersweet chocolate chips or chopped chocolate

note No need to soften your butter if you're using a stand mixer; only do so if you're using a hand mixer. The stand mixer can do more of the powerful work of breaking the brittle into smaller pieces. Be sure not to overpack your cups of flour here: that can make a big difference in how much these cookies spread.

There are several chocolate-chip-cookie recipes on the Smitten Kitchen website: There's the one that we thought was our favorite until we found our next favorite. There are crispy, chewy ones, chocolate-chunks-stuffed cookies finished with sea salt, and even a consummate one. But when asked which is my favorite, I always dodge answering ("Have you been to Levain?!" "Oh, look, a new coffee shop!"), because, although each of those does its job very well, none is accurately the very most perfect chocolate chip cookie *for me*. This one is. It has everything I've always wanted in one: Crunch. Caramel. Salt. Height. Crisp edges and just-gooey-enough centers. A flavor that isn't simply chocolate and brown sugar. No two-to-three-day rest in the fridge, as if cravings for chocolate chip cookies could be scheduled days in advance. I realize that not every-one wants to tuck a brittled heap of chopped walnuts into their chocolate chip cookies, but I think this recipe could convince you. Walnuts provide a depth of flavor and texture in this cookie without adding heaviness, and when these walnuts are first cloaked in a hard, crackly caramel, balancing their distant bitterness with toasted sweetness, they yield a level of chocolate-chip-cookie nirvana heretofore unseen in my kitchen.

Heat the oven to 350°F (175°C) and line two baking sheets, one small and one large, with parchment paper.

Make the brittle: Pour ⅔ cup granulated sugar into a medium-large skillet, place it over medium-high heat, and cook, without stirring, until the sugar is partially liquefied, about 3½ to 4 minutes. Whisk until all the unmelted sugar disappears into the caramel. Continue to cook the sugar until it is copper-colored and beginning to smoke; then turn the heat off and quickly stir in the walnuts.

Carefully—I know you're wearing pot holders, right?—pour the hot walnut brittle, leaving no melted sugar behind, onto the small lined baking sheet, and quickly use a spatula to spread the puddle as flat and thin as you can before it sets too much to move it. (This happens very fast, but don't worry if you don't get it completely flat; it's just a little more work to break it →

up when it's thick.) Sprinkle it with ¼ teaspoon flaky salt. Transfer this pan to the freezer to solidify for 10 to 15 minutes. No freezer space? The fridge works, too, but that could take closer to 30 minutes.

Make the cookies: Place the butter, light-brown sugar, remaining ⅓ cup granulated sugar, and remaining ¾ teaspoon flaky salt in the bowl of an electric mixer. Beat until the butter is softened and the mixture is light, scraping down the sides as needed. Add the egg and vanilla, and beat until combined. Sprinkle the baking soda and baking powder over the batter and beat them in thoroughly, scraping down the bowl midway and at the end. Add the flour, and mix until only a few floury patches remain.

Remove the chilled, solidified tray of walnut brittle from the freezer or fridge, and use a mallet, the handle of a chef's knife, or even the bottom of a heavy pot to smash it into bite-sized chunks. Pour the brittle chunks and chocolate into the bowl of dough, and mix briefly, just until they're dispersed throughout.

Scoop the cookies into 3-tablespoon-sized balls, spacing them 2 to 3 inches apart on the larger parchment-paper-lined baking sheet. Bake for 10 to 12 minutes, or until they're a deep golden brown at the edges. Transfer to a cooling rack to cool for at least 5 minutes before biting in (be warned: hot caramel is no friend to mouths).

notes

- Chocolate-chip-cookie recipes that insist you schedule chocolate-chip-cookie cravings in advance—or, worse, 2 to 3 days in advance—are the bane of my existence. I promise that these cookies are wonderful baked right away. But I'd be remiss if I didn't tell you that the batches of dough that chilled overnight in the fridge before being baked were even lovelier—more craggy in texture, less puffy. If you'd like to plan ahead, your chilled dough will be good in the fridge for up to 4 days. Leave it out at room temperature for 20 to 30 minutes before scooping, so you don't break your scoop on the cold dough. (Clearly, I've been there.)

- Because these cookies are caramel-studded, they'll probably not be perfectly round when they come out, and some will have puddled in different directions. You can leave them that way, of course, but if you want your cookies to be perfectly round again, while they're still hot, do the Cookie Scoot, a technique I learned from the talented Erin Clarkson at her blog, Cloudy Kitchen. Take a 4-inch round cookie cutter (or a glass with the same diameter), place it around a wayward-shaped cookie on the baking sheet the moment it comes out of the oven, and "scoot" the cutter around the cookie, pulling in the sides until it's tidy and round again.

bars

big crumb pie bars

*makes sixteen 2-inch
square bars*

crumbs

1 cup (8 ounces, or 225 grams)
unsalted butter, melted and
cooled slightly

½ cup (110 grams) packed
light-brown sugar

⅓ cup (65 grams) granulated
sugar

1 teaspoon (3 grams) kosher salt

1 large egg

2 teaspoons baking powder

3¼ cups (425 grams) all-purpose
flour

filling

3 cups (roughly 800 to 1000
grams) diced berries, stone fruit,
apples, or pears, but preferably
a mix of a couple

Juice of ½ lemon

¼ cup (50 grams) granulated
sugar

¼ teaspoon ground ginger,
cinnamon, or another pie spice
you like

1 tablespoon tapioca flour,
or 1½ tablespoons cornstarch

to finish (optional)

Confectioners' sugar, for dusting

Everyone loves pie bars. There is no happier, more welcome treat to bring to a summer picnic, potluck, or anything that involves a blanket at a park. You get pie, you get a cookie, and you get streusely crumbs. Yet about that last part: I don't actually want streusely crumbs. I don't want anything finely rubbled or cornmeal-looking. I want big boulder-like crumbs; I like crumbs that are their own pebbles of nearly distinct shortbread. To get this, we're going to put a lot of crumbs and a lot of fruit in a smaller pan, and bake them longer than thinner bars, and cut them smaller. These smaller, thicker squares take up less space in your bag (New Yorkers always consider real estate, naturally) and are even easier to take with you, by design.

Fruit choices: The best fruits here are anything you like in pie, diced. I've made these with strawberries and rhubarb, peach and blueberries, and peach and blackberries, but my absolute favorite, and what you see here, is a mix of whatever stone fruits I had to use up—peaches, apricots, plums, plumcots, and all the other hybrid varieties out there.

———

Heat the oven to 375°F (190°C). Lightly coat an 8-by-8-inch baking pan with nonstick spray, then line with two pieces of parchment paper in opposite directions, extending them up opposite sides to create a parchment sling. In a large bowl, whisk butter, sugars, and salt together. Whisk in the egg, then the baking powder. Stir in the flour and mix until all is dampened by the butter-sugar mix and in big crumbs.

Press about two-thirds of the crumb mixture (about 2⅔ cups, or 600 grams) across the bottom and up ½ inch (1¼ centimeters) of the sides of the prepared pan. Bake for 15 to 17 minutes, until the crumbs are lightly golden all over.

While the base bakes, combine the fruit, lemon juice, sugar, ginger, and tapioca flour in a bowl. Fill the bottom of the parbaked base with the fruit, leaving a ½-inch margin at the edges. Top with the remaining crumbs. If they're loose, you can grab tight fistfuls to make bigger clumps to scatter. →

big crumb pie bars *(continued)*

Return the pan to the oven for another 40 to 45 minutes, or until the edges are a deep golden brown and you can see the fruit juices bubbling up between some crumbs on top.

Let cool, either at room temperature or in the fridge; then use the parchment sides to lift the bars out of the pan and onto a cutting board. Cut into 2-inch squares, dust with confectioners' sugar, if using, and enjoy.

do ahead Bars will keep in the fridge for a week, which is where I find they stay the most crisp, too.

bee sting bars

makes 12 to 24 triangular bars

base

1 cup plus 2 tablespoons
(150 grams) all-purpose flour

½ teaspoon kosher salt

¼ cup (50 grams) granulated
sugar

½ cup (4 ounces, or 115 grams)
unsalted butter, cold is fine

½ teaspoon vanilla extract

topping

½ cup (4 ounces, or 115 grams)
unsalted butter, cold is fine

⅓ cup (65 grams) granulated
sugar

¼ cup (85 grams) mild-flavored
honey

2 tablespoons (30 grams)
heavy cream

¼ teaspoon kosher salt

½ teaspoon vanilla extract

2¼ cups (6¾ ounces,
or 195 grams) thinly sliced
almonds, lightly toasted

Flaky sea salt

note This recipe can be
doubled, using a 9-by-13-inch
pan.

My mother's favorite cake is a *Bienenstich,* or "bee sting cake," a German specialty with a crunchy almond-honey-butter caramel topping on a rich, yeasted cake that's (often, but not always) split and filled with a lush vanilla bean custard. The story goes that it's not an authentic *Bienenstich* unless a bee, drawn to the honey, has stung it. Alas, that will not be the only thing inauthentic about these bars; I've gotten rid of the cake entirely. Here I've transplanted the almond topping we always gush over to a simple shortbread bar, and the result is compact, buttery, caramelized bliss, excellent in holiday gift tins, where no bees can get to them.

Heat the oven to 350°F (175°C). Lightly coat an 8-by-8-inch baking pan with nonstick spray, then line it with two pieces of parchment paper in opposite directions, extending the pieces up over the opposite sides to create a parchment sling.

Make the shortbread: Combine the flour, salt, and sugar in the bowl of a food processor. Cut the butter into chunks, add it to the bowl along with the vanilla, then run the machine until the butter disappears into the flour, about 30 seconds. Press the dough into the prepared pan, pressing it up the sides just a little around the edges. Bake for 15 to 18 minutes, until the crust is lightly golden all over.

While it bakes, make the topping: In a medium saucepan over medium-high heat, heat the butter, sugar, honey, cream, and salt until the butter is melted. Simmer for 3 to 5 minutes, until the mixture becomes a shade darker (from a yellowish tone to a light beige), stirring from time to time. Stir in the vanilla and the almonds, and remove from the heat.

Dollop the almond-honey mixture over the cookie base in big spoonfuls, and then spread it into an even layer. Even if it's not perfectly evenly distributed, it levels out in the oven. Sprinkle a couple pinches of flaky sea salt on top.

Bake the bars: Bake for 15 to 20 minutes, or until the honey-almond topping is golden all over. Let cool completely; feel free to speed this up in the fridge, or outside on a cold day. Once cool, remove the bars with →

bee sting bars *(continued)*

the parchment sling, and use a sharp knife to cut them into the desired shape. Shown here are generous 2-by-3-inch rows, with each rectangle cut on the diagonal into two triangles, but when making these as part of a cookie tin, I cut them 3-by-4-inch, then into small triangles.

do ahead   Bars keep at room temperature for 3 days. In the fridge, they'll keep a week or longer, but are best brought back to room temperature before serving. They can be frozen between layers of parchment paper in an airtight container for 2 months.

luxe s'more bars

makes 16 luxe bars

crust

14 sheets (240 grams) graham crackers

2 tablespoons (25 grams) granulated sugar

Two pinches of kosher salt

½ cup (4 ounces, or 115 grams) unsalted butter, cut into cubes

filling

1 large egg

3 large egg yolks

½ cup (100 grams) granulated sugar

¼ teaspoon kosher salt

1¾ cups (400 grams) heavy cream (cold is fine)

4 ounces (115 grams) semisweet chocolate (60-percent range is perfect here), chopped

4 ounces (115 grams) milk chocolate, chopped

1 tablespoon (15 grams) unsalted butter

¼ teaspoon vanilla extract

meringue

3 large egg whites

¾ cup (150 grams) granulated sugar

Pinch of salt

½ teaspoon vanilla extract

These aren't s'mores. S'mores are for *children,* and I am a full "groan" (as my son once delightfully spelled it) adult. S'mores are for camping, and these need a hand mixer. No, this is a completely decadent chocolate-pudding-pie bar on a graham-cracker base with a toasted meringue frosting, and it exists for one single purpose: spoiling your friends.

I made these lush bars a few July Fourths ago. My plan had been to make chocolate-pudding bars with a plume of whipped cream on top, but I was bothered—more, perhaps, than I should be—by the leftover egg whites. So, instead, I whipped them into a vanilla meringue and then toasted the tops of the bars, cut them into wobbly squares, and brought them to a friend's yard. I felt certain that they were too rich, too lush, too messy. I mean, who needs this kind of gooey, over-the-top decadence?

Well, my friends do. These caused a commotion louder than the worst behavior that evening, and it wasn't because anyone was well behaved. "This needs to go in your next cookbook." "I am not working on another cookbook." "You need to get started working on one and put these in it." And . . . so, out of excuses, I did. I hope they cause a ruckus wherever you bring them, too.

———————

Make the crust: Heat your oven to 350°F (175°C). Lightly coat an 8-by-8-inch baking pan with nonstick spray, then line with two pieces of parchment paper in opposite directions, extending them up opposite sides to create a parchment sling. Coat the parchment lightly with nonstick spray.

Crumble the graham crackers into the work bowl of a food processor, and add 2 tablespoons granulated sugar and two pinches of kosher salt. Blend until the crackers are reduced to even crumbs. Add the diced butter, and pulse the machine until the butter disappears and the crumbs are easily pinched into clumps. Press the crumbs evenly across the bottom of your prepared pan. Bake for 10 minutes, or until the crumbs are a shade darker at the edges. Cool them on a rack while you prepare the chocolate layer. →

luxe s'more bars *(continued)*

Make the chocolate layer: Whisk the whole egg, the egg yolks, ½ cup granulated sugar, and ¼ teaspoon kosher salt in a medium-sized saucepan until thoroughly combined, 1 minute. Slowly drizzle in the cream, whisking the whole time. Warm the mixture over medium-low heat, stirring frequently, until it is thick enough to coat a spoon, about 7 to 10 minutes (or 177°F on an instant-read thermometer). Remove from heat and add both chocolates, a handful at a time, whisking until melted. Add the butter, and stir until that's melted, too. Stir in the vanilla.

Pour the chocolate layer over the graham crust, and smooth the top. Fully chill this layer, in the fridge for 1 to 2 hours or, if you're in a rush, in the freezer for about 30 minutes, but don't let it actually freeze solid.

Make the meringue: Combine the egg whites, ¾ cup granulated sugar, and pinch of salt in the metal bowl of a stand mixer or a heatproof bowl that you'll use with your hand mixer in a moment. Set the bowl over a pan of simmering water. Keep the mixture moving, whisking, until the sugar is completely melted and it's hot to the touch (or 160°F). Off the heat, add the vanilla, and use a stand or hand mixer to beat the mixture on moderately high speed until it's glossy and very stiff, about 2 to 3 minutes. Spoon the meringue over the cooled chocolate layer, and spread it in swirls with the back of a spoon. Use a kitchen torch or your oven's broiler to brown the meringue. Refrigerate the bars until you're almost ready to serve them.

To serve: Use a knife dipped into hot water to cut the bars into sixteen squares—they will look small, but they're very rich. Refrigerate any leftovers—which, honestly, would be unprecedented for these bars—for up to 5 days.

the blondie chipwich

makes 12 small ice cream sandwiches

½ cup (4 ounces, or 115 grams) unsalted butter

Scant 1 teaspoon (3 grams) kosher salt

1 cup (215 grams) packed light-brown sugar

3 tablespoons (45 grams) milk, any kind, cold is fine

1 large egg

1½ teaspoons vanilla extract

1 teaspoon baking powder

1 cup (130 grams) all-purpose flour

½ cup (3 ounces, or 85 grams) miniature chocolate chips, divided, plus more for dipping sandwiches

3 cups (580 grams) vanilla ice cream

The beach we go to in the summer has, as any good beach should, an ice cream stand. It took approximately five minutes for my kids to reintroduce their parents—via begging, with us only agreeing in exchange for a bite—to Chipwiches, those bliss-inducing chocolate-chip-cookie ice cream sandwiches. I have been closely, uh, *researching* these for a few summers now, and the more I "study" them, the more in awe I am of their brilliance, however manufactured: the perfect texture, the perfect level of sweetness, and just the right amount of salt to balance it all.

I'm also in awe because I learned the hard way how terrible homemade chocolate chip cookies are for ice cream sandwiches—the cookies freeze rock-hard, leading to ice cream squeezing out the sides, and our messy hands and sticky arms turned us into pieces of human fly tape one hot summer evening on my friend's roof in Greenpoint. I've since tried getting frozen cookies right in so many ways, and failed until my aha moment came: I noticed that cake layers don't freeze nearly as hard as cookies. Taking my favorite blondie recipe and giving it a cakier effect with baking powder and milk yields a blondie that we'd find too soft at room temperature but that is perfect from the freezer.

I have a few other tricks up my sleeve: I make these sandwiches out of blondies, so we don't have the mess and fuss of filling individual cookies. A single 9-by-13-inch pan makes exactly one dozen petite-looking but, trust me, quite filling sandwiches, and you can shape them right inside the pan, too. Miniature chocolate chips are less unappealingly crunchy when frozen. Bumping up the sugar and salt counteracts the flavor-dulling effect of freezing the cookie. A slightly lower baking temperature limits how much the blondies brown and crisp, which would be unpleasant once they were frozen. The one-bowl recipe comes together in about 5 minutes, and bakes in 15, but needs to chill overnight. So go! Go turn your freezer into the best beach ice cream stand on earth.

Make the cookie: Heat the oven to 325°F (165°C), and line the bottom of a 9-by-13-inch pan with parchment paper. Coat the parchment and the sides of the pan with nonstick spray. A little extra spray underneath the parchment helps it stay in place. $\rightarrow$

the blondie chipwich *(continued)*

note Yes, I of course tested this with browned butter, which I love in blondies, but I couldn't taste the nuance from the freezer, so it's not worth the extra step.

In a large bowl, melt the butter halfway, then stir until the butter finishes melting. (This keeps the temperature down.) Add the salt, brown sugar, and milk, and whisk until the mixture is smooth. If it's not cool yet, let it cool a bit more (you do not want the egg to scramble or the chips to melt) before adding the egg and vanilla and whisking until everything is combined. Sprinkle the batter with baking powder, and mix very well. Stir in the flour and about ⅓ cup of the chocolate chips, mixing until the flour disappears.

Spoon the blondie batter into the prepared pan in small dollops, and spread—an offset spatula is great here—into a thin, even layer. Sprinkle remaining chips on top.

Bake for 15 minutes, until the blondie is set but soft; transfer to a cooling rack. Let it cool completely in its pan. I transfer mine immediately to the freezer so that it cools quickly, in about 15 minutes. If your ice cream is rock-hard in the freezer, transfer it to the fridge for these 15 minutes so it will be easier to scoop.

Assemble the sandwiches: Once the cookie is cold to the touch, run a knife around it to loosen it from the pan, and use the parchment to slide it out of the pan. Cut it in half widthwise. Return the used parchment to the pan; and center it over one half of the pan—i.e., it will not cover the whole bottom but will extend up one short side of the pan. We will use it to help shape the sandwiches. Place one cookie half back in the pan upside down over the parchment, and press it firmly against the edge of the pan. Scoop the ice cream in small spoonfuls all over, and spread it evenly. Press the second cookie half, right side up, onto the ice cream. Use the sides of the pan and the parchment paper to help the ice cream keep its shape in the cookie, and place the pan in the freezer.

Freeze for 4 to 6 hours, minimum—for maximum ease and clean slices, ideally, overnight.

To finish: Once the ice cream is fully solid again, remove the blondie-and-ice-cream slab to a cutting board, and cut into twelve 2-inch squares. If you like, you can dip one or all sides into additional chocolate chips. Eat or return them to the freezer right away.

tarts, crisps,
and a well-deserved crème brûlée

raspberry crostata

dough

2 cups plus 3 tablespoons
(285 grams) all-purpose flour

½ cup (100 grams) granulated
sugar

1 teaspoon baking powder

1 teaspoon (3 grams) kosher salt

10 tablespoons (140 grams)
unsalted butter, cold, diced

1 large egg, plus 1 egg yolk
(save the white)

½ teaspoon vanilla extract,
or ¼ teaspoon almond extract

filling

1 cup (4½ ounces, or 130 grams)
fresh raspberries

½ cup (160 grams) raspberry jam

finish

1 egg white, reserved from dough

1 tablespoon (15 grams) coarse
or turbinado sugar

I have rarely found an intersection of raspberry jam and rich, buttery shortbread that I did not find to be exemplary, but I found the specific raspberry crostata of my affection, borderline obsession, at Via Carota, a beloved West Village restaurant. Their crostata di marmellata is gorgeously sturdy and fragrant. I know in time that they will write a cookbook and share their secrets, but I cannot wait that long, so I got to tinkering in my own kitchen until I landed on this, everything I want in a raspberry crostata we can all make at home with as little fussing as possible.

In testing, I found that the versions I made filled only with jam were too harshly sweet. Using a smaller amount of jam and adding a larger amount of mashed fresh raspberries yielded a perfect tart-sweetness, excellent texture, and better raspberry flavor. From there, you can fuss a little or not at all. Lattice strips are traditional, but I've also stamped out stars, hearts, and other shapes for the top and scattered them about, for ease and cuteness.

———————

Heat the oven to 375°F (190°C). If you're using a 9-inch round tart pan with a removable base, you're all set. (But if it does not have a nonstick coating, butter it or coat it with nonstick spray.) If you'd like to make this in an 8-inch square baking pan as bars, lightly coat an 8-by-8-inch baking pan with nonstick spray, then line it with two pieces of parchment paper in opposite directions, extending the pieces up over the opposite sides to create a parchment sling for easier removal later.

Make the dough:

In a food processor: Combine the flour, sugar, baking powder, and salt in the work bowl. Add the butter, and blend until it disappears completely and just begins to form sandy clumps. Add the whole egg, the yolk, and the vanilla or almond extract, and blend until the dough comes together in a few large clusters. $\rightarrow$

notes

- To make an Almond-Raspberry Crostata, you can replace ½ cup plus 3 tablespoons flour with 4 ounces or 115 grams (about 1 cup, but it's more consistently measured by weight) ground almonds (almond meal or flour). For this version, I always use the almond-extract option, and sometimes scatter some thinly sliced almonds over the lattice before baking.

- This is not a dough that you can easily weave into a lattice; it's not bendy and not worth fighting. I just crisscross the pieces—all in one direction, and all in the other on top— and it's just as gorgeous.

- If you'd like a slightly sweeter filling, use more jam and less fresh raspberries, ¾ cup of each.

In a stand mixer: Combine the flour, sugar, baking powder, and salt in the mixing bowl. With the machine on low speed, add the butter, and keep it running until the butter is incorporated. Add the whole egg, yolk, and vanilla or almond extract, and mix into an even dough.

For both methods: Roll a bit more than a third of the dough (1 heaped cup, or 220 grams) between two pieces of parchment paper into an even rectangle of about 8 by 11 inches. Slide the parchment onto a tray or board, and freeze for 10 minutes.

Press the remaining two-thirds to three-quarters of the dough (about 2 cups, or 415 grams) across the bottom and sides of the tart pan, or across the bottom and 1 inch up the sides of a square pan.

Bake (no weights needed) for 12 to 14 minutes, until the base is dry to the touch and barely golden at the edges.

While the crust parbakes, prepare the filling: Mash the raspberries with jam until the raspberries are mostly crushed.

Once the base is parbaked, transfer it to a rack, but leave the oven on. The sides will look a little slumpy, and the center puffed, but don't worry. If the sides have fully sunk, use the back of a spoon to press the dough back down across the center, creating a new space for the filling. Spoon the filling into the center, leaving the sides bare so that the top crust will adhere.

Remove the cold slab of dough from the freezer, peel back the top sheet of parchment, and replace it on the dough, to loosen it; then flip the dough and parchment over so it rests on the loosened side. Peel back and discard the top sheet of parchment paper. Cut the dough diagonally into 1-inch lattice strips, or use a cookie cutter to form a shape of your choice. Arrange the strips crisscrossed, or make a collage of shapes, over the filling. Trim the edges so that there's no overhang.

Beat the egg white until loose (if it's a struggle, add 1 teaspoon water), and brush it over the top lattice or shapes. Sprinkle with coarse sugar.

Bake the crostata: Bake for another 25 to 30 minutes, until it is a deep golden brown all over, which will ensure it has crisp edges. Cool it to room temperature, if you can bear it. Serve it in wedges.

do ahead Crostata keeps at room temperature for 4 days, or 1 week in the fridge.

mango curd tart

serves 8

crust

1 cup plus 2 tablespoons
(150 grams) all-purpose flour

½ teaspoon kosher salt

Finely grated zest of 1 lime

⅓ cup (40 grams) confectioners'
sugar

½ cup (4 ounces, or 115 grams)
unsalted butter, cold is fine,
cut into a few chunks

filling

1 cup puréed fresh mango
(from about 2 medium-large
yellow mangoes, 1 pound or
455 grams total), or scant 2 cups
(10¾ ounces, or 305 grams) in
a ½-inch dice

4 tablespoons (60 grams)
freshly squeezed lime juice
(from 2 medium limes)

¼ cup plus 3 tablespoons
(85 grams) granulated sugar

5 large egg yolks

⅛ teaspoon kosher salt

6 tablespoons (3 ounces,
or 85 grams) unsalted butter,
any temperature, in pieces

Whipped cream, for serving
(optional)

I know that lemon tarts are usually the darling of the pastry case, but I think it's time they shared the spotlight. Many years ago, I filled a wedding cake I made for friends with fresh mango curd, and it was so delicious, I vowed to find a way to make it the whole story in some future dessert. Ahem, well, fourteen years have passed, and, listen, I know I'm slow, but I wanted to get it exactly right. This is worth the wait. The crust is a lime-zest-flecked shortbread, the mango filling is rich, glossy, sweet-tart. It's the mangoiest mango dessert I've ever made or eaten, a velvety-smooth magnification of everything nuanced and delicious about my favorite fruit.

Make the crust: Heat the oven to 350°F (175°C). Combine the flour, salt, zest, and confectioners' sugar in the bowl of a food processor. Add the butter to the bowl, and run the machine until the butter is blended and the mixture forms large clumps. Don't worry if this doesn't happen right away; keep running the machine; it might take another 30 seconds for it to come together, but it will.

To shape the crust: Set two marble-sized pieces of dough aside, and transfer the rest of it to a 9-inch round tart pan with a removable bottom set on a large baking sheet (for drips and stability of use), and press the dough thinly, evenly, across the bottom and up the sides. Chill it in the freezer for 15 minutes, until it's solid.

Parbake the crust: Once the crust is firm, prick it all over with a fork. Coat a piece of foil with nonstick spray, and press it, oiled side down, tightly against the frozen crust, so it is fully molded to the shape. Bake the tart with the foil (no pie weights needed) for 20 minutes; then, carefully, gently, a little at a time, peel back the foil, and discard it. If cracks have formed in the dough, use the marbles of dough you set aside to patch it. Return the crust to the oven and bake for 5 minutes, until just golden at edges and dry to the touch. Rest the shell on a rack while you make the curd. Leave the oven on. →

Make the curd: In a food processor or high-speed blender, blend the mango, lime juice, granulated sugar, egg yolks, and salt until very smooth. For a silkier curd, pour the mixture through a fine-mesh strainer. Heat the curd in a saucepan, whisking over low heat, until it's beginning to thicken, at about 175°F to 180°F (80°C to 82°C), just below a simmer. (Don't let it boil.) Stir in the butter, one piece at a time, until it's melted.

Finish in the oven: Pour the curd into the prepared crust, and bake until the filling jiggles only in the center few inches when shimmied, about 15 minutes. Let it cool until it's fully chilled in the fridge, 3 to 4 hours.

To serve: Slide the tart ring off the base (this is easy to do if you first rest the pan on an upside-down bowl smaller than the tart). Dip a sharp knife into hot water for clean cuts, and slice the tart into wedges. Dollop with whipped cream, if desired.

note A thing I learned from making a wedding-cake-volume of mango curd is that the kind of mango you use is key. Acceptable as the Tommy Atkins variety (usually red, yellow, and green on the outside, larger and firmer) is for snacking, it's too stringy here. An Alphonso or other yellow-skinned, silky-fleshed mango that's fully ripe works much better, and tastes better, too. If it's too far from mango season where you are (often April through late June, although they might be in stores through July), look for a high-quality, nothing-else-added mango purée, sometimes sold frozen.

apple butterscotch crisp

serves 6 to 8

filling

2½ pounds (1.15 kilograms) baking apples (about 5 or 6 medium; my favorites are Mutsu, Granny Smith, Golden Delicious, or a mix thereof)

Juice of ½ lemon

1 cup (215 grams) packed dark-brown sugar

¼ cup (60 grams) water

½ teaspoon flaky sea salt, plus more to taste

2 tablespoons (30 grams) unsalted butter, cold is fine

¾ cup (170 grams) heavy cream

1 teaspoon vanilla extract

topping

½ cup (4 ounces, or 115 grams) unsalted butter, melted

½ teaspoon kosher salt

¼ cup (55 grams) packed dark-brown sugar

¼ cup (50 grams) granulated sugar

½ teaspoon ground cinnamon

¾ cup (75 grams) old-fashioned rolled oats

¾ cup (85 grams) chopped pecans

¾ cup plus 2 tablespoons (115 grams) all-purpose flour

Vanilla ice cream, to serve (not optional, sorry)

Here goes: I wish we'd all admit that apple-crisp recipes rarely work as well as they should. I mean, of course it's almost impossible for cinnamon baked apples with a buttery, nutty oat-and-brown-sugar topping to taste bad, but I wish more recipes owned up to the fact that the topping often burns before the apples reach bubbly, pielike perfection, especially if you like your apples in big wedges, as I do. You can fix this by covering the crisp midway with foil if it's getting too dark—every home cook enjoys leaning into a 400°F oven to mold a highly conductive metal against a scalding-hot dish, right? Or, you can parcook your apples before the topping is added, evening out the baking times for a truly failproof crisp.

That's where this headnote might have ended—but as I was sautéing apples in some brown sugar and butter on the stove to get them started, I realized that I was kind of making a butterscotch sauce. Why *kinda* make a butterscotch sauce if I could *really, actually* make a butterscotch sauce? Butterscotch—butter, brown sugar, vanilla, and salt—is one of the best substances on this earth, and surprisingly easy to make—so here we are going to use it twice, first to parcook and deeply infuse the apples with heady deliciousness; and later as the finishing touch on an apple crisp that's unsubtly striving to be the best apple crisp you've ever made.

Heat the oven to 400°F (205°C).

Prepare the apples: Peel, halve, and core the apples; then cut the halves into ½-inch-thick wedges. Toss them in a large bowl with the lemon juice, and set aside while you make the butterscotch.

Make the butterscotch: In a 12-inch heavy skillet, stir together the brown sugar, water, and salt. Turn the heat to medium-high and cook, without stirring, until it's dark brown and smells caramelized, about 7 to 8 minutes. Do not fret if it smokes; this is par for the course with butterscotch.

Reduce the heat to medium, and carefully (it's going to sizzle dramatically) whisk in the butter, and then the cream, being sure to mix everything well into the corners of the pan, and cook for another 3 to 4 minutes. Add the vanilla. You'll have a scant 1½ cups of butterscotch sauce. Remove →

note You're going to end up with twice the extra butterscotch sauce that you need to drizzle on the crisp—you're welcome. The sauce keeps in the fridge for a month and tastes good on everything from ice cream to oatmeal, pancakes, and spoons. From the fridge, it will be too thick to pour and might have separated; rewarm it for 10 seconds (watch carefully) in a microwave or briefly in a small saucepan on the stove, whisking until it's even and pourable.

from the heat just long enough to ladle half of it carefully into a spouted dish or bowl for later, and set that portion aside.

Parcook the apples: Keeping the heat at medium, add the apples to the remaining butterscotch in the pan, and cook, stirring frequently, until the apples begin to soften and become translucent, but aren't fully cooked, about 12 minutes.

If your skillet is ovenproof, you can keep the apples and butterscotch in it (but I prefer to proceed in a more snug dish). If it's not, transfer everything to a 2-quart baking dish; a deep-dish pie pan will work, too.

Make the topping: Mix all of the topping ingredients in a large bowl until the butter is evenly dispersed and the mixture is rubbly. Sprinkle the topping over the apples, and bake until the apples are tender, their juices visibly bubbling, and the topping is a light, nutty brown, about 20 minutes. Let it cool, if you can bear it, for 10 to 15 minutes before digging in.

To serve: Scoop the crisp into bowls and top with ice cream and a drizzle of the reserved butterscotch sauce. If your butterscotch sauce has cooled and firmed up, you can warm it up quickly in the microwave—check every 10 seconds, as it warms and bubbles up quickly—or in a small saucepan on the stove.

family-style crème brûlée

serves 4

1 vanilla bean, split lengthwise, or 1 teaspoon vanilla-bean paste and 1 teaspoon vanilla extract

⅓ cup (65 grams) granulated sugar, plus 2 tablespoons (25 grams) to finish

3 large egg yolks

1 large (whole) egg

1 tablespoon (15 grams) rum, Grand Marnier, or brandy (optional)

2 cups (475 grams) heavy cream

Heaped ¼ teaspoon kosher salt

This is crème brûlée for people who don't get enough crème brûlée in their lives—i.e., everyone, right?—but who don't want it to be a totally fussy-pants thing to make at home. I mean, who even owns a set of 6-ounce shallow ramekins that happen to fit inside another, larger dish for a water bath? Okay, hmm, well, I guess I do, but (1) I do not know where they are; please don't make me clean out the closet, and (2) I'm not normal. Instead, I drama-sized my crème brûlée, making it large enough for the whole family to dig into at once, but not so big that it requires special pans that few (normal) people have. I tried to keep the other parts as simple as possible. I use regular, everyday granulated sugar (which works best here, anyway). I don't use eight egg yolks, or even close. I tried very hard to get the maximum potential out of a single pint of heavy cream, so we didn't have to buy a second one just for, like, ⅓ cup. Finally, I even found a trick for brûléeing the sugar for people who don't keep blowtorches around (or those of us, like me, who have one but probably shouldn't be trusted with it). I hope that this recipe makes what seems like a fancy restaurant dish doable at home.

———

Heat the oven to 325°F (165°C) degrees. Place a small dish towel or washcloth in the bottom of a 9-by-13-inch or larger baking dish; this will keep the custard from rattling around while it cooks. Place a 1-quart shallow baking dish on top of the towel. Bring a pot of water to a boil.

Make the custard: If using a fresh vanilla bean, rub the seeds into the ⅓ cup granulated sugar to infuse it with the most possible flavor.

Whisk the yolks, the whole egg, and ⅓ cup sugar until very smooth and evenly combined. Add the vanilla paste, and vanilla extract and rum, if using, then slowly, slowly drizzle in the cream, whisking the whole time. For a perfect texture, pour through a fine-mesh strainer into a bowl, ideally one with a spout. →

Bake the custard: Pour the egg-and-cream mixture into the smaller baking dish placed on top of the towel. Carefully pour enough boiling water into the larger dish so that it reaches two-thirds of the height of your interior dish. Bake until the custard is just barely set and no longer jiggly in the center, about 35 to 45 minutes. The custard will be 170°F to 175°F (77°C to 79°C).

Remove the custard from the water, and cool it on a rack to room temperature, 2 to 3 hours; then chill completely, covered, for 4 hours, overnight, or up to 4 days.

Shortly before serving: When you're ready to eat it, sprinkle the surface evenly with the remaining 2 tablespoons granulated sugar. Use a kitchen blowtorch (see note for alternate suggestion) to melt the sugar into a crispy bronzed top.

Return the crème brûlée to the fridge one more time, just to take away the warmth from the blowtorch (or broiler), which will take about 15 minutes. Don't leave it there too long, or the crunchy caramelized sugar on top will dissolve.

We serve this family-style—i.e., we all dig in with our own spoons—and it's really fun. But you can also scoop it out into individual serving dishes, for more decorum.

notes

- No blowtorch? If your oven has a broiler, heat it, and toast the sugar-sprinkled custard under the broiler for 5 to 10 minutes, rotating it frequently for even color.

- No broiler? This method is a little more tedious, but it works if you have a gas stove. Heat a metal spoon for a minute over your stove's burner (obviously, you'll be wearing a pot holder when you do this) and get it very, very hot. Gently press it against the surface sugar; the heat will melt it. Reheat the spoon as needed when it cools off and is no longer melting the sugar. You can also do a second thin layer of sugar if you didn't get the caramelized crust you wanted with the first one.

easy drop berry shortcakes

serves 6 to 8

shortcakes

2¼ cups (295 grams) all-purpose flour

2¼ teaspoons baking powder

¾ teaspoon baking soda

3 tablespoons (40 grams) granulated sugar

½ teaspoon kosher salt

6 tablespoons (85 grams, or 3 ounces) unsalted butter, cold, cut into chunks

2 large egg yolks

¾ cup plus 2 tablespoons (200 grams) heavy cream

3 tablespoons (35 grams) coarse or turbinado sugar

to finish

1 pound (455 grams) strawberries or mixed berries, hulled, halved if large

2 tablespoons (25 grams) granulated sugar, or more to taste

1 tablespoon (15 grams) fresh lemon juice (optional)

1 cup (225 grams) heavy or whipping cream

This is the tall, craggy, crunchy-edged shortcake recipe I developed when I realized that the only ones I knew how to make were extraordinarily fussy, not at all in the spirit of a quick dessert necessary to celebrate berry season. These shortcakes require no rolling pins, round cutters, unusual ingredients, or, more pressingly, advanced planning to put together—yet they manage to be both soft and moist inside and sturdy enough to not dissolve into soggy nothingness under berry juices. Or, at least, not before you can eat them. The trickiest thing I've found about them? Not inhaling them plain, the moment they're cool enough to bite into.

Heat the oven to 400°F (205°C). Line a large baking sheet with parchment paper.

Make the shortcakes: In a large bowl, whisk together the flour, baking powder, baking soda, granulated sugar, and salt until thoroughly combined. Add the butter and, using your fingertips or a pastry blender, break it into small bits. (The largest should be no bigger than a small pea.) In a small bowl, whisk the yolks with a splash of cream, then pour the rest of the cream in, and whisk to combine. Pour this into the butter-flour mixture, and use a rubber spatula to mix and mash it together into one cohesive dough.

Divide the dough into six shortcakes (these will be large, 3½ to 3¾ inches wide and roughly 2 inches tall) or eight smaller ones. I do this by pressing the dough somewhat flat into the bottom of the bowl (to form a circle) and using a knife to divide it into pielike wedges. Place coarse or turbinado sugar in a small bowl. Roll each wedge of shortcake into a ball in your hands, and roll it through the coarse sugar, coating it except for a small area that you should leave bare. (The sugar underneath the shortcakes tends to burn, so better to leave it off.)

Place it, bare spot down, on the prepared baking sheet. Repeat with remaining wedges of dough. Bake for 10 to 13 minutes, until they're lightly golden all over. Let them cool completely on a tray or on a cooling rack. $\longrightarrow$

easy drop berry shortcakes *(continued)*

While the shortcakes cool, prepare the fruit and cream: Mix the berries, 2 tablespoons granulated sugar (more or less, to taste), and lemon juice, if desired, in a bowl and let macerate so that the juices run out.

In a larger bowl, beat the cream until soft peaks form. Add sugar to taste, or leave it unsweetened, if that's your preference.

To serve: Carefully split each cooled shortcake with a serrated knife. Spoon the berries and their juices over the bottom half. Heap generously with whipped cream. Place the shortcake "lid" on top. Eat immediately, and don't forget to share.

do ahead Shortcakes keep well for a day at room temperature. I prefer to keep them uncovered. On the second day, they're best if slightly rewarmed in a 325°F oven for 4 to 5 minutes.

cakes

better-than-classic pound cake

makes 1 loaf, or 8 to 10 slices

8 ounces (1 cup, or 225 grams) unsalted butter, melted and cooled slightly

1 cup (200 grams) plus 1 tablespoon (15 grams) granulated sugar, divided

½ cup (110 grams) turbinado or packed light-brown sugar

2 teaspoons (6 grams) kosher salt

3 large eggs

1 cup (240 grams) sour cream

1½ to 2 teaspoons vanilla extract (use smaller amount if you're using vanilla bean paste, too)

½ teaspoon vanilla bean paste (optional)

2 teaspoons baking powder

2 cups (260 grams) all-purpose flour

I want this to be the last pound-cake recipe you'll ever need. It tries to earn this crown in several ways: a craggy, crisp top that I constantly have to swat small and large hands away from picking off in barklike flecks (though I hardly blame them). It's buttery but not bland, thanks to sour cream, vanilla, and exactly the right amount of salt and sugar. And it's totally unpesky—no separated eggs, odd measurements—oh, and you're going to make this in one bowl, because I'm too lazy to make it in two and won't write the recipe any other way. Before you balk at the amount of sugar or butter, please note the towering proportions here; this is a *two-and-two-thirds-pound* pound cake. I don't make pound cakes that force you to look down into the pan to see them. I think pound cakes should dome tall and chaotic over the rim. They should make an entrance and feed the crowd that forms around them. This one is ready for her spotlight.

———————

Heat the oven to 350°F (175°C). Coat a 6-cup (check! see note) loaf pan well with nonstick spray or butter, and line with a sling of parchment paper that extends up the two long sides.

In a large bowl, whisk together melted butter, 1 cup granulated sugar and all of the turbinado sugar and salt. Add the eggs, one at a time. Add the sour cream, vanilla extract, and vanilla-bean paste, if using, and whisk until smooth. Sprinkle the baking powder over the surface of the batter, and whisk many more times than are needed to make it disappear; we want to make sure it's very well dispersed through the batter. Add the flour, and stir with a spatula until just combined.

Scrape the batter into the loaf pan, and drop the pan on the counter a couple times to release any trapped air. Smooth the top, and sprinkle with the remaining 1 tablespoon granulated sugar.

Bake for 1 hour and 10 to 15 minutes, until a skewer inserted all over—especially in the top third, where raw spots like to hide—comes out batter-free. Let it cool in the pan. Run a knife along the short sides of the cake, and use the parchment "sling" to remove the cake for slicing. $\rightarrow$

better-than-classic pound cake *(continued)*

notes

- Very key here is the size of your loaf pan, because this batter will fill out every speck of it before it is done. Mine holds 6 liquid cups; it's 8 by 4 inches on the bottom and 9 by 5 inches on the top. If yours is even slightly smaller, or you're nervous, go ahead and scoop out a little to make a mini-cake muffin or two. If you're still nervous, bake the cake on a larger tray to catch drips.
- This cake uses melted butter. Do not, I repeat, do not soften and whip the butter and sugar together as you would for other cakes. The crumb is way less rich.

do ahead This cake is good on the first day and gets better on the second and third. It keeps at room temperature for 5 days. I like to store it back in its loaf pan with the top uncovered (so it stays crisp). I press a piece of foil or plastic against the cut side only.

whole lemon poppy seed cake

serves 8

cake

1 medium-large (4½ to
5½ ounces, or 130 to
155 grams) lemon

1¼ cups (250 grams) granulated
sugar

½ cup (115 grams, or
8 tablespoons) unsalted
butter (cold is fine for a food
processor; at room temperature
for a blender)

3 large eggs

½ cup (120 grams) sour cream

¼ teaspoon fine sea salt

2 teaspoons baking powder

1⅔ cups (215 grams)
all-purpose flour

2 tablespoons poppy seeds,
plus more to decorate

glassy lemon glaze

½ cup (60 grams) confectioners'
sugar

1 tablespoon (15 grams) fresh
lemon juice, plus a little more if
needed

1 tablespoon (20 grams) corn
syrup, for shine

A simple lemon tea cake is the happiest thing. It's unchallenging—not everyone likes chocolate, nuts, or coffee in baked goods, but most people agree that a lemon cake is never unwelcome with tea, coffee, on a picnic, for a housewarming, or just as a sunny pick-me-up on a day that needs one. The only problem, if you're me and secretly quite lazy and impatient with recipes, is the fussiness of taking lemons apart. Measuring finely grated zest in tablespoons is maddening; the amount of juice you get per lemon varies by lemon and the tool you use to extract it but is scientifically proven to always come up short of the number of lemons you have left—and don't get me started on recipes that do not warn you to zest before juicing, or call for a misalignment of zest and juice, leading to several shivering, half-dried lemons glowering at me from the bottom of my produce drawer as we speak.

This recipe puts an end to such madness. Taking a page from my favorite Whole Lemon Bars from my first book, I made this lemon poppy seed cake on a whim by taking an entire lemon (just one!) and grinding it to a pulp, beating in the rest of the ingredients, and pulling from the oven the most remarkably dynamic cake I've ever eaten and honestly couldn't believe I made myself. Poppy seeds, with their faint, crackly nuttiness, are so good here (but, of course, you can skip them if you're a lemon purist). A glassy lemon glaze will also look like you did more work than you did, which is never the stated goal, but (buffs fingernails) we'll take it, right?

Heat the oven to 350°F (175°C). Coat an 8- or 9-inch cake pan with non-stick spray, and line the bottom with a circle of parchment paper.

Make the cake: Slice your lemon into thin wheels, and remove any seeds from the slices. Place them in the bowl of a food processor or a high-speed blender with the sugar, and blend, scraping down the sides as needed, until the lemon is as puréed as your machine can get it. Add the butter, and blend it completely into the lemon mixture. Add the eggs, one at a time, and blend until combined. Blend in the sour cream. Sprinkle the surface of the batter with salt and baking powder, and run the machine →

until they fully disappear, then 10 seconds longer. Add the flour and poppy seeds, and pulse the machine just until they disappear.

Pour the batter into the prepared pan, and smooth the top. Bake for 34 to 37 minutes in an 8-inch pan, or 28 to 33 minutes in a 9-inch pan, or until a toothpick inserted into the center comes out batter-free. Let it cool in the pan on a rack for 5 minutes.

Use this time to make the glaze: Whisk together the confectioners' sugar, 1 tablespoon lemon juice, and corn syrup in a medium bowl until smooth; add more lemon juice if needed, ½ teaspoon at a time, to get to a thick but pourable consistency.

Run a knife around the edge of the cake to loosen it. Flip it out onto the rack, remove the parchment paper if it's stuck, then flip it right side up again onto a cake plate. Pour the glaze onto the top center of the cake, and use a spoon or spatula to spread it evenly to the edges, which it will find its way over in drips. Decorate right away with poppy seeds because the glaze sets very quickly.

Let the cake cool completely to room temperature. Serve it in wedges.

do ahead The cake can be kept at room temperature, covered, for up to 5 days.

carrot cake with brown butter and no clutter

serves 8 to 10

cake

14 tablespoons (200 grams) unsalted butter, any temperature

2 cups (9.1 ounces, or 260 grams) packed carrot grated on the large holes of a box grater

¾ cup (160 grams) packed dark-brown sugar

½ cup (100 grams) granulated sugar

1 teaspoon vanilla extract

2 teaspoons (6 grams) kosher salt

1¼ teaspoons ground cinnamon

1 teaspoon ground ginger

1 teaspoon baking soda

1 teaspoon baking powder

3 large eggs

2 cups (260 grams) all-purpose flour

⅔ cup buttermilk

frosting

8 ounces (225 grams) cream cheese, softened

¾ cup (160 grams) dark-brown sugar

Pinch of salt

½ teaspoon vanilla extract

Can a cake be indignant? I recently read all of Beverly Cleary's Ramona Quimby books to my daughter, and the word "indignant" came up a lot, but always in a mildly charming way, a bit like the way I feel about this cake. This is a carrot cake that refuses to share its space with anything—not pineapple, not raisins, and no coconut, either. It's a carrot cake that demands you pay attention to the carrots and not hide them—as if they're too wholesome to be in cake—behind so many ingredients that, with your eyes closed, you'd never find them.

This story allows only a single plot twist, the realization that browning your melted butter doesn't just lend a nutty depth to the loaf, but turns a simple cream cheese frosting into something so phenomenal, I genuinely feared it was too good and would steal the spotlight from the cake. Fortunately, I returned to my senses—an excellent frosting is an established good thing!—and we are all the beneficiaries.

———————

Heat the oven to 350°F (175°C). Lightly coat a 6-cup or 9-by-5-inch loaf pan with nonstick spray.

Make the cake: In a large skillet, melt the butter over medium heat. It will melt, then foam, then turn clear golden, and finally start to turn brown and smell nutty. Stir frequently, scraping up any bits from the bottom as you do. As soon as you begin to see golden-brown flecks around the edges or bottom, turn the heat off. Keep stirring: the color will continue to darken until the solids are a fragrant nutty brown.

Place the grated carrot in a large bowl, and pour all but the last 2 tablespoons of brown butter over it (it's fine if the butter is still warm; set the remaining brown butter aside for the frosting). Thoroughly mix in the sugars, vanilla, salt, spices, and baking soda and powder. Whisk in the eggs, one at a time. Add half the flour, and stir until it's just combined. Add the buttermilk and mix, then stir in the remaining flour. Pour the batter into the prepared loaf pan, and smooth the top. Bake for 50 to 55 minutes, until a toothpick or tester inserted into the middle of the cake—but also into the top of the cake, closer to the dome—comes out batter-free. →

carrot cake with brown butter and no clutter (continued)

Let the cake cool completely in the pan on a rack.

When the cake cools, make the frosting: Combine cream cheese, brown sugar, salt, vanilla, and the remaining brown butter (including any brown butter sediment that might have stayed in the bowl) with a whisk or an electric hand mixer until lightened and evenly mixed.

Assemble and serve: Remove cooled carrot cake from pan using the parchment sling to aid you and transfer it to a plate. If you'd like it flatter on top for frosting, use a long serrated knife to horizontally cut the dome off the carrot cake. (That's a snack.) Dollop cream cheese frosting on the top and use a butter knife or small offset spatula to thickly spread it, swirling it as decoratively as you'd like. You could also place the frosting in a bag fitted with a large star tip and make messy dollops all over, as seen here.

Serve in slices. Leftovers keep in the fridge for up to a week.

devil's food cake with salted milk chocolate frosting

serves 8 to 10

cake

1⅓ cups (175 grams) all-purpose flour

⅔ cups (55 grams) cocoa powder, any kind

1½ teaspoons baking soda

¾ teaspoon baking powder

1 teaspoon (3 grams) kosher salt

6 tablespoons (90 grams) vegetable or another neutral oil

1⅓ cups (265 grams) granulated sugar

2 large eggs

1 teaspoon vanilla extract

¾ cup (175 grams) brewed coffee

¾ cup (170 grams) buttermilk

frosting

½ cup (4 ounces, or 115 grams) unsalted butter, at room temperature

½ cup (60 grams) confectioners' sugar, sifted if lumpy

¼ teaspoon kosher salt

3 ounces (85 grams) milk chocolate, melted and cooled to room temperature

½ teaspoon vanilla extract

Flaky sea salt, for between the layers

This cake is here to audition for the role of your new favorite chocolate birthday cake. It knows that what we want most of all is a plush dark-chocolate, hard-to-mess-up cake that can be made in a single bowl with no hard-to-get ingredients. A rich, classic frosting, sweet with just a hint of salt, is the perfect embellishment. It bakes in half an hour and cools quickly, knowing that most of us are in a hurry, and it keeps things really simple: a single 9-by-13-inch pan is divided into the easiest three-layer rectangular cake on earth. Why rectangular? Few things fit better in the bottom of a paper shopping bag than loaf-shaped cakes, optimizing this for subway commutes to see your favorite people. I've tweaked this one over the years from a few favorites, getting the levels exactly where I want them to be and then rearranging the steps so we could circumvent sifting while still using only one bowl. Because I'm surrounded by chocolate lovers—chocolate lovers with birthdays—this cake took no time to go into heavy rotation here.

———————

Heat the oven to 350°F (175°C). Coat a 9-by-13-inch rectangular cake pan with nonstick spray, and line the bottom with parchment paper.

Make the cake: In a large bowl, whisk together the flour, cocoa, baking soda, baking powder, and salt until evenly mixed.

Make a well in the center of the dry ingredients, and add the oil, sugar, eggs, and vanilla. Whisk until everything is evenly combined with the cocoa mixture; then whisk in the coffee and buttermilk.

Pour the batter into the prepared pan and bake the cake for 25 to 30 minutes, rotating the pan once at the 10-minute mark, so that the cake bakes as evenly as possible. The cake is done when a toothpick inserted into the center comes out clean and the top feels slightly dry. Run a knife around the cake to loosen it, and then let it cool in the pan for 5 minutes. →

note This is an old-fashioned chocolate cake, using oil instead of butter and a larger amount of liquid to achieve the perfect texture. The coffee will not make the cake taste like coffee; it just enhances the depth of the chocolate. I often use decaf (or even decaf instant) coffee when making it, just so I don't accidentally caffeinate anyone. However, almost any other liquid works here, too—tea, red wine, juice, or water.

Flip the cake out onto a rack, remove the parchment paper if it's stuck to the bottom, flip the cake back, and let it cool completely. Cooling the cake in the freezer has two benefits: it hurries the chilling along (takes only about 20 minutes), and this soft cake is easier to cut cleanly once it's firmer.

While the cake cools, make the frosting: In a food processor: Place the frosting ingredients in the work bowl, and blend until they're fully mixed and a little fluffy, scraping the frosting down as needed to mix evenly, about 2 minutes.

With a hand or stand mixer: Beat the butter, confectioners' sugar, and salt in a large bowl until the mixture is fluffy. Pour in the chocolate and vanilla, and beat until combined, then 1 more minute to whip it further.

To frost and serve: Cut the cooled cake crosswise into even thirds with a sharp serrated knife. Place the first layer on a platter, and cover the top with a third of the frosting; it will seem like a scant coating, but it's the perfect amount here. Sprinkle the layer with a pinch or two of flaky sea salt, and repeat twice. You can serve this right away, or, for super-clean edges, chill the whole cake until the frosting is firm, and trim the sides with your serrated knife.

do ahead This cake is fine at room temperature for a day. If you need it to last longer, keep it in the fridge. I often chill it if I'm taking it somewhere, so the firm frosting stays neat; it warms up as it travels.

strawberry summer stack cake

serves 12

cake

10 tablespoons (140 grams) unsalted butter, at room temperature

1½ cups (300 grams) plus 3 tablespoons (40 grams) granulated sugar

1½ teaspoons (4 grams) kosher salt

2 large eggs

1½ teaspoons vanilla extract

¾ cup (175 grams) milk, any kind

2¼ teaspoons baking powder

2½ cups plus 1 tablespoon (335 grams) all-purpose flour

2 pounds (905 grams) of the freshest, even a touch overripe, strawberries, hulled and halved

assembly

2 cups (475 grams) heavy cream

2 tablespoons (25 grams) granulated sugar

2 tablespoons (30 grams) sour cream or crème fraîche

1 teaspoon vanilla extract

note If you have 6-inch cake pans (and I think they're a wonderful investment for people who like to make layer cakes), you can halve everything for an equally celebratory three-layer cake for six people.

My birthday falls smack dab in the middle of strawberry season, and I've usually celebrated with a strawberry summer cake on my site that I've adapted over the years from a 2008 *Martha Stewart Living*. A staggering pound of fresh strawberries are baked on top of a layer of almost biscuitlike butter. In the oven, the berries collapse into jammy puddles. It's absolutely not summer until we've made this cake, but I've long felt that the only thing that could make it better was if it were an actual birthday cake—towering and party-ready.

I thought this would be a simple undertaking, but it turned out to be more complicated than stacking the cake in triplicate. The cake needed to be thinned in height, but then thickened in texture, to support the quilt of berries without becoming soggy. The whipped cream needed to be thick enough to support the layers—but not so thick that it seemed unpleasantly dry once some was absorbed into the cake. There were a few "dark" strawberry seasons in which I "forced" my friends and family to suffer through tests and tests of subpar strawberry layer cakes (violins, please), but the struggles were all worthwhile to land here: look at this rippling quilt of summer fruit.

One key thing about this cake: It's best after a rest in the fridge—a day, if you can bear it. I'm not saying it's not good right away, but it's *optimized* after a resting period. On the first day, you have strawberries and cake and cream. On the second, everything is settled and perfect. I'm a bit biased, but I think June birthdays deserve nothing less.

———————

Heat the oven to 350°F (175°C). Coat three 9-inch cake pans with nonstick spray or butter, and line the bottoms with rounds of parchment paper. (Don't have three 9-inch cake pans? Neither did I until about 5 minutes ago, and I did not let this keep me from making dozens of three-layer cakes. The batter can wait at room temperature until the cake pan or pans are free again.)

Prepare the cake layers: In a large bowl, beat the butter, 1½ cups of the granulated sugar, and salt together until the mixture is light and fluffy. Add the eggs and vanilla, and beat until they're combined. Add the →

milk, and mix until it's fully incorporated; it may look a little curdled, but don't fret, it will smooth out in a minute. Sprinkle the baking powder evenly over the batter, and beat it for 10 seconds longer than will seem necessary—this ensures that the baking powder is perfectly distributed. Scrape down the bowl. Add the flour, and mix just until everything is combined.

Divide the batter between the prepared pans (about 190 grams in each). Arrange the strawberries, cut side down, as snugly as you need to get them to fit, on top of the batter in each pan. Leave no strawberries behind, no matter how tight it seems on top. Sprinkle each pan with one of the remaining tablespoons of sugar; it will seem like a lot, but this helps the strawberries get jammy and gives the cake a great texture.

Bake for 30 minutes, or until a toothpick inserted around the strawberries in the cake comes out free of wet batter (gooey strawberries are a given and don't mean the cake is underbaked). Let the cake layers cool on a rack for 5 minutes, then run a knife around each to ensure that no strawberry juices are gluing the cake to the edge. You can cool the cakes the rest of the way in their pans, or flip them out onto a cooling rack (especially if you need to use the pan again for the remaining batter) to cool there. Cool to room temperature.

Assemble the cake: Beat the heavy cream, sugar, and vanilla together in a big bowl with an electric mixer until soft peaks form. Add the sour cream, 1 tablespoon at a time, beating the whole time. (This stabilizes the whipped cream and adds some depth of flavor.)

Place the first cake layer on a cake stand or platter, and cover it generously with one-third of the whipped cream. It will seem like too much, but the cake will absorb some of the cream as it rests. Repeat with the second and third layers. Any extra whipped cream can be saved in the fridge for serving.

To serve: Rest the cake in the fridge for 4 to 6 hours, if you can bear it, or overnight. The cake keeps in the fridge for 5 days, but the whipped cream will be the creamiest on the first 2. To serve, cut into generous wedges.

pumpkin snacking cake

serves 12 to 16

cake

2 cups (260 grams) all-purpose flour

1½ teaspoons baking soda

1 teaspoon (3 grams) kosher salt

¾ teaspoon ground cinnamon

A few fresh gratings of nutmeg

¼ teaspoon ground ginger

Two pinches of ground cloves

½ cup (115 grams) coconut oil, warmed just enough to liquefy, or ½ cup neutral oil

½ cup (100 grams) granulated sugar

½ cup (110 grams) packed light- or dark-brown sugar

¾ cup (185 grams) pumpkin purée (half a 15-ounce can)

¾ cup (175 grams) coconut milk (half a 15-ounce can)

1 tablespoon (15 grams) white vinegar

topping

½ cup (105 grams) cream cheese, nondairy if you'd like the cake to be vegan

½ cup (60 grams) confectioners' sugar

½ teaspoon vanilla extract

Cinnamon sugar, for dusting

I am not one of those "on a whim" bakers; I would get destroyed in a TV baking competition. I don't see flour, butter, and a cup of buttermilk and run with it. I like formulas. I like percentages. I research and plan. But I realized about two hours before we left for our big Thanksgiving dinner a few years ago—I am always in charge of desserts—that I had forgotten to make one for my sister, who is vegan (sorry, Allison!). She hardly complains, especially at a meal so devoted to turkey and butter, but I had an idea.

Have you ever heard of Wacky Cake—a.k.a. Cockeyed Cake, if you're a Peg Bracken fan (and, really, who is not?). It's an egg-free, butter-free, milk-free Depression-era chocolate cake that still manages to be as dark and moist as a cake with all of these things. I tinkered with the formula a bit, and this came out of the oven 45 minutes later, a plush, fragrant, perfect fall cake. Incredibly chuffed with my triumph, I went to the front of the room to collect my Star Baker medal, but, unfortunately, all I found there was a pile of dishes. Later, though, when this cake, with a crumb that was neither stodgy nor claggy, was demolished just as quickly as the pie and cheesecake (cheesecake!), I felt Mary Berry would approve, and that was enough for me.

Heat the oven to 350°F (175°C). Line the bottom of a 9-inch round or 8-inch square cake pan with a piece of parchment paper, and coat the bottoms and sides with nonstick cooking spray.

Whisk the flour, baking soda, salt, and spices in a bowl. Make a well in the center, and pour in the oil, sugars, pumpkin, coconut milk, and vinegar. Whisk until the batter is smooth—switch to a spoon or spatula midway if it's getting too thick to whisk.

Pour the batter into the prepared pan, and bake for 25 to 30 minutes, or until a toothpick inserted in the center comes out batter-free. Cool the cake in the pan on a wire rack for 10 minutes; then remove from the pan, and cool completely on a rack.

Once totally cool, whisk together the cream cheese (if it's cold, you might want to first mash it with a fork), confectioners' sugar, and vanilla. Spoon over the cake, swirling it out to the sides. Dust with a little cinnamon sugar.

Cut into 12 wedges, or 16 squares.

chocolate dulce puddle cakes

makes 2 small, single-serving cakes

2 teaspoons cocoa powder, plus more for dusting

4 tablespoons (55 grams) unsalted butter, cut into chunks, plus more for dishes

3 ounces (85 grams) bittersweet chocolate, roughly chopped

¼ teaspoon kosher salt, plus a couple pinches of flaky salt

1 tablespoon (15 grams) granulated sugar

1 large egg

1 egg yolk

4 teaspoons (25 grams) prepared dulce de leche, cold

Confectioners' sugar, to finish

note This recipe makes exactly two small cakes, but do know that, for a truly decadent party, I've scaled it up to a dozen—preparing them up to the point where you'd bake them, and then keeping them in the fridge until you do; all they'll need is a few extra minutes in the oven—and baked them in a friend's kitchen, along with the Raclette Tartiflette (page 211), on New Year's Eve.

Whatever you thought of lava cakes in their once-upon-a-time restaurant-menu ubiquity, I think we all need a recipe for one in our back pocket, for date nights, spoiling your kids or friends, or just yourself. My version replaces flour with a little cocoa to make it richer and gluten-free. I keep the sugar in the cake on the low end, because this version has even more of a surprise inside than molten chocolate ganache—a small puddle of sea-salt-flecked dulce de leche. This cake will make everyone think you are a magician, and there's no reason to tell them otherwise.

Heat the oven to 450°F (230°C). Butter two 6-ounce ramekins, making sure not to miss any spots. Spoon a little cocoa powder into each dish, pat it around so it coats the bottom and sides, and knock the excess out.

Place 4 tablespoons butter and chocolate in a medium heatproof bowl, and—either in the microwave or set over a pot of gently simmering water—heat until the butter and chocolate are about two-thirds melted, then whisk until they finish melting. (This ensures that the mixture is not too hot for you to add other ingredients.) Whisk in the kosher salt and granulated sugar. Whisk in the egg and yolk, and beat a good twenty to thirty extra times, to ensure that the mixture is very smooth, glossy, and a bit lightened; this step is important. Add the 2 teaspoons cocoa powder, and whisk until it's combined.

Spoon one-quarter of the batter into each baking dish. Center 2 teaspoons dulce de leche in each, and sprinkle it with a pinch of flaky sea salt. Cover the dulce with the remaining chocolate batter, nudging it around the dollop and sealing it in.

Bake for 10 minutes—the cakes will feel dry to the touch and smell amazing—and transfer them to a cooling rack for 2 minutes. Wearing pot holders, place a small dessert plate over your first ramekin. Flip the cake onto the plate, count to ten, then lift the cup off. Repeat with the second cake. Dust them with confectioners' sugar. Eat immediately.

sips and snacks

salt and pepper limeades

serves 2

4 or 5 limes

3 tablespoons (40 grams) granulated sugar

⅛ teaspoon kosher salt, plus 1 tablespoon (8 grams) for rims

A few grinds of black pepper, plus 1 teaspoon for the rims

1½ cups (360 grams) cold water

Ice

My single single-use appliance in the kitchen (after, ahem, the coffee-maker) is an electric citrus juicer. I'm not suggesting that anyone needs an electric citrus juicer in their kitchen to cook or eat well, I'm just saying that I personally do. I don't care for store-bought juices or flavored seltzers of any kind, but freshly squeezed grapefruit juice, orange juice, and lemonade make me happier than possibly even coffee. Limeade, in particular, is something that rarely tastes right from a store, but at home, it's piercing and impossibly refreshing on a hot day. A salt-and-pepper rim—usually reserved for margaritas, but why should they have all the fun?—is my favorite extra here, and I promise you will not regret adding it.

———

Use a peeler to remove the zest (just the green layer) from two limes, and add it to a bowl with the granulated sugar and ⅛ teaspoon kosher salt and a few grinds of black pepper. Use a wooden spoon or cocktail muddler to mash the zest and sugar together, trying to extract all the oils and flavor from the peels. The sugar will get pasty and translucent. Pour in the water, whisk to combine, and then continue stirring until all the sugar and salt are dissolved. You can also walk away for 5 minutes at this point. When you come back, whisk it again and, voilà, all the remaining sugar should have dissolved. Set one lime wedge aside, and juice the remaining limes until you have ½ cup lime juice. Add this to the bowl with the peels, and strain the mixture; discard the peels when you are finished.

Combine 1 tablespoon salt and 1 teaspoon black pepper on a small rimmed plate. Swipe the rims of two glasses with the reserved lime wedge, and dip them into the salt mixture. Carefully fill glasses two-thirds full with ice, and pour in the limeade. Finish each glass with a grind of black pepper.

apple cider old-fashioned

makes 6 cocktails

1 quart (4 cups, or 950 grams) regular or spiced fresh apple cider

½ teaspoon pumpkin or apple pie spice blend (if the cider isn't spiced)

12 shakes orange or Angostura bitters

2 cups (475 grams) rye or bourbon whiskey, plus up to ½ cup more

Ice

Fresh apple slices, for garnish, if you wish

note Because apple ciders can range in sweetness, the concentrate will, too, and you may feel that you need more or less of it to get the drink to its correct bracing but lightly sweet flavor.

This is my take on my husband's favorite fall cocktail, the Old-Fashioned. In a classic Old-Fashioned, a cube of sugar is muddled with bitters and water before whiskey is added. It's garnished with an orange slice, orange peel, or cocktail cherry. It's delicious the way it is, but I like it even more when I replace the sugar cube with some homemade apple syrup. I make this by taking a container of spiced apple cider and cooking it down to a concentrated syrup. It takes about 30 minutes, but it's largely hands-off until the end, when you need to watch so it doesn't reduce too far. Once it's cooled, I stir in orange bitters and whiskey, and it tastes—and I don't even mean to dramatize—like a crisp October day in an apple orchard followed by a cozy evening by the fire. Since this is a bit of a process, it makes more sense to make a larger batch of the cocktail, a carafe that keeps for at least a month in the fridge, perfect for bringing to friends' houses as a homemade gift.

———

Boil the apple cider and spice, if using, in a 3-to-4-quart saucepan over high heat until it is a shade darker and syrupy, reduced to about ⅔ cup in volume. This takes about 25 to 30 minutes on my stove. Stir occasionally, especially near the end, when you want to make sure it doesn't cook off too far. (If it does, it won't ruin the drink, but the texture can be thicker and harder to keep mixed.) Let it cool to room temperature; then whisk in the bitters. In a thin stream, slowly whisk in the whiskey until it's evenly combined. Taste, and add more whiskey, up to ½ cup, if desired. Transfer the mixture to a lidded carafe, and chill thoroughly until you're ready to serve.

To serve: Place one large or a few smaller ice cubes in an Old-Fashioned glass (6 ounces). If the apple cider has settled in the carafe, give it another stir, and pour it over the ice. Garnish with an apple slice, if using, and toast the new season.

white russian slush punch

6 ounces (¾ cup, or 180 grams) half-and-half, or ½ cup milk plus ¼ cup heavy cream

1 tablespoon confectioners' sugar

4 ounces (½ cup, or 115 grams) vodka

3 ounces (6 tablespoons, or 85 grams) coffee liqueur, such as Kahlúa or Tia Maria

This is a crossover episode between two of my favorite old-school drinks-bordering-on-dessert cocktails, a White Russian and milk punch, a milk-based brandy or bourbon beverage with a little sugar and vanilla that reached the height of its popularity in the eighteenth century. Here, I adapt this with the trifecta of cream, vodka, and coffee liqueur in a White Russian. Why slush it? An icy top layer isn't traditional, but I love the experience of tucking into a snowy cocktail on a snowy day, especially when snug and warm inside.

Combine the half-and-half and confectioners' sugar in a small spouted pourer. Divide the vodka and coffee liqueur between two Old-Fashioned glasses, and stir. Slowly pour in the half-and-half over the back of a spoon, trying to disturb the vodka liqueur as little as possible. Transfer the glasses to the freezer, and freeze for 1 hour, or until a thin icy layer appears on top. Break through it with a spoon and give each drink half a stir, to ruffle the ice up before sipping.

three savory snacks

One of the first times I threw a cocktail party, I made a tremendous number of miniature savory snacks, like tarts, little toasts with things on them (canapés, I suppose they're more articulately called), hors d'oeuvres, crackers, all from scratch. It was . . . terrible. Making a million tiny things is an absurd amount of work, only for your guests, despite your herculean efforts, to really still need a slice, burger, or at minimum disco fries when you're done.

I still love making party snacks, but only if they're easy: throw-together-able, back-pocket recipes. These are three I return to time and time again. The olives are an amalgamation of every bowl of restaurant olives I've ever loved: citrus-scented, pistachio-crunched, a little spicy. The almonds are the kind I'd find as part of a cheese plate and then hope nobody noticed that I finished them first, because I'm always craving contrast. And the feta . . . sigh. If you've never had roasted feta with honey, olive oil, salt, pepper flakes, and sprigs of thyme, I'm actually so jealous that you're about to eat it for the first time because there's nothing like it. All types of feta work, but Bulgarian and French taste, to me, the creamiest once baked, so grab one if you can. And by all means: have more parties, especially now that the snacks are the easiest part.

honey thyme baked feta

serves 4 as a snack or appetizer

8-ounce (225-gram) block firm feta, drained

¼ cup (85 grams) honey

2 tablespoons (25 grams) olive oil, plus more for serving

6 sprigs fresh thyme

Red-pepper flakes, to taste

Flaky sea salt

Crisp flatbread crackers, for serving

Heat the oven to 400°F (205°C). Place the feta in a baking dish just a little larger than it, about 2 to 3 cups. Pour the honey over and around the block, and add 2 tablespoons olive oil. Season the block and the honey with red-pepper flakes, and scatter with the whole thyme sprigs. Bake for 10 minutes, or until the block is warmed through and tender; transfer to the broiler, and cook until it's dark on top. Remove the feta from the oven, drizzle with a final glug/pour/spoonful of olive oil, and sprinkle with sea salt. Eat right away, with small spoons to scoop the honey and thyme onto crackers.

spicy crushed olives with pistachios

**4 strips of orange zest,
removed with a vegetable peeler
(save the fruit for a snack)**

**½ cup (60 grams) shelled
roasted, salted pistachios**

**½ teaspoon red-pepper flakes,
plus more to taste**

**1 tablespoon finely chopped
fresh rosemary**

**2 tablespoons (25 grams)
olive oil, plus more as needed**

Flaky sea salt

**2 cups (270 grams) large green
(ideally Castelvetrano) olives,
crushed and pitted**

On a cutting board, slice the orange zest into thin matchsticks. Chop the pistachios into tiny pieces, and transfer the orange zest, pistachios, pepper flakes, rosemary, and olive oil to a medium bowl. Stir to combine, seasoning well with salt. Add the olives, and stir to coat evenly, adding more olive oil and/or salt to taste.

toasted sesame almonds

serves 4 as a snack or appetizer

2 tablespoons (25 grams) packed
light- or dark-brown sugar

2 tablespoons (25 grams)
granulated sugar

2 teaspoons (6 grams) kosher
salt

½ teaspoon ground cayenne

3 tablespoons (25 grams)
white sesame seeds,
or 1½ tablespoons each white
and black sesame seeds

1 large egg white

2 teaspoons soy sauce

3 cups (425 grams) unsalted
almonds

Toasted sesame oil, to finish

Heat the oven to 300°F (150°C). Line a large baking sheet with parchment paper. Combine the sugars, salt, cayenne, and sesame seeds in a bowl. In a second bowl, beat the egg white with the soy sauce until the mixture is even. Add the almonds to the egg-white bowl, and stir to coat them evenly. Sprinkle the sugar-seed mixture over the almonds, and stir to combine. Transfer the almonds to the prepared sheet in a single layer, and bake for 30 minutes, checking once or twice to make sure they're cooking evenly, and stirring if they're not. Pull the nuts from the oven, drizzle very lightly with sesame oil, and let them cool completely in the pan. Once they're cool, put the almonds in a bowl or jar, breaking up any that stick together.

chocolate olive oil spread

makes 1 cup spread

4 ounces (115 grams) dark chocolate (semi- or bittersweet), roughly chopped

½ cup (105 grams) olive oil

½ cup (60 grams) confectioners' sugar

¼ cup (20 grams) cocoa powder, any kind

Flaky sea salt

do ahead The spread keeps at room temperature for 2 weeks, or 4 weeks in the fridge, covered. Fully chilled, the mixture will be solid, and you'll want to bring it back to room temperature to make it spreadable. You can hasten this along in the microwave for 10 seconds; stir thoroughly afterward. If your kitchen runs warm, you might find that the mixture has liquefied in the jar. Do not fret; just use the fridge-cooling process described in the recipe to return it to the correct consistency.

Because my devotion to butter, cream, and triple-cream dairy products is irrefutable, and my family's devotion to chocolate-hazelnut spread is omnipresent, I hope you know I do not make this statement without considering the implications: I think this chocolate and olive oil spread is better than every one of these things. This started as an all-purpose chocolate breakfast spread, a wonderful host gift, also wonderful for gifting yourself, and while it's not unwelcome in the morning, it's also welcome—I'd humbly like to argue—at all times, most especially on a piece of bread at 4:00 p.m., when a chocolate craving reliably hits.

The most persnickety thing about this is its sensitivity to temperature. We keep it in a jar at room temperature (while it's officially good for one week, I've found it often lasts longer), but when the apartment is warm, it's liquid, and when the apartment is too cold, it's solid. There's a fix for both—a little fridge time, a little stirring when it's too loose; a quick burst in the microwave and a stir when it's too firm—and while this makes it more finicky than a jar of mass-produced chocolate spread, I think you'll agree that it's worth this effort and more.

———

In a medium saucepan, melt the chocolate and olive oil together over medium-low heat, whisking until they're evenly combined. Whisk in the confectioners' sugar and cocoa until the mixture is smooth. It will be liquid, and needs to cool to become a spread. There are two ways to do this.

Room temperature: You can leave it out at room temperature for several (4 to 6) hours, faster in a cooler kitchen and slower in a warmer one.

Fridge: You can also cool this in the fridge, but it requires more monitoring. After 15 minutes, remove from the fridge and thoroughly whisk the mixture until it's even. Repeat this every 5 minutes (it shouldn't take more than 30 minutes total) until a spreadable consistency forms.

Both methods: Spoon the mixture into its final jar for storage, and sprinkle the surface with flaky sea salt, to taste.

To serve: We love this best spread on a baguette for breakfast, with a bowl of fresh berries on the side.

acknowledgments

To everyone who comes to Smitten Kitchen to read, to cook, to comment, to share, to welcome these recipes into your home and come back with stories of how it went and who ate what and used the word *keepers* so many times in comments that you, essentially, named this book for me: Thank you. You make this so much fun.

A huge thank-you to everyone at **Knopf,** especially Reagan Arthur, Sarah New, Morgan Hamilton, Kathy Hourigan, Andy Hughes, Kathleen Fridella, Cassandra Pappas, Lisa Montebello, and Kelly Blair, who have worked so hard—through pandemics and snags, precedented (me, bad with deadlines) and unprecedented (global pandemic, shipping crisis)—to get this book out in the world. It takes a village. I am lucky to have such a strong one on my side.

To **Lexy Bloom,** thank you for your tireless patience, calm, and unwavering vision for this book.

To **Alison Fargis,** for giving my projects and whims your all.

To **Sara Eagle,** for a decade of keeping me organized, supported, and focused on what matters. It will be impossible to fill your impeccable shoes, but I'm glad you set the bar so high.

To **Rachel Gorman,** for being the best addition to my kitchen. Nearly every one of these recipes has been improved by your presence, patience, and opinions.

To **Barrett Washburne and Lauren Radel,** I still don't know how you did it, but you pulled off the momentous feat of stunningly styling an entire book of recipes from a control freak who's used to doing everything herself in her crappy kitchen *and* you made it fun. Thank you.

To **Sandy Gluck,** for your careful recipe testing—and local deliveries.

To **Tess Le Moing,** thank you for the kitchen assistance.

To **Anna Painter,** for almost two decades of great conversation and for coaxing me off the chicken-and-crouton ledge.

To **Jessie Sheehan,** for your consistent cheer and caring as much about pot roast as I do.

To **Renu Blankinship,** for cookie dates, butter chickpea guidance, and constant inspiration.

To both my families: Thank you for your endless support, babysitting, recipe tasting, and for seemingly accepting, ten years in, that the book will be done when it's done and there's no need to ask when that will be.

To **Anna and Jacob:** Thanks for all of the recipe tasting and savagely honest reviews. I am so proud of the people you're becoming.

To **Alex Perelman,** my favorite person, the best date, and the very definition of a keeper.

index

(Page references in *italics* refer to illustrations)

A NOTE ABOUT THE AUTHOR

DEB PERELMAN is a self-taught home cook, a photographer, and the creator of smittenkitchen.com. She is the author of the *New York Times* best sellers *The Smitten Kitchen Cookbook,* which won the IACP Julia Child Award, and *Smitten Kitchen Every Day.* Perelman lives in New York City with her husband, son, and daughter.